THE AMERICAN CONSTITUTION AND THE ADMINISTRATIVE STATE

Constitutionalism in the Late 20th Century

Edited by
Richard J. Stillman II

With a Foreword by
Frederick C. Mosher

Series Editor
Kenneth W. Thompson

Volume II
In the Miller Center Bicentennial Series
on Constitutionalism

UNIVERSITY
PRESS OF
AMERICA

The Miller Center

Lanham • New York • London

University of Virginia

Preface and foreword copyright 1989 by
The White Burkett Miller Center of Public Affairs
University of Virginia

University Press of America®, Inc.

4720 Boston Way
Lanham, MD 20706

3 Henrietta Street
London WC2E 8LU England

British Cataloging in Publication Information Available

The contents of this work originally appeared in *Public Administrative Review*,
January/February, 1987, Volume 47, No. 1
Copyright 1987 by Public Administrative Review

Library of Congress Cataloging-in-Publication Data

The American Constitution and the administrative state : constitutionalism in the late 20th century / edited by Richard J. Stillman II ; with a foreword by Frederick C. Mosher.
    p.   cm. — (Miller Center bicentennial series on constitutionalism ; v. 2)
    "The contents of this work originally appeared in Public Administrative review, January/February, 1987, volume 47, no. 1"—T.p. verso.
    1. Administrative agencies—United States—Management—History. 2. United States—Politics and government. 3. United States—Constitutional history.
    I. Stillman, Richard Joseph, 1943– . II. Series.
JK411.A63   1989   353.07'09—dc20   89–33136 CIP

ISBN 0–8191–7465–3 (alk. paper)
ISBN 0–8191–7466–1 (pbk.: alk. paper)

The views expressed by the author(s) of this publication do not necessarily represent the opinions of the Miller Center. We hold to Jefferson's dictum that: "Truth is the proper and sufficient antagonist to error, and has nothing to fear from the conflict, unless by human interposition, disarmed of her natural weapons, free argument and debate."

Co-published by arrangement with
The White Burkett Miller Center of Public Affairs,
University of Virginia

This University Press of America book is produced on acid-free paper.
The paper used in this publication meets the minimum requirements of
American National Standard for Information Sciences—Permanence of Paper
for Printed Library Materials, ANSI Z39.48–1984. ∞

Table of Contents

Preface

This volume is the second in a Bicentennial Series on Constitutionalism of the White Burkett Miller Center of Public Affairs. It follows an introductory volume entitled *Constitutionalism: Founding and Future* that looks back to the historical setting and the views of some of the founders and lead to the challenges of constitutionalism in the future.

Volume III seeks to analyze leading political theories and theorists and their relationship to the U.S. Constitution. Such theorists include Madison, Jefferson, conservative British and American theorists, and legal writers whose philosophies influenced the Constitution. It also considers theories concerning such issues as slavery and the Constitution.

Volumes IV-VII are addressed to the impact of the American Constitution abroad and its interaction with constitutions in other world regions. Volume IV concerns the U.S. Constitution and the constitutions of Asia. Volume V deals with the U.S. Constitution and constitutionalism in Africa. Volume VI has as its focus the U.S. Constitution and constitutionalism in Europe. Volume VII will examine the U.S. Constitution and the constitutions of Latin America. Finally, this volume will include essays on concepts such as prudence and constitutional breakthroughs.

Foreword

It has long seemed to me remarkable that the Constitution of the United States contains so little—so very, very little—about the administration of the government. The word *administration* does not appear, nor does *management, implementation, policy-making, direction, budget, civil service,* and a lot of the other words we regularly buzz. True, the *executive power,* whatever that may include, is vested in the President. And there are some specifics: the President is commander-in-chief; with advice and consent, he makes treaties and top level appointments; he can demand the *opinion* of the heads of departments on matters within their purview. Most of all, he must "take care that the laws be faithfully executed." This last power may be taken to mean *administer,* but it may also be, and has often been, interpreted to mean *inspect and report,* especially since in the Constitution the expression appears soon after the stipulation that the President tell Congress about the state of the union.

Maybe the framers could not agree on what to say—so said very little. Maybe they feared that more specificity would frighten themselves from signing and the states from ratifying. After all, chief executives—kings and royal governors—were not very popular in the United States in the eighteenth century. Maybe they thought that administrative matters were so subject to changing requirements that they should be left to the new government as it evolved. Probably, there was a combination of these factors. Americans, particularly students of government, should agree that we have been the beneficiaries of their restraint. Difficult as it often seems to bring about change of purpose or structure or performance in government from year to year, how much harder, and more dangerous, it would be if we had to amend the Constitution every significant time! Many

American states and foreign governments have suffered from such rigidities in their constitutions.

As Don Price has so ably pointed out,[1] most of our operative constitution is unwritten, built upon or deduced from, or quite outside, the written document. Further, most of the specifics of the interface between the written Constitution and federal administration are, in at least one sense, indirect; they have been developed pragmatically from the broad constitutional powers and constraints provided the Congress and the President. However, the vast majority of federal activities involve administrative agencies and people when they are conceived and planned as well as when they are performed. So in a second sense, the interface is direct and immediate. Administration is why and where and when and what and how and by whom things are done.

The subject of this volume is at the meeting point between the Constitution and human and organizational behavior. It is not less than constitutional law on the one hand nor public administration on the other. It is old values and principles, grown and adapted, as they are confronted with new and rapidly changing situations and with technologies unimaginable two hundred—or twenty—years ago. The essays that follow treat various aspects of this meeting ground. They are not histories but provocative and thoughtful discussions of old problems as they appear in the late 1980s. Their authors represent a variety of perspectives in terms of geography, field of interest, and nature and extent of experience. They are among the most astute students of the topics they treat—such as the relations of political and career executives, or the new, new federalism, the relations of the judiciary with public administrators, or the impact of computers on the powers of the executive and legislative branches.

The papers were initially prepared and published in the *Public Administration Review* to celebrate the bicentennial anniversary of the drafting and signing of the Constitution in 1787.[2] They are of such enduring merit and value that they are here republished in book form. And there are two reasons why 1989 is a particularly appropriate year for this republication. The first is that 1789 was the year that the Constitutional government and its administration became a reality. The first electors of the first President and Vice

President were chosen in January of that year; in February they made their selections; in April the first Congress under the Constitution convened and the electoral votes were counted; and in May President Washington and Vice President Adams were inaugurated. During the summer of 1789, the Congress enacted the laws and appropriations to establish the departments of government, and soon thereafter the President named the heads of those agencies. In September the Supreme Court was established by law, and the President nominated its first members in the months following. Thus in most respects, the government was created and operating in the course of nine months, the normal term of a human baby. Two of the original thirteen states had not yet ratified the Constitution.

Would that there were half such speed today!

The second reason that 1789 was such an important year is that in September the Congress adopted and transmitted to the states twelve proposed amendments to the Constitution. Of these, the ten which were ratified by the requisite number of states[3] constitute what was even then known as the Bill of Rights: one—some think the most important one—of the three distinguishing pillars of the Constitution.[4]

1789 was therefore, like 1775 and 1787, a major landmark of American history; the year that our government started to work and the year that a significant element of our system, the Bill of Rights, was initiated. It is fitting that we herein note and celebrate the bicentennial anniversary of that year.

Charlottesville, Va.   Frederick C. Mosher
November, 1988

ENDNOTES

1. In *America's Unwritten Constitution* (Baton Rouge: Louisiana State University Press, 1983).

2. In the January 1987 edition (47,1).

3. The two that were not ratified did not concern individual rights.

4. The other two are the division and allocation of powers among the executive, legislative, and judicial branches and the federal system of national and state governments.

The Constitutional Bicentennial
and the Centennial of the
American Administrative State

RICHARD J. STILLMAN II*

Two significant anniversaries for Americans occur in 1987: the bicentennial of the U.S. Constitution and the centennial of the founding of the administrative state. Both hold very special meanings for the public administration community. Two hundred years ago, in May 1987, delegates met in Philadelphia to draft a document that they hoped would create a new nation. One hundred years ago, in February 1887, Congress enacted the Interstate Commerce Act, the first of many regulatory bodies which would serve as central building blocks of the modern administrative state.

The first event is of course well known. Convening a constitutional convention to found a new nation is the sort

---

* **Richard J. Stillman II** is Professor of Government and Politics at George Mason University. Among books which he has written and edited are: *The Rise of the City Manager; Public Administration: Concepts and Cases; Results-Oriented Budgeting; The Effective Local Manager* (with Wayne Anderson and Chet Newland); *Basic Documents of American Public Administration Since 1950; A Search for Public Administration: The Ideas and Career of Dwight Waldo* (with Brack Brown); and *Public Bureaucracy in America.*

of event that occurs rarely in human history, and so beyond any question 1787 was one of the most significant years in U.S. history. It even rivals several other key dates in importance—1492, 1607, 1776, 1803, 1812, 1861, 1917, 1933, 1941, and 1945—because it represents the central political event in the life of Americans. Washington, Hamilton, Madison, Franklin, and the other 51 Framers, as we all know, labored hard throughout the hot Philadelphia summer from May 25 to September 17, 1787, to draft a written Constitution to replace the faulty Articles of Confederation (which was actually the *first* U.S. Constitution). Their collective wisdom provided the nation with a strong, resilient charter which would guide America's development from obscurity to world power and global leadership. Their labors also resulted in a bold, creative document, very different from any others up to that time, which would serve as the fundamental law of the land. With its adoption and the addition of the Bill of Rights in 1791, the Constitution shifted the basis of political authority—fundamentally and permanently—from a weak confederation to a federal republic based on popular rule.[1] Remember, the Constitution begins, "We the people. . . ." That decisive shift to popular-based rule makes the Constitution perhaps the most revolutionary document of all times, though the sober-minded, realistic Framers of 1787 were hardly wild-eyed revolutionaries.

The Constitution opened an entirely new chapter in history. America would never look quite the same after the Founders performed their handiwork. Nor would the world. Popular sovereignty shortly became the very backbone of U.S. society; some would even say, arguably "the American Way." As Tocqueville rightly observed 43 years after "The Grand Convention" of 1787, "The people reign in the American political world as the Deity does in the Universe. They are the cause the aim of all things; everything comes from them and everything is absorbed by them."[2] Here America set the model for the rest of western society to follow. Rightly ought 1787, not 1776, be cited as the date when shots from the American soil were really heard round the world?

Novus Ordo Seculorum

The Constitution of 1787 radically altered the basis of political order and hence changed the world for the better, but also according to Stephen Skowronek, "The political and intellectual achievement of the men who met in Philadelphia in 1787 was to formulate and legitimize an organizational framework that bypassed both the European and revolutionary designs."[3]   While the Europeans, especially on the Continent, were moving towards more centralized forms of governance, the Framers chose not to follow their lead. Rather, they selected deliberately a different governmental pattern by which to secure individual liberties.   The Constitution reflects a unique institutional order, a "Novus Ordo Seculorum," according to the motto on the U.S. seal: a balanced Lockean republic, modelled on Montesquieu's ideals of division of power, and the importance of federal design that constrained central government with certain powers left to the states or the people.

This "New Order of the Ages" was a genuine "first" in the advancement of the science of government.   It was boldly an American original which ranks ahead of even such U.S. technological "firsts" as splitting the atom or landing men on the moon; for it proved a self-governing republic could work within the context of a large, heterogeneous society (recall, only a few small, compact states like Switzerland up to that time operated as free, self-governing republics).   The new constitutional order also formulated possibly the most difficult government to administer with its ample internal checks and balances, strictly enumerated legislative powers, specified individual rights, limited institutional functions, decentralized authority and representative governance.   No nation before—and few since—have tried to order their governmental affairs in this manner and then make them work!   As Henry Steele Commager stressed,[4] the Europeans had talked about all these ideas, but it was the Americans who put such concepts into practice.   Another principal reason to celebrate the Constitution's splendid achievements?

Still one more justification for this bicentennial tribute, and perhaps the most important, the Constitution survived!   Through a bloody civil war, two world wars, numerous other military engagements, and countless political, economic, and social upheavals, the U.S. Constitution has endured for two centuries as the fundamental law of the land. The genius of the Constitution, as numerous scholars have observed, is precisely its adaptability to radically changing conditions. As the central governing instrument, it has stretched its capacities for rule from a tiny eighteenth century republic of 3 million people bordering the Atlantic to a twentieth century global superpower of 240 million.

The Founders wisely left room, a lot of room, for change. Perhaps they recognized that change was indeed the only permanent condition in American life and so they institutionalized processes to accommodate change, massive changes, by establishing a formal process for amending the Constitution and by creating an independent judiciary with scope for constitutional interpretation (also "firsts" for the science of government). Even then, the amendment process and truly "landmark court decisions" have been relied upon infrequently throughout U.S. history. Yet, those two elements have given enough elasticity to the Constitution to allow it to outlast all others. The U.S. Constitution is now the oldest written constitution in the world, outdistancing most by a very long stretch. As Mark Cannon recently pointed out,[5] two-thirds of the world's 160 national constitutions have been adopted or revised since 1970. Only 14 predate World War Two. The average nation has had two constitutions since 1945, and some, as in the cases of Syria and Thailand, have ratified nine written constitutions within the last 40 years!

Even more remarkable, the Constitution not only survives but remains a meaningful, central document for government, "the supreme law of the land." One only needs to recall the experience of the Weimar Republic or look to many communist states or third world nations to recognize, in the words of William G. Andrews, that it is very possible to have "constitutions without constitutionalism."[6] It is an all too common, unfortunate spectacle in world affairs today when authoritarian regimes use written constitutions to mask their despotism. But any one who doubts the U.S. Constitution's vitality and relevance to contemporary events only need read the Supreme Court's rationale in 1986 for stroking down a key provision of the Gramm-Rudman-Hollings "balanced budget" legislation. Yes, the words of this document are vitally alive, meaningful *and important* to the

American people in 1987. "The hard core of the American tradition," as Clinton Rossiter once observed, "is a belief in constitutional government."

Those may be good reasons for this tribute to the "birthing" of the U.S. Constitution (and there are no doubt many more good reasons, such as promoting political education, developing a sense of the past, honor for great deeds, respect for law, and the like), but why choose to take note of the centennial of the rise of the administrative state, beginning with the formation in the Interstate Commerce Commission[7] in 1887? Why praise the initiation and growth of public bureaucracy? Red tape, regulation, and all that? Aren't we overdoing things a bit? Rather, should we not mourn its start? Damn its origins? Certainly, the 1980s are not noted for effusive enthusiasm over governmental organizations or their antecedents!

The Rise of the Administrative State

Granted, 1887 does not hold the same emotional or dramatic appeal as 1787. No grand convention met somewhere in closed session to found a new nation. No ringing preambles were dedicated to "promoting the general welfare." No grand national debate occurred, containing a brilliant set of *Federalist Papers*, over the central issues of founding a new constitutional order.

No fundamental law was framed, only another statute was written into the law books. The administrative state began much less auspiciously—and some might say ignominiously—with the aggressive agitation by aggrieved midwest farmers over what they viewed as imposition of unfair, gouging rates by monopolistic railroads. It was a nasty fight, almost a classic Marxian economic contest between classes. An economic squeeze in the 1870s fanned the prairie fires of the Granger Movement that led to numerous prolonged legal contests in the courts as well as legislative efforts on the state level to impose effective public controls over the irresponsible, unchecked use of private power by these corporate entities.[8] For more than a decade such legal-legislative efforts had failed to accomplish much.

The year, 1887, marked the passage of a weak but vital national legislation which for the first time aimed to remedy these deep-rooted, intense socio-economic problems. The Interstate Commerce Commission (ICC) became a model for subsequent regulatory commissions and in the broader sense, started the rise of a vast administrative complex now called by many names (some with slightly differing meanings—and *all* none too flattering): the "regulatory state," "bureaucratic state," "welfare state," "corporate state," and for purposes here, the "administrative state."

Thus, 1887 is a seminal date in American history, and a good case can be made for giving it just as serious reflection—if not praise—as 1787. Why? For one reason, modern society would not be possible without an administrative state. In the same year that the ICC was begun, a young political science professor at Bryn Mawr College, named Woodrow Wilson, published the first "conscious" American essay on the subject of public administration, arguing prophetically that this new discipline was needed because "it was getting to be harder to run a constitution than to frame one."[9] How correct he was then, and, even more, how true his comments rings today!

In 1987 the United States is a vast, heterogenous, urbanized nation, bound together in a massive, complicated industrial economy, exhibiting many special interests and national requirements, with major international and security responsibilities. To carry out these varied tasks today, administrative machinery is not merely useful but essential. Large, powerful public organizations have been formed since 1887 to service critical public requirements at many levels of U.S. government. Indeed, civilized life within a constitutional democracy like that of the United States would be hard to comprehend without the services of a modern administrative state. American society requires its modern administrative state to carry out such vitally complex tasks as space exploration, national defense, public education, regulation of industry, macro-micro economic planning, protection of the environment, and support for scientific research.

On another level, 1887 is an important date because it, like 1787, may have made freedom—*real* freedom—possible. What kind of liberty would the poor, aged, sick, young, old, *or* any American citizen have without the protections—economic, political, and social—accorded through numerous public organizations? What kind of freedom would workers *or* business enterprise *or* the consumer have without some mediation or constraint impinging upon private power via public regulation? Freedom endures, it can reasonably be suggested, in modern, urbanized, industrialized societies precisely because of the variety of administrative checks and balances imposed on the marketplace by numerous public organizations. The Constitution wisely and correctly set up a federal republic to negate public power in order to protect individual liberty, but perhaps unwisely and incorrectly it ignored the consequences of unchecked *private power.*

Some would and have argued convincingly that the administrative state provided a much needed constitutional corrective, offering enhanced individual freedom through the *positive* enlargement of the public sphere to check and balance unrestrained private power on individuals, groups, and the society as a whole. It effectively supplemented, not supplanted the Constitution by extending constitutional protections in accordance to the new imperatives of the twentieth century, particularly in the realm of private power. Child labor laws, meat inspection, public health standards, and fire codes helped to make society safer, more secure, and more humane. Now, whether the U.S. Constitution would have failed or would have been radically revised without this corrective to the unfettered reign of the private marketplace is anyone's guess. Yet, it is a safe bet that the U.S. Constitution would have been different without the rise of the administrative state. My hunch is that the administrative state allowed the U.S. Constitution *and freedom* to survive and prosper in the modern age. Regrettably, the United States has produced few eloquent theorists, such as T. H. Green in England, to make that point, although John Rohr's recent book, *To Run a Constitution, The Legitimacy of the Administrative State,* takes a bold and original first step in that direction.[10]

Finally, a third reason to take note of 1887: the administrative state, in the words of Don K. Price, has become part of the fabric of our "unwritten constitution."[11] It, along with the Constitution, is now the central means of governance in society. For better or worse, or better *and* worse, complex rules, routines, hierarchies, procedures, budgets, organizations, and professional expertise in various fields of public policy govern people's lives as much as the form and content of the U.S. Constitution. This machinery decides critical and significant political choices in society involving, using Lasswell's apt phrase, "who gets what, when, how." Acronyms such as DOD, FAA, OMB, or FTC symbolize this vast, complicated, and largely hidden administrative apparatus which has been created over the course of the last century to help chart the direction of the American nation.

Knowingly or not, Americans are governed by a modern administrative state which has developed alongside and within constitutional democracy. People's lives, fortunes, and futures are today decided by *both* the Constitution and an administrative state. Grafting this "unwritten constitution" into our written document (remember, the U.S. Constitution says nothing about bureaucracy, budgets, personnel rules, civil service, or legislative oversight, and it does not use even the term, "executive branch") was a substantial accomplishment, perhaps matching some of the brilliant achievements of the Philadelphia Convention in 1787. Relatively unknown founders of the administrative state—i.e., Dorman Eaton, Charles A. Beard, Emory Upton, Henry Bruere, Elihu Root, Richard Childs, A. E. Buck, Charles Francis Adams, Frederick A. Cleveland, Ernst Freund, Frank J. Goodnow, William E. Mosher, Luther Gulick, Louis Brownlow, and others—deserve recognition for their remarkable success as Founders of this endeavor. They wisely conceived and astutely crafted such new institutional inventions as the council-manager plan, the Executive Office of the President, administrative law, regulatory reform, the general staff concept, public service training, executive budgets, audit procedures, research bureaus, and the civil service. Their lasting handiwork in reframing American government ought to be acknowledged as *important* for society's continued survival and for the constitutional order's vitality in 1987.

Why This Volume is Different

However, the contents of this volume are not devoted to praising the Founders of 1787 or 1887. Other journals and texts during the bicentennial no doubt are devoted to recognizing the accomplishments of the Founders. These essays do not even look carefully at the events of 1787 or 1887. The history of the Constitutional Convention as well as the ICC are well-chronicled elsewhere by many distinguished scholarly authorities. This volume does not even probe what many would deem important specific, more technical, constitutional, or administrative questions like due process or regulatory enforcement. Again, others are offering that sort of useful analysis in 1987.

Rather, this volume of original articles is designed to provide a distinctive examination of the relationship between the Constitution and the administrative state and of the resulting prospects and problems for *both* in this bicentennial era and beyond. Except for a few notable books, this key connection between the Constitution and administration seems so far to have been overlooked by many of the scholarly bicentennial deliberations. Project '87, for example, the major constitutional bicentennial program developed jointly during the past decade by the American Political Science Association and the American Historical Association lists the 13 enduring constitutional issues upon which it concentrates attention, but none specifically mentions the relevant problems pertaining to the dilemmas of constitutional-administrative interconnections. This volume helps to fill that void in the bicentennial discussions by studying critical problems at the interstices of the Constitution and administration which thus far have been dealt with in only a few books, most notably, besides John A. Rohr's study cited above, Don K. Price's *America's Unwritten Constitution: Science, Religion, and Political Responsibility*; James Sundquist's *Constitutional Reform and Effective Government*; and Ralph Chandler's forthcoming *A Centennial History of the American Administrative State.*[12]

The specific topics of these essays were chosen because they were deemed to be significant issues involving key constitutional-administrative relationships such as leadership, organization, political appointments, budgets, federalism, separation of powers, and the like. Certainly not *all* the salient issues can be covered here. Regrettably space limits preclude such comprehensive coverage. But some of the major "relational issues" are found in the following pages, such as: What critical antecedents, from a comparative perspective of world history, gave rise to the U.S. Constitution and the administrative system? How does the constitutional principle of separation of powers "square" with the politics-administrative dichotomy—one of the key building blocks of the administrative state? Are there historic constitutional roots to the contemporary popular hostility toward bureaucrats? What constitutional challenges do public executives face in exercising leadership roles in the 1980s and beyond? Do administrative trends in budgeting and computer utilization raise profound constitutional issues? And, conversely, where and how do constitutional ideas like federalism and judicial oversight raise significant dilemmas for contemporary administration? In short, how well—or poorly—do the Constitution's concepts and practices mix and "mesh" with administration?

Authors were selected to write on these and other topics because of their particular recognized expertise and understanding of the specific topics under review. All writers have been given a relatively free hand in deciding how to tackle their respective assignments, issues to examine, interpretations of problems, and proposed solutions. Thus, as one would expect, a rich diversity of themes, ideas, styles, and points of view emerge from the following pages. It would be impossible—even foolhardy—to try to summarize or categorize them concisely, yet each essay in this volume:

- relates to the overall theme involving the "interface" between the U.S. Constitution and administrative state;

- focuses upon some important past, present, and future aspects of the interconnections between the two realms;

- summarizes and synthesizes current scholarly research on that particular topic;

- where possible, touches on all three levels of government;

- attempts to offer different, creative, even bold, interpretations of issues;

- raises numerous points which deserve further attention by scholars, students, and practitioners in the field.

In summary, this is a volume of reflective, original essays on critical issues concerned with important past, present, and future relationships and interactions between the Constitution and the administrative state. The opening four essays address important historical perspectives on these relational questions; they deal with their origins from a comparative perspective and probe such problems as separation of powers, the politics-administration dichotomy, the image of bureaucrats, and organizational forms. The central articles in this collection focus on current aspects of constitutional-administrative dilemmas pertaining to leadership, political appointee-careerist relationships, budgets, federalism, use of computers in government, and the judiciary. One of the two concluding essays looks toward future problems and prospects involving public-private relationships and public investment. The final essay, by Luther Gulick, presents his current reflections on time and public administration.

In selecting the particular topics to analyze and authors to write for this volume, the editor relied heavily on invaluable advice and guidance from several distinguished members of the public administration community. Help is gratefully acknowledged from James W. Fesler, Paul C. Light, Frederick C. Mosher, Deil S. Wright, Naomi B. Lynn, James L. Sundquist, Don K. Price, Wayne F. Anderson, James P. Pfiffner, and the late Kenneth Howard in the early planning stages of the development of this issue. Dwight Waldo took on the onerous chore of reading, reviewing, and providing "second opinions" on every first draft. To these and many other helpful reviews of individual essays as well as the authors themselves who labored diligently and without complaint on this project for nearly two years, the editor owes a great debt of gratitude.

Ultimately, the hope is that readers will find these essays timely, enjoyable, illuminating, and instructive. Fundamental purposes also are that these essays will be a suitable tribute to honor the remarkable achievements of 1787 and 1887 and that they will advance understanding of both.

ENDNOTES

1.   Gordon S. Wood, *The Creation of the American Republic, 1776-1787* (Chapel Hill: UNC Press, 1969). Also useful is Jack N. Rakove, *The Beginnings of National Politics* (New York: Alfred A. Knopf, 1979).

2.   Alex de Tocqueville, *Democracy in America*, 2 vols. (New York: Vintage Books, 1945), vol. I, p. 59.

3.   Stephen Skowronek, *Building a New American State: The Expansion of National Administrative Capacities, 1877-1920* (New York: Cambridge University Press, 1982), p. 21.

4.   Henry Steele Commager, *Empire of Reason: How Europe Imagined and America Realized the Enlightenment* (New York: Doubleday, 1977).

5.   Mark W. Cannon, "Why Celebrate the Constitution?" *National Forum*, vol. 64 (Fall 1984), p. 3.

6.   William G. Andrews, *Constitutions and Constitutionalism*, (New York: D. Van Nostrand Co., Inc., 1968), p. 22.

7.   A equally good case can be advanced for celebrating 1883 as "the birthing" of the administrative state with the passage of the Civil Service Act (Pendleton Act) of 1883. Since any administrative system requires a trained cadre of personnel, the precise date is thus open to debate involving the founding of the administrative state, but a strong case can be made for 1887 given the primary importance of the ICC to creation of national regulatory authority, without which the American administrative system would have limited scope, influence, and structure today. I realize that the debate on this point is an open, ongoing one and certainly I do not mean to imply that this offers *the last* words on the subject. For a recent outstanding discussion of this problem, see Paul Van Riper, "The

American Administrative State: Wilson and the Founders—An Unorthodox View," *Public Administration Review*, vol. 43 (November/December 1983), pp. 477-490.

8. Several excellent discussions of the birth of the Interstate Commerce Commission are available. Two good ones are Ari and Olive Hoogenboom, *A History of the ICC: From Panacea to Palliative* (New York: Norton, 1976) and Thomas K. McCraw, *Prophets of Regulation* (Cambridge: Harvard University Press, 1984).

9. Woodrow Wilson, "The Study of Administration," *Political Science Quarterly*, vol. 2 (June 1887), pp. 197-222.

10. Unfortunately, America has never produced a political thinker on a par with T.H. Green, who argued eloquently in such writings as *The Principles of Political Obligation* (1886) that many liberties are guarded effectively only in a well-ordered administrative state. American theorists generally have tended to overlook—or to be hostile towards—the administrative state, although research and reflections during this bicentennial era may help to change that. As noted, John A. Rohr has made a major contribution in that direction: *To Run A Constitution: The Legitimacy of the Administrative State* (Lawrence: University Press of Kansas, 1986).

11. Don K. Price, *America's Unwritten Constitution: Science, Religion, and Political Responsibility* (Baton Rouge: Louisiana State University Press, 1983).

12. Price, *supra*; Rohr, *supra*; James L. Sundquist, *Constitutional Reform and Effective Government* (Washington: The Brookings Institution, 1986); Ralph Chandler, *A Centennial History of the American Administrative State* (New York: Macmillan Publishing Co., 1987).

CHAPTER ONE

American Constitutional and Administrative Systems in Comparative Perspective

FERREL HEADY[*]

Caveats About Comparisons

Some cautions must be kept in mind when American constitutional and administrative systems are examined from a comparative perspective.

The most important is that to a remarkable extent the course of political development in the United States has been influenced by internal rather than external factors. The resulting constitutional and administrative amalgam is a product which is uniquely American, even though it can be traced historically to diverse origins and more recently has furnished a pattern influential in political choices made by other countries scattered around the globe.

A focus on comparative aspects means that these indigenous forces can be treated only incidentally, despite

---

[*] **Ferrel Heady** since 1981 has been Professor Emeritus of Public Administration and Political Science at the University of New Mexico, where he was Academic Vice President (1967-68) and President (1968-75). Previously he was director of the Institute of Public Administration at the University of Michigan. He is a member of the National Academy of Public Administration and was president of the American Society for Public Administration (1969-70). He is the author of *Public Administration: A Comparative Perspective* (3rd ed., 1984).

their overall significance in shaping American politics. Other contributors to this symposium will be able to concentrate on the impact of such factors as geographical distance from Europe; a colonial population made up largely of individuals who had made a personal choice to cut their ties with the Old World and were determined to resist governmental intrusions affecting their lives; the opportunity to move from frontier to frontier in settling most of a continent; the surge of growth during the American industrial revolution resulting from westward expansion, the influx of immigrants, improved communication and transportation, the spread of manufacturing, and increasing urbanization; and the consequent social and economic crises which demanded governmental responses.[1]

Another caveat is that in making comparisons it must be recognized that during the whole course of American history neither the constitutional nor the administrative system has ever been based on the existence of full consensus. Although basic characteristics can be identified, these mask a welter of differences in objectives sought, in understandings as to the intent of choices formally agreed upon, and in subsequent interpretations as to the meaning of these choices.

A further complication is that constitutional and administrative systems are dynamic, not static. In the American case, each system existed in embryonic form before taking definite shape, has subsequently gone through a series of changes, and will continue to evolve. To make comparative analysis manageable, it helps to have only a limited number of chronological checkpoints, rather than to give equal attention to changes over short time intervals.

The bicentennial and centennial anniversaries being celebrated in 1987 conveniently provide such checkpoints. The roots of American constitutionalism and of American public administration undoubtedly were formed earlier, but each system has a date which is commonly accepted as marking when the system emerged in a clearly recognizable form. Tracing the birth of the constitutional system to the Constitutional Convention of 1787 is relatively easy. Dating the emergence of the "American administrative state" is more controversial. The linkage is most frequently to the decade of the 1880s and specifically to the year 1887, because during that one year the Interstate Commerce Commission was created and Woodrow Wilson's essay on "the

Study of Public Administration" was published, but such specificity is more and more subject to challenge. The significance of Wilson's essay has been debated recently at length.[2] Crenson contends that the bureaucratization of the federal government took place earlier, during the Jacksonian era.[3] Skowronek argues that the most crucial systemic transformation came later, around the turn of the twentieth century.[4] Thus, 1887 is a date of convenience rather than certainty.

Finally, leadership in shaping the constitutional and administrative systems has been differentiated, not unified. The most influential molders of each system have usually been different people, working at different times, and drawing upon different precedents.

Among framers of the constitutional system, the primary figures were James Madison, Alexander Hamilton, and Thomas Jefferson.[5] Identification of the primary shapers of the American administrative state during the following century is more difficult. A short list would include civil service reformers such as Dorman B. Eaton and scholars such as Woodrow Wilson and Frank J. Goodnow, with the former also of course being influential as a public official later in his career.

A few of these individuals were actively involved in both the constitutional and administrative spheres. This is particularly true of Hamilton and Jefferson in the first group and of Wilson in the second.[6] Hamilton had a fully developed view about executive and administrative functions under the new constitution and was able to have more impact than anyone else in the design of the administrative machinery in the early years. Jefferson, who held widely different opinions on matters of administration, was in position of influence over a much longer time and eventually had an equivalent impact largely negating that of Hamilton, whose views were in part resurrected later as the administrative state took shape. Wilson, first as a scholar and then as chief executive at both state and national levels, was a major force in changing the constitutional system from what he called "congressional government" toward a readjustment which gave more emphasis to an enhanced role for the presidency.[7]

With these caveats as background, the focus here is a comparative treatment, in both historical and contemporary terms, of the constitutional and administrative systems which have evolved in the United States during the two centuries since independence.

Antecedents for American Systems

The architects of the American constitutional and administrative systems, in a process which was sometimes explicit but often implicit, drew upon a wide variety of historical precedents considered to be relevant for the American setting. The main interest here is to identify the most important of these external factors and to indicate how they have influenced American constitutional and administrative development. The analysis of historical antecedents is based on a simplified classification of dominant types of political regimes during successive eras in the history of the Western world and on identification of their prime characteristics which have helped to shape American institutions and practices.[8]

Ancient and Classical Empires and City-States

During the long period from the rise of Sumerian civilization to the gradual breakup of the Roman Empire and the subsequent transition to feudalism, the ancient and classical societies of the Fertile Crescent and the Mediterranean Basin were generally structured either as traditional empires or as city-states. These two political system types differed in scale and in their value orientations. The empires were larger in their territorial sweep, valued order and stability, and devoted a great deal of effort to the administrative tasks of making governance effective. The city-states were smaller in size, provided considerable freedom for individuals and groups, and (especially in Greece) were forums for speculation on political issues with relatively little attention being given to administrative matters.

In view of their chronological and geographical remoteness, these systems understandably have had a relatively minor and mainly indirect impact on American institutions. City-state characteristics such as limited scale, negotiated cooperative arrangements, and amateurism in administration appealed to the framers of the American constitutional system, but they were most interested in how the political experience of confederations of city-states might be instructive to constitution makers seeking the best way to bind a cluster of quasi-sovereign late eighteenth century states into a new nation. Advocates of the proposed federal system such as Madison and Hamilton scrutinized ancient confederacies and emphasized their overall inadequacies for attainment of political continuity.[9] Jefferson, on the other hand, had initial reservations about the federal arrangements in the 1787 document and never disavowed his characterization of the confederation system as the best government "existing or that ever did exist."[10] Later in his career he became increasingly concerned about what he viewed as evidence of encroachment by the federal government beyond its primary responsibility for foreign affairs into the domestic concerns of state governments, and he continued to describe the American Union as a confederation, with neither the federal government nor the states being superior in power.[11] Thus at this early stage in constitutional development, philosophical differences among shapers of the American system were reflected in their interpretations and applications of classical history.

The empires of the ancient world attracted less interest, since they had despotic and monarchical characteristics considered incompatible with American political values. The Roman Empire was recognized, nevertheless, for its contributions to law and administrative technology, and certainly it was the progenitor of organizational concepts and practices concerning matters such as hierarchy and professionalism which were kept alive during the medieval period by the Roman Catholic Church and reappeared in the governmental sphere after the Renaissance as Western European absolutist monarchies matured. These, in turn, nurtured the development of cameralism and other forms of a European "science" of administration admired by Wilson and other architects of the American administrative state.

European Feudalism

The impact on the United States of the lengthy feudal period in Europe is to some extent masked and indirect, transmitted to the societies of the New World as transplants of the colonial powers of Western Europe. As Reinhard Bendix has pointed out, "the overall similarity of the

Western European experience" arose "from the common legacies of European feudalism,"[12] which were in turn inherited by the colonies. The imprinted lesson from the feudal "dark ages" was that the societal fragmentation characteristic of feudalism had inflicted a tremendous setback to the level of social life achieved during the heyday of the Roman Empire. This had both constitutional and administrative implications for the newly independent former English colonies, emphasizing as it did the necessity for organizing a political entity with endowments of territory and resources sufficient to develop adequate governing capacities to assure survival. Some specific features of feudalism may also have appealed to American decision-makers. For example, the contractual interrelationships of feudalism were compatible with the social compact views of the constitutional framers, and feudal vertical authority arrangements were consistent with the concepts of those who shaped the American administrative system.

The remoteness in time of European feudalism and the absence of a feudal period in the historical experience of the English colonies are more significant, however, than any traceable feudal influences. Tocqueville noted many years ago that Americans had the great advantage of attaining democracy "without the suffering of a democratic revolution" and that they "were born equal instead of becoming so."[13] Hartz stresses that America skipped the feudal stage of history, so that the outstanding thing about the 1776 revolution was "not the freedom to which it led, but the established feudal structure it did not have to destroy." The result was national acceptance of a "Lockian creed" which included "the reality of atomistic social freedom" as the master assumption of American political thought and which insisted that the power of the state must be limited.[14] Huntington attributes the weakness of political institutions in the United States to the absence of feudalism and to the resulting freedom from the need to counter it, thus contributing to a consensus in an "American Creed" that is "basically antigovernment."[15] These are major consequences of what is essentially the absence rather than the presence of feudalism in American history.

European Absolutist Monarchies

Over a period of four centuries, the medieval political patterns of feudalism were gradually transformed, at different rates in different parts of Europe, into the absolutist monarchies of the sixteenth to eighteenth centuries, culminating in regimes such as those in Prussia under a succession of four kings who ruled from 1640 through 1780 and in France during the reign of Louis XIV and his successors from the middle part of the seventeenth century to the French Revolution. These regimes were made possible by successful efforts to vest sovereignty in the monarch (partly by citing the Roman imperial precedent); by exploiting powers of taxation to secure resources of the monarchy; by adopting mercantilism as basic policy for the control of economic activities; and by expanding, centralizing, and professionalizing governmental administration.[16]

Such monarchies were dominant in continental Europe during the period when the United States gained independence, experimented under the Articles of Confederation, adopted the 1787 Constitution, and installed the initial national system of administration. They were natural reference points for reactions, both negative and positive. With regard to constitutional issues, they naturally were viewed almost universally as models to be avoided rather than emulated. As exemplars of administration, they received a mixed reaction both initially and later on. Hamilton's administrative doctrines, which emphasized executive energy, responsibility and power and which led to the crucial decision during Washington's presidency to have the central government create its own agencies of administration rather than rely on state agencies, reflect his basic acceptance of the European pattern. Jefferson, on the other hand, repeatedly warned against such European models, identified centralized government with arbitrariness and oppression, advocated narrow limits for the range of government programs, and condemned steps taken by the national government during the first decade after adoption of the constitution as an intrusion on states' rights.[17] During the terms of Jefferson and his successors early in the nineteenth century, patterns of administration were gradually changed so that by the time Tocqueville arrived as a foreign observer in the 1830s Jeffersonian preferences had largely replaced those of Hamilton.

Revived interest in and acceptance of the administrative achievements of these European monarchies came when the American administrative state was taking shape in the late nineteenth century, receiving special attention in the writings of Woodrow Wilson.[18]   He regarded the systematic study of administration as a recent phenomenon which had produced a "science of administration" as the latest fruit of a much older "science of politics."   Credit had to be given primarily to Europeans in Germany and France for this "foreign science" employing only "foreign tongues."   The lead had been taken by governments with rulers who were absolute but enlightened.   Hence this science was "adapted to the needs of a compact state, and made to fit highly centralized forms of government. . . ." Wilson cited Prussia under Frederick the Great and his successors as the prime example where administration had been "most studied and most nearly perfected."   His second example was French administration derived from the French monarchy and recast by Napoleon as an absolute ruler.

A cardinal point in Wilson's presentation was that a democratic country such as the United States could safely utilize the administrative science developed by absolutist regimes without running the risk of becoming like them politically as well.   Conceding that the United States would not want "Prussia's history for the sake of having Prussia's administrative skill," he saw no such risk and urged no delay in "naturalizing this much-to-be-desired science of administration."   The recurring American interest in administrative science, although taking varied forms, has its source in the experience of these European monarchies.

The British Polity

Among external influences, those of British origin have been cumulatively most important.   Over the whole course of American constitutional and administrative development, Great Britain has been a prime role model, parent figure, and source of political ideas.   Both the constitutional and administrative systems in the United States reflect dependence upon, rebellion against, and deliberate modification of British precedents.

Caldwell identifies three pre-independence sources for American political and administrative institutions and practices: English laws and history, colonial experience, and "the general body of political thought and theories pertaining to the republics of classical antiquity."[19] The first two of these ensured that the initial constitutional and administrative arrangements in the United States would be variations on the British pattern and that the two systems would be more alike than different.

The main political changes from the British model which were incorporated in the U.S. Constitution are familiar and need not be discussed in detail. They include substitution of a republic for the monarchy, a federal system for a unitary one, and a constitutionally-based separation of powers for parliamentary supremacy. The list of political and institutional continuities is longer and probably more significant, including as it does such items as the English common law tradition, the concept of limits on the scope of government authority contained in contractual agreements between rulers and ruled, representation through officials chosen by popular election, and guarantees of individual rights against governmental encroachment.[20]

Samuel P. Huntington makes a strong case that one episode in English history—the Puritan Revolution of the mid-seventeenth century—deserves special attention as pivotal in understanding the origins of American politics. Calling it "the single most important formative event of American political history," he asserts that "Puritan radicalism spread and diffused to become the core of a credo for a new society. England had a Puritan revolution without creating a Puritan society; America created a Puritan society without enduring a Puritan revolution." American Protestantism, according to this view, has evolved in such a way that nowhere else in the world "are church and state more firmly separated institutionally and religious and political ideas and symbols more closely interwoven in national beliefs." The recurring periods of "creedal passion" that have become part of the pattern of American politics are thus traced to the English Puritan Revolution.[21]

Historian Henry Steele Commager may have overstated the point when he said at the time of the bicentennial of the American Revolution that "every major political institution that we have today was invented before the year 1800,"[22] but the major constitutional and political borrowing that we did from Great Britain does seem to have occurred by that time.

With regard to administrative emulation, the situation is different. According to Barry D. Karl, "the British may have had more persistent impact as a greater variety of levels" in influencing American administrative theory and practice than any other foreign source.[23] He gives some illustrations, without attempting to provide a complete catalogue. Leonard White also has pointed out the significance of English forms and procedures and has provided instances of reliance on them during the Federalist and Jacksonian periods. Undoubtedly the most dramatic and far-reaching example of what Paul Van Riper calls "Americanizing a foreign invention" was the civil service reform movement which culminated in adoption of the Pendleton Act in 1883. These efforts consisted essentially of adapting to the American scene the results of British experience following the Northcote-Trevelyan reforms of the 1850s.[24] A more current instance of this continuing reliance on British civil service precedents was the establishment in 1978 of the Senior Executive Service, after several earlier unsuccessful efforts along the same lines.

Contemporary Nation-States

The United States has deservedly been called the "first new nation,"[25] but its birth was soon followed by the post-revolution transformation in France which replaced the monarchy with the nation as the source of legitimacy, and since the late eighteenth century the number of such modern political entities has grown to more than 150 in the world today, with the most rapid rate of increase taking place since World War II. Presumably these contemporary nations might, during the course of American history, have been a source of both constitutional and administrative borrowing by the United States, but the record indicates that this has been so only to a quite limited extent and that it has been mostly confined to the field of administration.

The United States Constitution often became a model for constitution making elsewhere, but the American constitutional system as it has evolved has been little affected by foreign innovations.

On the administrative side, the situation is more complicated, although again overall the United States, in its relationships with contemporary nation-states, has been more of an exporter than an importer of administrative theory and technology. During the first century after independence, until the American administrative state had taken shape, there appears to have been a considerable interest in European practices which were regarded as more advanced and could be copied. Leonard White reported that during the Jacksonian period in particular "both Congress and the executive branch began to make specific investigations of foreign experience as a guide to administrative and technical improvement," and he gave numerous illustrations in such diverse fields as steam navigation safety, customs warehousing systems, operation of postal systems, and management of public printing.[26] The mid-nineteenth century civil service reform movement was probably the most impressive single instance of such borrowing and adaptation.

During the century of the American administrative state since the 1880s, this attitude of receptivity has waned except for sporadic examples such as the attraction in recent years to the institution of the Scandinavian ombudsman, interest shown in the operations of government corporations in countries where they have been more widely used than here, and recent attention given to management methods in Japan because of Japanese competitive successes. Instead, the United States became a source for the export of administrative technology, particularly through the massive technical assistance programs of the post-World War II years.

American Systems as Models

The constitutional and administrative amalgam which has been put together in the United States during the more than two centuries since independence consists of a complex of interdependent ingredients. Identification of the most important of these elements is no easy task, and analysts are likely to differ in their selections. In my view, the three most significant features are constitutionalism, federalism, and presidentialism.[27]

Emphasis on these features is not intended to downgrade the importance of others which might be included or substituted—such as, for example, separation of powers, judicial review, pluralism, natural rights of man, or limitations on governmental powers.[28]   Obviously, those chosen are in part dependent upon or require the existence of some of the other ingredients.   Presidentialism is a product of the separation of powers.   Judicial review rests on a claim that it is necessary to have a final arbiter for constitutional interpretation.   Individual rights need constitutional protection against invasion by the government of the day.   A federal system must be based on some prearrangements as to the distribution of governmental powers. And so forth.

A comparative perspective points toward this stress on constitutionalism, federalism, and presidentialism.   These elements, as well as some of the others mentioned, are not unique in the sense that they are found only in this country.   In fact, many of them can be discovered in numerous other contemporary nations.   This choice in a comparative analysis is based on two considerations.   One is that these aspects if the American experience are the ones that seem to have been most attractive as models to other countries in the shaping of their own constitutional and administrative systems.   The other is that the American amalgam is unique in the way these features have been blended and reblended during the course of national development, so that although some of these specific elements may be found elsewhere, they are unlikely to operate in identical ways.   Each of these dominant elements was the result of a deliberate choice in 1787 as to constitutional arrangements, and each has had an identifiable effect on the operation of the administrative system.   The exact meaning of these elements in the constitutional system has not remained constant over time, however, nor has their impact on the conduct of administration always been the same.

Constitutionalism

A constitution in the sense of a set of fundamental laws and principles guiding and controlling state operations exists in all present-day nations. American constitutionalism has the more precise meaning of a written constitutional document conferring and limiting governmental powers. The 1787 Constitution was the pioneering national effort at

constitutionalism in this sense, although of course it had
antecedents during colonial times and in the Articles of
Confederation.

This historical preference is in large part explained by
what seemed to be the essentiality of a written constitution
for installation and maintenance of the other two main
features of the constitutional system—federalism and the
separation of powers in the central government that
fostered presidentialism.

The fact that the Constitution of the United States is
by far the most long-lived example of constitutionalism is
partly because of its brevity and partly because of its
adaptability. Although only 26 formal amendments have
been added (the first ten almost immediately after adoption
of the Constitution), the meaning of key constitutional
provisions has changed over time through judicial
interpretations and reinterpretations. None of these
modifications, however, has altered the basic pattern. In
essence, the constitutional system has had two centuries of
continuity.

Although the American administrative system must
conform to constitutional requirements, remarkably little in
the document itself directly affects the pattern of public
administration. Constitutional responsibility is assigned to
the President as chief executive officer to ensure that the
laws be "faithfully executed" and the heads of major
executive departments are appointed (with Senate
confirmation) by and serve "at the pleasure" of the
President. The regular legislative process, involving both
Congress and the President, is used for most decisions
concerning the structure and management of administrative
agencies. These provisions raise no basic constitutional
barrier to change in the administrative system, so that even
such a major modification as creation of the "administrative
state" a century ago required no formal constitutional
amendment and could not be challenged successfully on
constitutional grounds.

During the last two centuries, the United States
Constitution has been the model for many written
constitutions adopted by other nations. Acceptance of the
concept of constitutionalism elsewhere may or may not have
meant inclusion of specific features of the American
Constitution. No detailed analysis of similarities and
differences can be attempted here. The most obvious

contrast between the American and other constitutions is its relative longevity. For example, the 1958 French Fifth Republic Constitution is the sixteenth during an almost identical period of two centuries since 1789, and the Bolivian Constitution of 1967, which has only intermittently actually been operative, is the sixteenth in that country since independence from Spain in 1825. Despite the popularity of the American Constitution as a model, its staying power has not been matched elsewhere.

Federalism

American federalism was the direct outgrowth of the failure of confederate arrangements under the Articles of Confederation. Based on the legitimizing concept of popular sovereignty, constitutional powers were conferred on both the national and the state governments, using a method of allocation which enumerated the powers of the national government, denied certain powers to both national and state governments, and reserved other powers to the states. Although this approach appeared and was undoubtedly originally intended to favor the states over the center, this advantage has been gradually overcome by judicial interpretation in response to the march of events. The long-range trend has been toward enhancement of the role of the national government and a growing intermingling of central and state government policies and programs. From the beginning, the national government has maintained its own administrative machinery rather than relying on state agencies for the execution of national policy, but in recent decades the operating administrative system has become a more and more complicated network of intergovernmental cooperative relationships.

Similar formal federal systems have been installed in only about one out of seven contemporary nations, and in some instances federalism is more a facade than a reality. But these countries tend to be both large in size and populous, covering over half the earth's territory and containing over a third of its people. The list contains nations as diverse as Australia and Canada within the British Commonwealth, the German Federal Republic in western Europe, the U.S.S.R., and numerous Third World countries (including Argentina, Brazil, Mexico, India, Nigeria, and Tanzania). American federalism provided the prototype but many of these systems differ from the American model in significant respects, due either to initial intent or subsequent developments in the country concerned.[29]

Presidentialism

The presidency as an institution has become the most distinctive feature of both the American constitutional and administrative systems. Presidentialism is the indirect consequence of acceptance by American constitution makers of Montesquieu's doctrine of a tripartite separation of governmental powers into legislative, executive, and judicial branches. As the elected head of the executive branch, the president of the United States has emerged,due to the constitutional scope of the office and the course of national development, as an extremely powerful force in both political and administrative affairs.

This has happened even though the presidency as an institution has had its ups and downs as the executive branch has competed for power and with the legislative and judicial branches. Presidential prerogatives have been enhanced during times of crisis and during the terms of individuals who have been "strong" presidents. Perhaps the greatest contrast to date is between the "congressional government" of the post-Civil War period and the "imperial presidency" of the late 1960s and early 1970s. As this century draws to a close, the trend lines are unclear as to the future of presidentialism, even in the United States. The presidential system is not likely to be abandoned, but in operation it has demonstrated weaknesses which will demand attention and possible reform. Presidentialism is the element in the American constitutional-administrative amalgam that is most vulnerable and most subject to future change.

Meanwhile, presidentialism has been the American governmental innovation most widely copied or adapted on a global basis, particularly by nations of the Third World, over 30 of which now have presidential constitutions. Among democratic regimes, the presidential and parliamentary options are the primary alternatives for allocating policy-making authority and assigning responsibility for administrative implementation, with the mixed parliamentary-presidential system pioneered by the French Fifth Republic as a third possibility. These presidential democracies have included developing countries such as Costa Rica and Venezuela for some time, with others such as Argentina, Brazil, and Uruguay being added more recently. However, a considerably larger number of Third World countries with presidential constitutions in fact have had or now have authoritarian or at best semi-competitive regimes, including numerous African nations and such Latin American countries as Paraguay, Chile, and Mexico. Clearly, in many instances, other nations have adopted presidential systems constitutionally patterned after the American model, without success in making the system function as it does in the United States. Presidentialism will be even more on trial in the future in such settings than in the country where it originated.[30]

Comparative Relationships

In summary, a transition has occurred over time in the relationship between American constitutional and administrative systems and their foreign counterparts. During the formative stage of American institutions and practices, external influences were exerted from numerous historical and contemporary sources. When these were combined with even more powerful internal forces, the result was a distinctly American product, with features unlike any foreign precedents or counterparts. In turn, American innovations (particularly in constitutionalism, federalism, and presidentialism) became models for other countries, often with unanticipated consequences differing from experience in the United States. This record indicates that although initially external factors affect the formation of national constitutional and administrative systems, each nation can be expected to put its own imprint on foreign institutions and practices whether they are inherited, imposed, borrowed, or adapted.

ENDNOTES

1. Major sources on these factors include: Louis Hartz, *The Liberal Tradition in America* (New York: Harcourt Brace Jovanovich, 1955); James E. Anderson, *Politics and the Economy* (Boston: Little, Brown & Co., 1966); Samuel P. Huntington, *American Politics: The Promise of Disharmony* (Cambridge: Harvard University Press, 1981); Kenneth M. Dolbeare, *American Public Policy: A Citizen's Guide* (New York: McGraw-Hill, 1982); Frederick C. Mosher, *Democracy and the Public Service*, 2nd ed. (New York: Oxford University Press, 1982); Douglas Yates, *Bureaucratic Democracy: The Search for Democracy and Efficiency in American Government* (Cambridge: Harvard University Press, 1982); Don K. Price, *America's Unwritten Constitution* (Baton Rouge: Louisiana State University Press, 1983); Barry D. Karl, *The Uneasy State* (Chicago: The University of Chicago Press, 1983); Robert H. Horwitz, ed., *The Moral Foundations of the American Republic*, 3rd ed. (Charlottesville: The University Press of Virginia, 1985); and John A. Rohr, *To Run a Constitution: The Legitimacy of the Administrative State* (Lawrence: University Press of Kansas, 1986).

2. For example, see Paul P. Van Riper, "The Politics-Administration Dichotomy: Concept or Reality?" in Jack Rabin and James S. Bowman, eds., *Politics and Administration: Woodrow Wilson and the Study of Public Administration* (New York: Marcel Dekker, Inc., 1984), pp. 203-218; and Kent A. Kirwan, "Woodrow Wilson and the Study of Public Administration: Response to Van Riper," 21 pp. mimeo, prepared for the annual meeting of the American Political Science Association in New Orleans, September 1, 1985.

3. Matthew A. Crenson, *The Federal Machine: Beginnings of Bureaucracy in Jacksonian America* (Baltimore: The Johns Hopkins University Press, 1975).

4.   Stephen Skowronek, *Building a New American State: The Expansion of National Administrative Capacities, 1877-1920* (Cambridge: Cambridge University Press, 1982).

5.   Morton J. Frisch has provided an informative analysis of the views of all three in "The Constitutional Understanding of Thomas Jefferson," 7 pp. mimeo, prepared for the annual meeting of the American Political Science Association in New Orleans, August 31, 1985.

6.   For an exploration of differences on constitutional and administrative issues between the Founding Fathers and leaders of the Progressive era such as Wilson, see Jeffrey Leigh Sedgwick, "Of Centennials and Bicentennials: Reflections on the Foundations of American Public Administration," 17 pp. mimeo, prepared for the annual meeting of the American Political Science Association in New Orleans, August 29-September 1, 1985.

7.   See Henry A. Turner, "Woodrow Wilson as an Administrator," 32 pp. mimeo, prepared for the annual conference of the American Society for Public Administration in Anaheim, April 13-16, 1986.

8.   For a brief historical review, see Ferrel Heady, *Public Administration: A Comparative Perspective*, 3d ed., rev. (New York: Marcel Dekker, Inc., 1984), Chapter 4. The only comprehensive historical account (in two volumes) is E.N. Gladden, *A History of Public Administration* (London: Frank Cass, 1972).

9.   No. 18 of the *Federalist Papers* contains this analysis; Nos. 19 and 20 were devoted to more recent confederations in Germany, Poland, Switzerland, and the Netherlands.

10. Letter to Edward Carrington, August 4, 1787, *The Works of Thomas Jefferson*, Paul Leicester Ford, ed. (New York: G.P. Putnam's Sons, 1904), vol. V, p. 318.

11. Lynton K. Caldwell, *The Administrative Theories of Hamilton and Jefferson* (Chicago: University of Chicago Press, 1944), pp. 142-145.

12. Reinhard Bendix, *Nation-Building and Citizenship* (New York: John Wiley & Sons, Inc., 1964), p. 101.

13. Alexis de Tocqueville, *Democracy in America*, J.P. Mayer, ed. (Garden City, NY: Doubleday & Company, Inc., 1969), p. 509.

14. Hartz, *op. cit.*, pp. 9, 35, 61, 62.

15. Huntington, *op. cit.*, pp. 39-41.

16. For a general overview, refer to Ernest Barker, *The Development of Public Services in Western Europe* (London: Oxford University Press, 1944); for details with regard to England, see G. R. Elton, *The Tudor Revolution in Government* (Cambridge: Cambridge University Press, 1962).

17. For specifics, refer to Caldwell, *The Administrative Theories of Hamilton and Jefferson, op. cit.*, pp. 126-137.

18. I have written a more detailed analysis of Wilson as a comparativist in the study of administration, which will be included in Part VI, Chapter 15, "Comparative Public Administration," in a forthcoming volume, *A Centennial History of the American Administrative State*, edited by Ralph C. Chandler (New York: The Macmillan Company, 1987).

19. Lynton K. Caldwell, "Novus Ordo Seclorum: The Heritage of American Public Administration," *Public Administration Review*, vol. 29 (September/October 1976), pp. 476-488, at p. 477.

20. The relationship of American to British constitutional development has been recently reviewed by J. R. Pole in *The Gift of Government: Political Responsibility from the English Restoration to American Independence* (Athens: The University of Georgia Press, 1983).

21.   Huntington, *op. cit.*, pp. 153, 154, 158.

22.   "America's Impact on the World 1776-1976: The Revolution as a World Ideal," *Saturday Review* (December 13, 1975), p. 110.

23.   "Public Administration and American History: A Century of Professionalism," *Public Administration Review*, vol. 36 (September/October 1976), pp. 489-503, at p. 493.

24.   Full details are provided by Van Riper in his *History of the United States Civil Service* (Evanston, IL, and White Plains, NY: Row, Peterson and Company, 1958).

25.   Seymour Martin Lipset, *The First New Nation; The United States in Historical and Comparative Perspective* (New York: Basic Books, 1963).

26.   *The Jacksonians* (New York: The Macmillan Company, 1956), pp. 531-533.

27.   A fuller treatment of these features considered comparatively is in a chapter on public administration in the United States which I have written for inclusion in a forthcoming volume, *Public Administration in Developed Democracies*, edited by Donald C. Rowat (Monticello, NY: Marcel Dekker, 1987).

28.   See Carl J. Friedrich, *The Impact of American Constitutionalism Abroad* (Boston: Boston University Press, 1967).

29.   For recent summaries of some of these variations, refer to Gabriel A. Almond and G. Bingham Powell, Jr., eds., *Comparative Politics Today*, 3d ed. (Boston: Little, Brown and Company, 1984), pp. 98-101.

30.   See Fred W. Riggs, "Bureaucratic Power and Administrative Change," in Karl W. Deutsch and Mattei Dogan, eds., *Interplay of Similarities and Contrasts Among Nations* (Berkeley: University of California Press), in press.

CHAPTER TWO

Doctrines and Developments: Separation of Powers, the Politics–Administration Dichotomy, and the Rise of the Administrative State

LAURENCE J. O'TOOLE, JR.*

During the last century, two of the most important ideas of American government have repeatedly crossed paths. The venerable notion of separation of powers, borrowed and amplified by the founders from some classic themes of Western political thought, has had to confront the rise of the administrative state in the United States in a period when the politics-administration dichotomy in its various forms was employed to explain, justify, and advance fundamental changes in the nation's living constitution. This essay explores the interplay between the two, with the object of helping to clarify the place of administration in the nation's public life.

Separation of powers, an idea crystallized at the time of Montesquieu and even before, is not, of course, the only important principle imbedded in the American constitutional framework; but it has certainly been one of the most significant for administration. Yet among the framers there

---

* **Laurence J. O'Toole, Jr.,** is Professor of Political Science at Auburn University. His primary research interests include the history and theory of American public administration, implementation, and regulatory administration.

were discernable differences in emphasis—for example, in the eloquent but not entirely consistent disquisitions by Madison and Hamilton in *The Federalist*, and in the heated debates at the constitutional convention itself.[1]

The first articles of the constitution clearly delineate three branches of the national government and assign apparently-distinct functions to each.   Much of that fundamental document, however, indicates the multitudinous fashions in which the separateness of these powers, or at least of the three institutions, is softened by the need for joint action.   As the political currents were to change thereafter, so the different branches would rise or decline in initiative and primacy.

What the founders did not much specify formally was the place of administration in this arrangement.   Although the subject was significantly addressed in *The Federalist*,[2] it is frequently noted that the word administration does not appear in the constitution.   The basic document makes reference to "executive departments" (Article II, Section 2) but indicates nothing about their functions or any prescribed patterns for supervision.

In the first decades of the new nation's existence there certainly were clashes between the branches on many matters, from political appointments to judicial review. However, for the most part the activities of U.S. administrative agencies were not a prime focus of these actions.   As the nineteenth century wore on, however, and especially as the problems with the patronage system became more apparent and the perception of a need for skillful administration grew among the reformers, the hallowed doctrine of separation of powers began to receive reexamination and some critique.

By the late nineteenth century, Congress was ascendant.   Hamilton's admonitions notwithstanding, there had been a succession of weak Presidents; the national legislature, through its committee system, the House Speaker, and the chamber's detailed involvement in patronage, appropriations, and administrative affairs, was without doubt preeminent—even if widely regarded as of marginal competence and propriety.[3]

Yet, as students of public administration are well aware, near the turn of the century a series of reforms created fundamental alterations.   These signalled and helped to promote the rise of the administrative state, and they often constituted efforts to emphasize the executive at all levels in the system. Indeed, as Waldo observed nearly 40 years ago, "Generally speaking, students of administration have been hostile to the tripartite separation of powers."[4] Yet the realities of the American context—including the continuing attractiveness of the pluralist ideal,[5] the institutional jealously of Congress and other American legislature, and the pull of grass-roots rhetoric with its critique of the implicit elitism in the thrust for reform—meant that the rise of the administrative state in this nation accompanied no radical weakening of the legislature or the salience of representativeness.[6] Instead, many of the most significant policies contributing to the emergence of modern public administration either were ambiguous on the separation of powers issue or explicitly incorporated a consideration of the legislature into plans for strengthening the executive. In fact, the rise of the administrative state occurred ironically: the reformers, many of whom had little patience with the classic doctrine of separation of powers and sought instead a politics-administration distinction, actually achieved a restoration of some power to a branch weak at that time (the executive) and, thus, a reinvigoration of the interbranch competition that had frustrated them.

Yet it would be too simple to portray the movement for public administration as an effort by reformers to assist the executive in reasserting authority by invoking the politics-administration dichotomy. Even the earliest self-conscious students of administration attempted to develop some rather sophisticated perspectives on politics-administration and separation of powers (see below). Furthermore, especially after the early efforts and certainly by the 1920s and the 1930s, some prominent exponents of reform linked the operations of the growing administrative state most directly to the authority and supervision of the legislature.[7] W. F. Willoughby, one of the experts on administrative thought during the early twentieth century, forcefully developed this position.[8] The most obvious overt conflict between the two groups of administrative experts, asserting executive or legislative eminence respectively, occurred over the reorganization proposals fostered by Roosevelt in the 1930s and supported by his Committee on Administrative Management. The consideration of this set of recommendations featured a rival study conducted under the Brookings Institution's auspices and reaching—from the supposedly identical administrative science—markedly different conclusions about the structure of federal administration.[9]

The important points for present purposes are these: the framers created a certain ambivalence in the status and direction of American public administration. At the time of the rise of the administrative state, this ambivalence—when combined with the power of Congress and the set of problems and challenges confronting the nation—fueled among reformers a dissatisfaction with prevailing doctrine though no revolutionary fervor to upset the overall system.[10] The leaders of the movement focused upon a distinction between politics and administration as a way both to render comprehensible and also, it must be said, to legitimate the unmistakable phenomenon before them. The bulk of the literature and the movement nurtured executive power in this context, though this was not a unanimously-held position. The politics-administration framework seemed to hold the promise of uniting the reformers. As indicated below, some of the major policies that helped to institutionalize the American administrative state are buttressed by the dichotomy even when they do not consistently support a strengthened executive.

To develop some understanding of the impact of these two venerable doctrines on the important developments of the past century, I first briefly survey how the reformers of the American public administration movement dealt with the separation of powers principle and fashioned the distinction between politics and administration, and then see how these ideas operated as several of the most important national policies of the administrative state were established. This essay closes with some observations on the current status of these constructs and on the theory and practice of American public administration.

Politics and Administration

So much has been said on the subjects of politics and administration, and the links and distinctions between these, that in an essay of this size and scope the issues cannot be adequately summarized—let alone settled. One can only tough lightly on a few major ideas.

The most significant point is that at the time of the movement for administrative reform the concept of an analytical distinction between politics and administration seemed sensible and enlightening to many. The division was, roughly, between deciding and executing. It was easy for matters quickly to become more complicated, however. The notion of "politics," even as utilized by seminal thinkers, was often employed ambiguously (sometimes referring to mere partisanship, for instance in rhetoric on civil service reform).[11] The boundary between political and administrative functions was sometimes, especially later, crudely interpreted as a suggestion that the two functions could be separated into distinct institutions—an idea different from those expressed in some of the early classic works. Also, many advocates of the politics-administration distinction did not really assume that there was or could ever be a strict dichotomy between the two; rather, they asserted even in the era of orthodoxy that these blend and mix in complex fashions.[12]

Still, at a time when the separation of powers seemed a source of some of the difficulties plaguing public service, the dichotomy in its less rigid form appeared as an innovative and promising development. Even a crude version could provide some support for the emergence of the administrative state, and many of the early thinkers developed more discerning analyses. This construct seemed a way to show how some traditionally worthy goals could be achieved in an era during which government seemed threatened by the forces of mass-based democracy, crude partisanship, and political infighting.

This type of argument, that there could be identified two distinguishable spheres of government, one of which could be significantly "removed from the hurry and strife of politics"[13] and handled through the application of technique toward the ends of efficient and wise public action, attracted disparate followers. In his famous *Politics and Administration*, Goodnow attacked the traditional separation of powers; and argued that "there are two distinct functions of government, and . . . their differentiation results in a differentiation, though less complete, of the organs of government provided by the formal governmental system." For Goodnow, *some* aspects of administration "should be subjected to the control of the function of politics" (ultimately via political parties), but "the fact is . . . that there is a large part of administration which is unconnected with politics, which should therefore be relieved very largely, if not altogether, from the control of political bodies."[14] W. F. Willoughby, though convinced that in Congress lay the source of administrative authority and though desirous of developing a case that the American government was actually a composite of five, not three, powers, also reached a position similar to that of other reformers on the dichotomy issue: administration could be usefully distinguished from executive and other clearly political functions; and certain reforms intended to rationalize and depoliticize administration were worth supporting.[15]

Despite the rhetorical ammunition directed against the traditional version of the separation of powers idea, however, the reformers may have been less exercised about the presumed flaws in the handiwork of the founders than about nineteenth-century political developments: the evolving role of parties in the system, the shifts in control between branches, the development of a strong and yet fragmented committee system in Congress, and the apparent inattention to the increased national responsibilities that seemed so obvious to the reformers themselves. These developments were not foreordained by the framing document generally or the separation of powers doctrine itself. Instead, they comprised part of the fabric of the nation's "unwritten constitution" of the period.[16]

Focusing on the weakness of conventional formulations of the separation of powers argument and finding common ground in support for the dichotomy, many of the reformers used a simple version of the newer doctrine to help support a variety of administrative developments. Yet, as is clear from the examples discussed below, *both* constructs influenced the actual shape of these innovations.

The Pendleton Act

Perhaps nowhere are both the congruence and the tension between these two crucial constructs more apparent than in what is often regarded as the first major national policy on administrative reform, the Pendleton or Civil Service Act of 1883.

This law, of course, was neither the first nor the last word on federal personnel policy. Some notions of merit played a part in executive appointments from the earliest days of the republic. Also, even during the bleakest times of the spoils period, there were halting efforts toward improvement. (In 1871, for instance, legislation authorized the President to establish regulations for a merit system; the attempt was abortive.) On the other hand, the mere enactment of the official policy embodied in the Pendleton Act guaranteed nothing. Proponents struggled for decades before it became clear that the system would have some permanence.[17] Nevertheless, by authorizing a competitively-selected merit system, limiting the political activity allowed therein, allocating responsibility for administration of the process to a Civil Service Commission insulated from the chief executive while also authorizing some presidential role in the personnel function, the United States established a unique and unmistakably American framework—one that provided elements of support for *both* separation of powers and the dichotomy.

How? For decades before Pendleton, President and Congress had been tied in a viselike grip both to each other and to the process of personnel appointments. Neither could afford to neglect the opportunities occasioned by the flood of patronage, nor could their parties. Yet the selection process became increasingly burdensome with the passage of time and growth in bureaucracy. The struggles between the two branches, which reached constitutional proportions at the time of the impeachment of Andrew Johnson, threatened to grow worse.

Allen Schick has commented with regard to presidential-congressional relations in more recent times that although "divided political leadership" and "pervasive mistrust of executive power" stimulate the legislature to seek control, "neither Congress nor the Executive Branch relishes perpetual collision."[18] Civil service reform, by relieving both branches simultaneously though gradually of the patronage function, allowed for each to retreat to a more tolerable—even if uncertain—stance. Thus, although the Act represented "the first institutional recognition of the President" as "the active head of the administrative system,"[19] reform also helped to preserve a separation of powers.

The 1883 action also and even more obviously represented an effort to enact the dichotomy. By insulating through the commission mechanism the civil service and various aspects of its administration from the overtly political actors in government, the Pendleton Act erected a kind of politics-administration border. Although the legislation did not establish a presumption in favor of lifetime government careers for merit appointees, it did distinguish positions tied to political matters from those administrative openings to be filled by competitive exams. Furthermore, the Act provided authority by which later presidents were able to restrict the political activities of civil servants, far in advance of the Hatch Acts (see below). The 1883 reforms did decisively initiate the decline of federal patronage and the gradual weakening of party machines on a national scale. *Partisan* politics was no longer to be inextricably tied to the country's administrative apparatus; and thus the goal of a civil service of elevated moral status, if not one designed carefully after the British model or one engineered for effective management,[20] seemed within reach.

In short, therefore, the single change enacted through Pendleton worked simultaneously to advance several aims. Kaufman's analysis of the cycles of American public administration makes reference to three core values that have been differentially prominent in various historical periods.[21] Civil service abetted two of these, executive leadership and neutral competence, as well as helped to reinvigorate separation of powers. The civil service system, revised and reviled though it has been, has thus hewn true to several salient political ideals.

The Budget and Accounting Act of 1921

The legislative event that triggered the modernization of the nation's system of public finances, the Budget and Accounting Act of 1921, has been characterized by one authority as "probably the greatest landmark of our administrative history except for the Constitution itself."[22]

Why might this significance be attributed to such a policy? The system for handling *any* nation's public fiscal policy is bound to be important, of course, and the U.S. had entered this century as the only major Western industrial country without a real budget. The American treasury, long unstrained by demands placed upon it, had finally begun to sink into frequent deficit near the end of the nineteenth century. And a decision on this subject would necessitate a reconsideration of some fundamental, constitutionally-based principles like separation of powers and the proper place of administration in the political system.

Congress was charged by the founders with the lead responsibility in this sphere (Article I, Sections 7-9) and remained understandably protective of the jurisdiction. Through the nineteenth century and until the reform period itself, budget requests of individual agencies found their way to Congress without coordination or alteration by the executive.[23] For a portion of the 1800s, Congress sought a rational appropriations process by establishing a central committee jurisdiction for crucial spending decisions, but late in the century that had given way to multiple fiefdoms even within the House itself.

The impetus for financial reform at the national level was the strongly-felt need for a budget. As with civil service reform, part of the stimulus for this later idea arose from a concern about corruption—in this case, initially, municipal corruption. The desire was to attack this problem by strengthening city executives, in general and especially on budget matters; the effort fed a growing movement on the national level.[24]

The last and most important of several study groups on the budget matter was President Taft's Commission on Economy and Efficiency, appointed in 1910. Its membership included several prominent figures in the movement for reform, including such stalwarts as Frederick A. Cleveland of the New York Bureau of Municipal Research, Frank Goodnow, and W. F. Willoughby. The Commission reported, predictably, in favor of the executive budget, but the report said virtually nothing about the role of the legislature.

The proposal encountered resistance in Congress. For years the issue remained on the national agenda. Some support for the executive budget was maintained by the two major political parties, and the Institute for Government Research (later renamed Brookings), under Willoughby's direction, produced studies and publications promoting the idea. Finally, Congress acted. In 1919 congressional hearings were conducted on budget legislation, and the House (in 1920) and Senate (1922) reorganized themselves internally for more coordinated legislative consideration of money matters   On the subject of the reform legislation, "the principal advocate outside the Congress was unquestionably W. F. Willoughby," who had also done much of the drafting of the major proposals under consideration; in 1920, a reform package was lopsidedly supported in Congress, partially because of public support and despite misgivings voiced by a number of lawmakers about granting such a role to the President in the budget process.[25]   That earlier reformer Woodrow Wilson, who had become President, vetoed the measure out of a concern about the possible unconstitutionality of a provision limiting his removal power over a new officer, a comptroller general. In the following year, after the election of Warren Harding, a similar bill was enacted.

The legislation not only established an executive budget but also aimed at reorganizing and strengthening another aspect of national policy. Since the first years of the republic, the responsibility for ensuring accountability in the exercise of federal spending power had had its locus in the Department of the Treasury. The new policy shifted these existing activities to a General Accounting Office (GAO) to be headed by a comptroller general appointed by the president for a fixed single term of 15 years and held directly answerable to Congress.

The Act required an annual executive budget to be proposed by the president to Congress. Assisting in this task would be a Bureau of the Budget within Treasury (later moved to the Executive Office of the President). The law also required GAO audits of agencies, thus effectively removing this function from the executive. The importance of this portion of the policy, then, lay not in the activities it authorized but in the seriousness with which it invested the separation of powers concept itself.   As Mosher recapitulates on the matter of the independent audit, "this idea was a latecomer, added probably to gain congressional support as a counterbalance to the granting of powers and staff to the president for initiating the budget."[26]

In fact, this aspect of the policy proved in practice to be no mere sop to parochial legislative interests. The Act conferred a broad grant of authority to the Office, not only a licence to conduct audits. Today the GAO is nine times as large as the somewhat more heralded OMB, and the former performs analyses and studies that can have a profound impact on federal policy.[27]

This law was thus crafted by and approved with the support of those who were protective of legislative prerogatives and the separation of powers principle more generally, as well as reformers who sought unsullied administration and an enlarged sphere for a strengthened executive. That the new law represented a careful, perhaps tentative, melding of these potentially-contradictory elements is demonstrated in the person of its major author, Willoughby. For he, as indicated earlier, had developed views on the separation of powers doctrine that both accorded a major role to Congress in the conduct of the nation's affairs and also identified the task of administration as one that "strictly speaking involves the making of no decisions of a political character."[28]

In this fashion, then, by institutionalizing administrative expertise reporting to both the executive and legislature, the Act sought a reconciliation between these two important principles. That these early reformers were unsuccessful in effecting a permanent resolution of such complex questions—as future controversies and actions like impoundment, off-budget decision-making, congressional budget reform, and the contemporary separation-of-powers furor over Gramm-Rudman attest—is not to slight their efforts or the importance of their product, which remains the nation's fundamental policy statement on this subject.

The Hatch Acts

Civil service reform as enacted in 1883 was designed to square with multiple values and to embrace divergent tendencies. One of the concerns addressed in that policy was political neutrality for the nation's civil servants. Neutrality seemed an almost-necessary component of the politics-administration dichotomy as applied to personnel matters; and, as discussed above, neutrality on matters of partisanship held the prospect of helping to disentangle the legislature and executive from the ultimately-unproductive patronage struggle.

The Pendleton Act had established rules detailing the proscribed political activities of those in the executive service, and the law authorized the President to formulate

regulations for members of the competitive service as well.
In 1907, President Theodore Roosevelt approved Civil Service
Rule I, which constrained the permissible political activities
of those in the protected service.

That some of these restrictions were aimed at real
abuses by candidates and the major parties is beyond
doubt.[29] And it is important to note the context of these
limitations. *Any* effort to regulate the political activities of
civil servants is likely to spring in significant measure from
the desire to separate politics in a policy-determining sense
from administration. (The British system, for instance,
entails restrictions designed to control the inappropriate
expression of partiality deep within the bureaucratic
apparatus, while still allowing civil servants substantial
freedom for political expression.) The uniquely American
approach to the neutrality question, on the other hand, can
only be understood as an effort to incorporate a dichotomy
that would also deal with partisanship from the political
branches.

By the 1930s, the regulations enacted near the turn of
the century had generated thousands of cases requiring
rulings by the Commission, and emerging from this plethora
of individual decisions was an elaborate and complex policy
on the subject of the political rights, protections, and
prohibitions of federal employees. Yet with the
developments accompanying the New Deal, this restrictive
stability was challenged. Many reports circulated of
partisan abuses, as the proportion of the bureaucracy
included in the protected service markedly declined.[30]

Anti-New Deal sentiment within Congress contributed
significantly to the backing for legislative proposals to deal
with the problem. The 1939 Hatch Act prohibited many
permanent federal employees from participating in certain
partisan political activities and also barred political
superiors from enticing or coercing partisan support from
the bureaucracy. In 1940 the Act was extended by
amendment, the most important aspect of which was to
include under federal restrictions the state and local
employees who helped to administer programs. Yet one
cannot interpret the Hatch Acts as a simple manifestation of
the anti-New Deal view. There seemed to be considerable
support for legitimating earlier practice into permanent and
more comprehensive legislation.[31] As part of the
congressional debates, serious consideration was given to

prohibiting only coerced, not voluntary, political activity on the part of federal employees. However, this option was narrowly defeated, a major concern being that it might be impossible to distinguish in practice between the two, thus allowing a loophole through which could slip the influence of partisanship once again.

The issue was not firmly settled by this enactment, however. Periodically, recommendations for dramatic relaxation of the policy have surfaced. Indeed, during the 1970s a major challenge was mounted against the Hatch Act. Reacting to persistent prodding from critics, including several public employee organizations, Congress in 1976 approved a significant weakening of the rules. Yet this measure was vetoed by President Gerald Ford, who expressed concern about the dangers of a politicized civil service. No other such initiative has been able to command the necessary support in Congress.

The Hatch Acts have stood the tests of time and constitutionality, despite long and heated arguments. Indeed, this is especially noteworthy, since it constitutes the "one major exception" to the Supreme Court's "reluctance to uphold flat, across-the-board special restrictions on [public employees'] rights."[32] Yet one could hardly say that consensus exists. The activity of public employee unions and organizations often flouts the Hatch Act restrictions. The fact that the policy clearly restricts constitutionally-established freedom of speech for one sizable category of citizens often stimulates resentment. Those who study the impact of this policy find much to criticize.[33] And while there has been no major overhaul of the Hatch Acts' policy of political neutrality, an attenuation of the policy's effects has occurred over time.[34] For instance, there are currently more than 3,000 noncareer executive branch appointments, a number substantially larger than in Britain, West Germany, Canada, or Australia; and only a minority of these involve policy-crucial responsibilities. The 1978 Civil Service Reform Act removed a number of central personnel controls and created a Senior Executive Service, 10 percent of which by law may consist of political appointees. Additionally, occasional efforts by political leaders, e.g., during the Nixon years or through the operations of the Office of Personnel Management under the Reagan administration, indicate the continuing appeal of the idea of a partisan civil service to those who would directly benefit. But there is no denying that the oft-maligned Hatch Acts and the predecessor regulations represent quite clearly an American effort to accommodate the neutrality goal, embraced by the politics-administration dichotomy, in a system of party competition, fragmentation, and separation of powers.

The Government Corporation Control Act of 1945

Typically neglected in analyses of the major policies that have institutionalized the American administrative state in the twentieth century is the Government Corporation Control Act. Perhaps this relative obscurity is fitting, since the point of the law was to come to grips with a sector of modern government that is itself frequently far removed from the limelight.

The New Deal period, which marked in many respects the fruition of the modern administrative state in the United States, spawned a large number of government corporations at the national level. There were numerous earlier examples, but this peculiar species was especially attractive during the 1930s, when the inauguration of many such experimental and innovative units seemed warranted by circumstances. Many varieties of the corporate form with numerous combinations of formal powers were used to address specific problems; yet as the structure was repeatedly adopted for use, the question of accountability presented itself.

In the vague policy context prior to legislation, a government corporation could be established without congressional approval. Given the substantial independence of which these units were capable, the possibility existed that the executive could utilize this mechanism to gain decisive influence and autonomy. Additionally, corporations held the potential to operate free of much oversight even from the President. For this reason especially, some of the major administrative examinations of the federal structure, such as those conducted by the Brownlow Committee and the first Hoover Commission, criticized corporate autonomy in the public sphere.

Establishing a corporation with substantial independence from the political branches and from the usual oversight procedures and policies provides an opportunity, at least, for administration to be exercised free of partisan considerations. But what of democratic government?[35] It is true that some early reformers were enthusiastic proponents of the independent government corporation. W. F. Willoughby sought to justify them by invoking Congress as the real authority and arguing that the executive ought to have no direct role.[36] Yet in practice, *neither* political organ was a channel of accountability. Even before the Roosevelt era the Supreme Court validated corporations' independence from the executive (via the Treasury) and the legislature (via GAO).[37] By executive order Roosevelt required the corporations to "submit their annual accounts to GAO,"[38] but most ignored the directive.

Legislative action to force some degree of uniformity and formal accountability was the consequence. The 1945 Act assisted the tasks of executive and legislature in their previously-established separate spheres of financial control, without stultifying the flexibility and independence that had allowed for "businesslike" exercise of administration. Under the terms of the policy, corporations typically must submit annual budget plans to Congress and must undergo the "normal" appropriations process to receive funds in excess of the generated revenues. The GAO conducts business-type audits (though the Office cannot disallow expenses) on an annual basis. And the Treasury oversees some aspects of how the corporations manage their funds.

Proponents of congressional control over administration and presidential subservience did not find the Act to their liking, some complaining that the law represented victory for the forces favoring executive integration and control.[39] Yet, through its execution, the advantages of the corporate form have been retained, while legitimate ties to the branches have also been developed. In this sphere, at least, the constructs have been reconciled in practice, and it is thus understandable that Seidman labelled the policy "one of the most significant developments in the art of public administration."[40]

Political Constructs and the Contemporary Administrative State: An Assessment

The bulk of this essay has been devoted to an examination of two doctrines that have markedly shaped the character of American administrative operations in the past.

Yet the fact that the analysis is so heavily based in history is not artifice of the present bicentennial occasion. It was during the rise of the administrative state—when constitutional principle faced the need to confront and adjust to circumstances—that the need for a political theory of American public administration seemed most sorely pressing. The reformers fashioned an administrative orthodoxy as they sought to deal with necessity. At the heart of that perspective was the politics-administration distinction, a construct *not* neatly consistent with the venerable separation of powers notion, but one innovative and compelling enough that those with different views about the operations of the governmental branches could reconcile those differences around the enactment of several basic policies that now form the core of the modern administrative system.

Today, nearly every student of American public administration is taught the bankruptcy of the simple version of the dichotomy. The prevailing view among constitutional experts is that focusing on the *separation* of powers in the national government's structure neglects the important reality of sharing.[41] Further, the administrative sphere is populated by regulatory agencies in which separation is even more a distortion than elsewhere. Also, some sophisticated students of contemporary American politics and administration note that there may be other separations or disjunctions in the structure of the government that are as important as the formally-established distinctions among the branches.[42]

In short, the dichotomy has collapsed; and despite new insights regarding separation of powers, theoretical advance has been relatively slight.[43] Yet, as this paper demonstrates, it would be incorrect to conclude that these constructs are merely fictions or dogmas that paraded as truths in an earlier era but have served no useful purpose. Rather, these ideas helped earlier generations of reformers fashion an administrative state that, despite its flaws, remains remarkably true to the American constitutional heritage and experience. The brief analyses of the policies referenced in this article suggest as much. As for improvements on this basic design? Progress of consequence would require some conscious attention to the political theory of public administration. Recent years have not been totally bereft of such efforts.[44] However, none has commanded the widespread support that would probably be necessary to effect significant redirection. As Mosher has observed, "on the theoretical plane, the finding of a viable substitute [for the dichotomy] may well be the number one problem of public administration today."[45]

The principles and ideas of earlier days have had an undeniable impact on the practice of public administration. Improvements in such practice must likely await, or accompany, theoretical developments as yet unforeseen. Meanwhile, it would be most unwise to take from our administrative history the lesson that since those ideas were flawed, nothing would be lost by dismantling the policies, practices, and institutions constructed on behalf of those notions. Recent unfortunate experience in such fields as personnel reform, e.g., the revisions in federal practice since 1978, suggests the wisdom of reexamining anew the historical and theoretical roots of the administrative state, especially with regard to their complex links with American constitutional development.[46] Far from being a sterile academic exercise, such retrospective examinations offer practical wisdom for those who seek resolution of some of the most vexing current difficulties.

ENDNOTES

1. For an illuminating discussion of the European origins of the separation of powers doctrine, especially as it emerged through the evolving notions of interests and their checks and balance in both political and economic spheres, see Albert O. Hirschman, *The Passions and the Interests: Political Arguments for Capitalism Before Its Triumph* (Princeton: Princeton University Press, 1977), esp. pp. 30-31.

2. John A. Rohr, *To Run a Constitution: The Legitimacy of the Administrative State* (Lawrence: University Press of Kansas, 1986). See especially *The Federalist Papers* (New York: Mentor, 1961), nos. 69-77.

3. E.g., Leonard D. White, *The Republican Era* (New York: Macmillan, 1958).

4. Dwight Waldo, *The Administrative State*, 2d ed. (New York: Holmes and Meier, 1984), pp. 104-105.

5. William E. Nelson, *The Roots of American Bureaucracy, 1830-1900* (Cambridge: Harvard University Press, 1982).

6. Cf. David H. Rosenbloom, "Public Administrative Theory and the Separation of Powers," *Public Administration Review*, vol. 43 (May/June 1983), pp. 219-27.

7. "This opinion distinguished between the presidential power to 'take care that the laws be faithfully executed' . . . and the actual execution of them, which, it held, is legally under the direction of Congress." Frederick C. Mosher, ed., *Basic Literature of American Public Administration, 1787-1950* (New York: Holmes & Meier, 1981), pp. 119.

8. See, e.g., *The Government of Modern States* (New York: Appleton-Century, 1919). He, however, was not alone. Willoughby, for instance, became director of Brookings, an institution that advocated the position of congressional primacy during the early period. Others, like Marshall Dimock, also became known for asserting and defending the administrative-legislative connection.

9. President's Committee on Administrative Management, *Report of the Committee* (Washington: Government Printing Office, 1937); U.S. Congress, Hearings before the Joint Committee on Government Organization, 75th Congress, 1st session, February-April 1937; see Barry D. Karl, *Executive Reorganization and Reform in the New Deal* (Cambridge: Harvard University Press, 1963). James Garnett's article in this issue of the *Review* focuses on the reorganization.

10. Laurence J. O'Toole, Jr., "American Public Administration and the Idea of Reform," *Administration and Society*, vol. 16 (August 1984), pp. 141-66. Cf. Stephen Skowronek, *Building a New American State: The Expansion of National Administrative Capacities,*

1877-1920 (Cambridge: Cambridge University Press, 1982).

11. Cf. Kent Aiken Kirwan, "The Crisis of Identity in the Study of Public Administration," *Polity*, vol. 9 (Spring 1977), pp. 321-43; and Paul P. Van Riper, "The American Administrative State: Wilson and the Founders—An Unorthodox View," *Public Administration Review*, vol. 43 (November/December 1983), pp. 477-90.

12. For instance, see Luther Gulick, "Politics, Administration, and the New Deal," *Annals*, vol. 169 (September 1933), pp. 55-66.

13. Woodrow Wilson, "The Study of Administration," *Political Science Quarterly*, vol. 2 (June 1887), pp. 197-222. Reprinted in vol. 56 (December 1941), p. 493.

14. *Politics and Administration* (New York: Russell and Russell, 1900), pp. 18, 78, 85.

15. *The Government of Modern States.*

16. Don K. Price, *America's Unwritten Constitution* (Baton Rouge: Louisiana State University Press, 1983), p. 9.

17. White, *The Republican Era*, pp. 279-87, 303-46. See also Paul R. Van Riper, *History of the United States Civil Service* (Evanston: Row, Peterson, 1958).

18. "Congress and the 'Details' of Administration," *Public Administration Review*, vol. 36 (September/October 1976), pp. 516-28.

19. White, *The Republican Era*, p. 346.

20. David H. Rosenbloom, "Politics and Public Personnel Administration: The Legacy of 1883," in Rosenbloom, ed., *Centenary Issues of the Pendleton Act of 1883* (New York: Marcel Dekker, 1982) p. 4; cf. Hugh Heclo, *A Government of Strangers* (Washington: Brookings, 1977). For an insightful discussion of the development of federal personnel policy, and in particular the tie between the commission form and American separation

of powers, see Chester A. Newland, "Crucial Issues for Public Personnel Professionals," *Public Personnel Management*, vol. 13 (1984), pp. 15-46.

21. Herbert Kaufman, "Administrative Decentralization and Political Power," *Public Administration Review*, vol. 29 (January/February 1969), pp. 3-15.

22. Herbert Emmerich, *Federal Organization and Administrative Management* (University: University of Alabama Press, 1971), pp. 40-41.

23. Jesse Burkhead, *Government Budgeting* (New York: Wiley, 1956), pp. 10-11; Louis Fisher, *Presidential Spending Power* (Princeton: Princeton University Press, 1975); and Frederick C. Mosher, *A Tale of Two Agencies* (Baton Rouge: Louisiana State University Press, 1984), p. 15. The extent of executive impotence in the national government at this time has sometimes been exaggerated. See e.g., Howard E. Shuman, *Politics and the Budget: The Struggle between the President and Congress* (Englewood Cliffs: Prentice-Hall, 1984), p. 23.

24. Burkhead, *Government Budgeting*, pp. 13-15, 17; Mosher, *Tale of Two Agencies*, p. 6.

25. Mosher, *Tale of Two Agencies*, pp. 27-28.

26. *Ibid.*, p. 3.

27. *U.S. Budget, 1986, Appendix* (Washington: Government Printing Office, 1985); Frederick C. Mosher, *The GAO* (Boulder: Westview, 1979); Mosher, *Tale of Two Agencies*; and Joseph Pois, *Watchdog of the Potomac* (Washington: University Press of America, 1979).

28. *Government of Modern States*, p. 385. On the first matter, he even explicitly drew the analogy that the legislature was like the board of directors for the United States, exercising "final authority" in a supervisory capacity. *Ibid.*, p. 351. Of course the influence of business and its ideas on the reformers and on the development of the dichotomy itself is

well-known.   See,   for   instance,   Waldo,   *The Administrative State*, pp. 38-39.

29. Otto Kirchheimer. "The Historical and Comparative Background of the Hatch Law," *Public Policy*, vol. 2 (1941 annual), p. 354.

30. See e.g., Leon D. Epstein, "Political Sterilization of Civil Servants: The United States and Great Britain," *Public Administration Review*, vol. 10 (Autumn 1950), p. 282.

31. Henry Rose, "A Critical Look at the Hatch Act," *Harvard Law Review*, vol. 75 (January 1962), pp. 510-26. See also Section 15 of the 1940 amendments.

32. David H. Rosenbloom, "Public Personnel Administration and the Constitution: An Emergent Approach," *Public Administration Review*, vol. 35 (January/February 1975), pp. 52-59.

33. E.g., Commission on Political Activity of Government Personnel, *A Commission Report*, 3 vols. (Washington: Government Printing Office, 1968). See also Charles O. Jones, "Reevaluating the Hatch Act: A Report on the Commission on Political Activity of Government Personnel," *Public Administration Review*, vol. 29 (May/June 1969), pp. 249-54.

34. Heclo, *A Government of Strangers*. It is worth noting that a careful examination of this question would require distinguishing foreign and domestic affairs. The relations between policy and administration in the two spheres is quite distinct, with the former more complex and confusing than even this discussion suggests.

35. Annmarie Hauck Walsh, *The Public's Business* (Cambridge: MIT Press, 1978), p. 38. Cf. Harold Seidman, "The Government Corporation: Organization and Controls," *Public Administration Review*, vol. 14 (Summer 1954), pp. 183-92; and Jameson W. Doig, "If I See a Murderous Fellow Sharpening a Knife Cleverly: The Wilsonian Dichotomy and the Public Authority

Tradition," in Jack Rabin and James S. Bowman, eds., *Politics and Administration* (New York: Marcel Dekker, 1984), pp. 175-99.

36. *Principles of Public Administration* (Baltimore: Johns Hopkins, 1927).

37. *Skinner and Eddy Corp. v. McCarl*, 275 U.S. 1 (1927).

38. Walsh, *The Public's Business*, p. 282.

39. For expressions of concern for preserving corporate autonomy see, e.g., C. Herman Pritchett, "The Paradox of the Government Corporation," *Public Administration Review*, vol. 1 (Summer 1941), pp. 381-89; and Marshall E. Dimock, "Government Corporations: A Focus of Policy and Administration, I and II," *American Political Science Review*, vol. 43 (October and December 1949), pp. 899-921, 1145-64.

40. Harold Seidman, "The Theory of the Autonomous Government Corporation: A Critical Appraisal," *Public Administration Review*, vol. 12 (Spring 1962), pp. 89-96. See also Seidman, *Politics, Position and Power*, 4th ed. (New York: Oxford University Press, 1986).

41. E.g., Louis Fisher, *The Politics of Shared Power* (Washington: Congressional Quarterly Press, 1981). Yet note that the decision rendering the one-house congressional veto unconstitutional, *Immigration and Naturalization Service v. Chadha*, 77 L. Ed. 2d 317 (1983), reinforces the continuing importance of separation of powers in the modern constitutional scheme.

42. See Henry J. Merry's analysis of *Five-Branch Government* (Urbana: University of Illinois Press, 1980). Cf. Heclo, *Government of Strangers*.

43. As Waldo has observed recently, "The period since the mid-1940s has not been an exciting one for theory that bears upon the separation of power, at least in any direct way." *Administrative State*, p. xlii.

44. Examples include the "new public administration" as well as the work of the public choice theorists.

45. *Democracy and the Public Service*, 2d. ed. (New York: Oxford University Press, 1982), p. 8.

46. Newland, "Crucial Issues," pp. 27-28.

CHAPTER THREE

The American Bureaucrat: A History of a Sheep in Wolves' Clothing

BARRY D. KARL[*]

For most of American history the terms "bureaucrat" and "bureaucracy" have been used in popular discourse as epithets, when they have been used at all. Although both terms have achieved a certain amount of academic credibility in American social science over the last 30 or 40 years, it is an acceptance which is grudging. That is true, in many respects, even in the worlds of political science and public administration where the influence of European theory since the end of World War II has brought about a broader understanding of comparative administrative practices. Nonetheless, in the sophisticated professions that now constitute the complex fields of journalism and political commentary the terms are part of a political language that has evolved in American political life. They evoke negative images. Even when they appear in debates that are ostensibly about deregulation and the role of the state in the life of the citizen, they are in fact expressions of an American suspicion of government that goes back to our

---

[*] Barry D. Karl is the Norman and Edna Freehling Professor of History at the University of Chicago. He is also a professor in the College and a member of the Committee on Public Policy Studies. He is the author of *Executive Reorganization and Reform in the New Deal, Charles E. Merriam and the Study of Politics*, and *The Uneasy State: The United States from 1915 to 1945.*

national origins. Americans believed that power was essentially corrupting long before Lord Acton articulated the idea for them; and "bureaucracy" is a term that can easily be used to describe the inherent corruption of power.

Revolutionary Origins: The Two Revolutions

The framers of the Constitution of 1787 and the authors of the *Federalist Papers* had already adopted British attitudes toward reform politics that lumped political parties, patronage, and self-interest together as enemies of the public virtues which they defined as Republican. Their revolution had been a rebellion against George III's failure to become the hero of their Republican ideal, the monarch who could see through the factionalism of his parliament and his ministers and restore virtue to the state. The subsequent development of political parties in the new nation was thus an unwanted consequence of their state building not simply an unintended one. The fact that the framers' ultimate acceptance of the grim reality of party difference required a major constitutional change in the method of selecting the president and vice president is often lost in the now familiar experience with partisan political contests.[1]

The election of Andrew Jackson in 1828 signified a major reshaping of politics and an acceptance of party practices. As Matthew Crenson has pointed out so effectively, the Jacksonian administrators were indeed a newer breed than Leonard White had believed them to be. They objected to the personal control which Federalist and Jeffersonian bureaucrats had used to maintain and justify their sense of their own public virtue. They sought a definition of Republican virtue that could be verified by public records and made accountable, in every sense of the term, to public judgment.[2]

In time even the new system would be perceived as corrupt, in the standard sense of the term. Rotation in office, or spoils, depending on where one stood on the democratic reform spectrum, formalized the establishment of a two-tiered system of political management. One tier used party organization and the distribution of offices as its base, while the other depended on elite figures chosen from traditional elite families, as well as the newer elites of business, banking, the law, and the emerging professions. In some parts of the country, notably New England and the coastal South where the traditions of politics allowed for the selection of individuals from the old elite to run for office, the two merged. But by the middle of the nineteenth century one could see in most parts of the country—and particularly in the rapidly expanding cities of the nation—a growing distinction between politicians who controlled political offices and business and professional elites who alternated between cautious support of candidates who met their standards and the angry organizing of reform opposition to defeat those who did not. The distinction between politics and administration rested on social and economic realities that went back to the beginning of the nation's partisan political organization.

The profound character of that distinction is part of what makes the idea of bureaucracy in the United States so complexly different from European conceptions of bureaucracy. On the continent bureaucracy developed prior to and independent of the growth of mass democracy. In England the emergence of a civil service elite which shared and supported upper class values reflected a different tradition of parliamentary control that was both Republican and elitist before mass democracy entered the scene. Without going through the complex distinctions that mark debates about the development of British politics in the eighteenth century, it is still important to point out again that such debates were part of the background of the framers of early American governments. It is just as important to remind ourselves of the changes produced by Jacksonian democracy, for the embedding of the conflict between mass democracy and elite professionalism in the American political structure is what really shapes the American meaning of bureaucracy and American attitudes toward it.

Hostility to the term itself has distinctive Anglo-American roots. Thomas Carlyle's reference to it as "the continental nuisance" became the often-repeated source quotation in definitions in English dictionaries and encyclopedias.[3] The substitution of the term "civil servant" was probably an attempt to articulate the sense of public control which made it possible to argue that such service was the fulfillment of a public trust, not an opportunity for independent, self-serving aggrandizement.

For American reformers the term "administration" served to focus a kind of pragmatic attention on the governing process. The term became part of an elite reform vocabulary, however, one which appealed primarily to the post-Civil War reformers who had begun to designate efficient government as the opposite of partisan political government. The Civil Service reform movement adopted the rhetoric of public service to attack, in effect, the basic party structure that had developed. Designations like "stalwart" and "regular" were used by reformers as criticisms of the party machinery which, from their perspective, violated the logic of good government, if not the practice, even if party adherents rejected their criticisms. Adherence to party for committed party regulars was not simply the recognition of the personal benefits bought by party loyalty but an acknowledgement of the function which party membership had played in supporting and maintaining the national union.

Administration and the Progressives

Woodrow Wilson's essay, "The Study of Administration," appeared in 1887 and established not only the field but the clear articulation of contrasts and comparisons with European and British government which Wilson's generation of genteel reformers created to mark the parameters of an appropriate democratic bureaucracy, however contradictory such a phrase might have seemed to them.

Wilson viewed Prussian government as "despotic," although he was willing to express a certain amount of admiration for Frederick the Great and the influence of Stein in Prussia, "where the leadership of one statesman imbued with true public spirit transformed arrogant and perfunctory bureaux into public-spirited instruments of just government."[4] The development of administration in France by Napoleon is Wilson's second example of "the perfecting of civil machinery by the single will of an absolute ruler before the dawn of the constitutional era."[5]

The revolutionary era in France, he warns us, was an era of "constitution-*writing*," not one of "constitution-*making*, a distinction which prepares us for the basic historical difference between England and Europe that Wilson and his teachers at the Johns Hopkins University had taught as the unique foundation of Anglo-American democracy. England's Henry II, Wilson tells us, had attempted to establish a system of despotic administrative efficiency through his control of the administration of justice; but the thrust of his endeavors had been blunted by the "errant" administration of the "impulsive" Richard and turned back by the "weak, despicable" John. As Wilson puts it, "Parliament became king before any English monarch had had the practical genius or the enlightened conscience to devise just and lasting forms for the civil service of the state."[6]

Fortunately for his argument, Wilson stops his review of the English monarchy short of the Tudors to make the point he needs to make, namely, that "The English race, consequently, has long and successfully studied the curbing of executive power to the constant neglect of the art of perfecting executive methods. . . . It has been more concerned to render government just and moderate than to make it facile, well-ordered, and effective." Also, to make certain that the lessons are not lost, he throws one final brickbat at central Europe. "We should not like to have had Prussia's history for the sake of having Prussia's administrative skill; and Prussia's particular system of administration would quite suffocate us. It is better to be untrained and free than to be servile and systematic."[7] The cliches that were to be used to justify the Anglo-American alliance in the First World War were already well in place by 1887.

In a sense, Wilson's argument provides a historical and constitutional rationale for a movement which had, since shortly after the Civil War, been attempting to cope with the consequences which reformers now saw in the Jack-sonian revolution in government and administration. For Wilson's era, as indeed for the Progressive era as a whole, Andrew Jackson was not viewed as the hero he had been for Bancroft or that he was destined to become again for the New Deal historians. Administrative historians have been inclined to see the post Civil War period as a period of chaos brought about by political expansion and corruption. They were not prepared to consider it a period of the extension of pre-war Jacksonian individualism and self-interest into an era of national industrialization which raised serious questions about the limits of that approach for the creation of a national order. William Graham Sumner's descriptions of Jackson, like Wilson's use, tend to emphasize the raw frontier quality of Jackson's background, his presumed ignorance of banking and finance, and his willful opportunism. Jacksonians, after all, were the Yuppies of their era, eager for their share of the growing national pie whatever the cost to previous owners of the pie or the efficiency they claimed as justification for their ownership.[8]

Wilson, like many of his reform-minded contemporaries, tended to look upon Jacksonian reform as having over-extended the legislative process. While they would not have put it in terms of limiting democracy ("unforseen tendencies of democracy" was the way E. L. Godkin put it), they did argue that bloated, chaotic legislatures hobbled effective executives. Electing rather than appointing administrative offices and officers, such as school boards and superintendents, coroners, and other executives who are not expected to have technical training, did not lead to efficient, intelligent administration or to the exercise of responsibility. The so-called "short-ballot" was, in effect, a way of limiting voter input in the administrative process, an acknowledgement of the boundaries of popular democracy. Efforts to reform the House of Representatives and break the power of the Speaker, like reformers' efforts to obtain direct elections of senators, are the best examples of the complex relation they saw between political participation and efficient government.

Wilson and his generation of administrative reformers were articulating a problem that was to plague not only the Progressive movement and the history of reform ever since but also those historians who sought to understand the relation between theories of democracy and administrative reform. The problem rests on some fundamental issues that may require a simpler articulation than they deserve. A bluntly stated sequence of assertions might help.

Industrialization and technology require trained personnel and efficient methods of administrative management. The historical association of such methods and such personnel are with elite systems of government. Whether one designates such governments as benevolent despotisms or administrative states, they still require the limitation of democratic participation, if only by placing intellectual, certifiable restrictions on access to authority as well as on methods of exercising.

The paradox can thus be stated in ways which Wilson and his generation were unable to state it for themselves.

In order to survive in the modern world, democratic governments must find ways of adopting methods associated with despotic governments, and they must do it within the rhetorical frameworks defined by the democratic revolutions of the eighteenth and early nineteenth centuries. That might not have been so difficult had those frameworks stayed the same through the nineteenth century. Democratic theory, in its eighteenth century guise, had also accepted the classical theorists' view of democracy as a potentially dangerous force and had established a complex range of limits on participatory democracy.

By the end of the nineteenth century the progress of democratic thought had produced a wide range of populist and socialist conceptions that were far more radical. Whether or not one chooses to think of it as a paradox, it seems nonetheless true that the pressures of technological, scientific advance on conceptions of participatory democracy and self-government produced the confrontation with which we are now familiar: mass democracy versus class leadership. The use of the term "class" is itself open to controversy in American life where the relation among intellectual leadership, wealth, and the educational institutions that tend to provide the states and the nation with its leaders is far more complex an issue than it is elsewhere in the world.[9]

The fact that the potential class confrontation has always been clearer in Europe than it is for Americans has made it difficult for American theorists to cope with it. Bureaucracy and bureaucrats were familiar figures in European government. Every revolution against the traditional state has raised the question of the role of the bureaucracy, whether it be in the administration of the Nazi regime or the structure of revolutionary Marxist states of Eastern Europe and the Soviet Union. Americans have coped with the introduction of the bureaucratic state by castigating it all the while and attempting to place upon it every limitation of which they could think.

Wilson's identification of what he was now calling the "science" of administration with despotic European governments was going to haunt many of his followers in the years after World War I, when the identification of efficiency with totalitarianism plagued efforts at administrative reform and governmental planning. Yet it is clear in Wilson's writings that he recognizes the necessity of strong leadership, that he requires of leaders an unswerving commitment to their ideals and a force of character which makes them less the followers of public opinion than the creators of it. His essay, "Leaders of Men," is, in some respects, a shocking document, filled with what generations today would consider "macho" images of leaders and leadership, but images which historians would clearly identify with Nietzschean and Hegelian categories understood by Wilson's generation.[10]

Wilson and his generation of Progressive leaders were trying to create a British-like, upper-middle class elite, to put themselves in control of it, and to co-opt others into it as a means of stabilizing the wildly growing American society of the late nineteenth century. One can trace the careers of men and women from upper class backgrounds who adopt careers in politics or reform management as their method of using family wealth. At the same time, there is an expansion of voting publics, a transformation in attitudes toward party loyalty, and a whole raft of changes in politics traceable to urbanization, industrialization, communication, rapid technological change, and the uses of the educational system from kindergarten through graduate school as a route of access to power. The question is, what does the period say about attitudes toward bureaucracy, and I summarize my points here to make that clear.

First, the identification of administration with continental despotism may have turned out to be an unfortunate way to introduce the topic. Although other writers on administrative reform continued to look admiringly toward Germany and the management of German cities, some, like Herbert Croly, rejected both the British and the German models entirely. World War I, the Russian Revolution of 1917, and the development of fascism in the 1920s and 1930s gave those whose interests would be threatened by efficient administration an effective weapon to use, namely, that it was foreign and that it represented what was increasingly being called "totalitarian rule."

Secondly, the inability of American proponents of effective administration to cope with the fact that American definitions of democracy excluded sophisticated conceptions of a public interest elite capable being responsible to the national interest as a whole was bound to give reformers difficulty. In the years after World War I men like Walter Lippmann would attempt to use ideas current in British politics and formulated there by Graham Wallas to talk about the public's limited focus, its preoccupation with self-interest, and its lack of profound contact with all of the issues involved in governing a nation state to avoid as far as they could the more pessimistic continental approach to public psychology exemplified by Sorel. British and American publics were neither neurotic, animalistic, nor stupid. They were busy with their own interests. John Dewey's *The Public and Its Problems* became the American description of the potentiality of popular reform politics.[11]

Thirdly, even enthusiasts like Wilson, who saw the need for new administrative forms, were profoundly committed to what they felt were the origins of American democracy in the country's state and local governments, not in the federal government in Washington. The generation that still celebrated the Fourth of July as a secular holiday and revered the Constitution of 1787 as a biblical document had also experienced the hard reality of the Civil War and accepted the compromises that concluded it. Wilson looked on the disenfranchisement of Negro voters as a good thing, not simply as expedient. His Freedom in 1912 was a virtual glorification of localism, politically as well as economically.

Louis Brandeis was in some respects the philosophic architect of Wilson's commitment to localism. It is perhaps not surprising that Brandeis's favorite model was an Englishman, Sir Alfred Zimmern, a disciple of Lord Acton in his belief not only that absolute power corrupted absolutely, but that the chief protection against the exercise of such power was the natural community of individuals whose commitment to a common culture and a common democratic ideal enabled them to govern one another. Adopting an ideal that Wilson was later to defend in his support of the post-war division of Europe into small, culturally cohesive states, and which Brandeis himself would use in his support of Zionism, Brandeis built a whole economic and political philosophy around an argument that is insufficiently described in the phrase "the curse of bigness" with which he is perhaps most associated.

Finally, the Anglo-American unwillingness to use the term "bureaucracy" in anything but a pejorative sense was rooted not only in its association with continental despotism but with the threat that centralization itself posed for self-government. Both British and American political theorists believed that participation in government was essential to the maintenance of democracy. What classical theorists like

Plato and Rousseau expressed by questioning the geographical size of the state and the number of citizens who could comprise its population, modern theorists had to adjust to conceptions of class, definitions of appropriate local units, levels of education, and perceptions of geography that made classical views of space irrelevant. Technology had revolutionized perceptions of space, time, and the role of government. Participatory democracy had to be adjusted to that revolution. Benthamite and Jacksonian ideas of representation had become the new answer. But Englishmen had a class of citizens whose commitment to responsible participation in government had built a tradition of service that could aid in the transition from class democracy to mass democracy.

Americans had such a class, and they would continue to use it; but it was based on local family leadership in states and cities, not on an accepted national leadership. The Adams family, the Lodges, Roosevelts, Tafts, Stevensons, and Kennedys, to name only the best known and most obvious, could get control of the national system, from time to time, but only to the extent that they were willing to allow themselves to be used by the managers of a national political network who suspected their elite backgrounds and would work to keep them under control.

American public administration, then, was controlled from the earliest years of democratic development in the United States by factors that rarely received consistent public attention. The unwillingness of Americans to believe that administration might be an elite function requiring education, a family tradition of public service, and an independent income that made it possible to live and raise one's family on a public salary governed the way public administration developed, and it complicated beyond belief, almost, its relation to politics as a career. The new version of the two-tiered system, one based on voluntarism and service, the other on a free-wheeling sense of utility that critics would see as corrupt when the details surfaced in periodic public inquiries, produced the system that, by the 1920s, had become the American way of preserving self-government. The alliance between elite reformers and the professional politicians who managed the structure of partisan politics had been confirmed.

It is important to point out that only recently have writers in American political science begun to examine and

question the role of administrative elites. Stephen
Skowronek raises the issue in a very significant piece of
work, even though in his concentration on those areas
where the transformation most significantly failed—Civil
Service, railroads, and the military—he may overlook the
continuities as well as the historical unsolvability of the
problem.[12]

Two World Wars and the Transformation
of Administration

Between 1920 and 1950 at least three major influences
transformed the field of public administration in the United
States and its relation to English and European theory. The
first was the ascendancy of professional training in the
various fields of public service. The Progressive Era
practice of looking to experts as administrators as well as
advisers was expanded dramatically. The second was the
growing awareness elsewhere in the world of the influence
of conceptions of industrial management in designing public
policy and the gradual and reluctant acceptance of that
influence by the leaders in American public administration.
One has only to compare the influence of Frederick Winslow
Taylor and Henry Ford in Europe with their political and
administrative influence in the United States to see the
extent of that reluctance.[13] Yet, as Judith Merkle has
pointed out, Taylor was far more a product of traditional
Protestant conceptions of middle-class responsibility for
maintaining a democratic system than his German and Soviet
admirers thought him to be.[14]

The third influence is the growing impact, from the
late 1930 onward, of continental theories of bureaucracy and
social organization, an impact traceable at least in part to
the so-called "Atlantic migrations" of continental social
scientists in the wake of the fascist revolutions of the
1920s and 1930s. Max Weber had visited the United States
in 1904, and efforts had been made to translate some of his
writings in the 1920s; but not until the end of World War II
did his influence on American social science take a serious
turn.[15]

The creation of the idea of policy science and the
exploration of its implications by such scholars as Edward
Shils was the culmination of a movement in American

society that began with Woodrow Wilson and his generation of academicians in economics and political science who deliberately began working to formulate ideas that would influence policy-makers in government.[16]   Richard Ely, E. R. A. Seligman, and John R. Commons spent their careers struggling with what often seemed, at least to some of them, an endless battle of educating the nation's leaders in politics and business not only to use their services but to follow their plans and programs. Thorstein Veblen spent his time castigating those same leaders but seeded the profession with students whose influence carried through the New Deal.

    Even before the seeming collapse of traditional business practices in the Crash of 1929 and the Depression, business leaders like Owen D. Young, Samuel Insull, and Herbert Hoover were searching for ways of establishing a new and larger conception of business responsibility for guiding the social order and utilizing the new academicians to provide ideas.[17]   Through the New Deal and into the Truman administration the notion of "on tap but not on top" was accepted by academicians and political leaders as a way of restating the staff-line distinction in American terms; but by the Eisenhower administration the distinction had begun to blur under the pressure, chiefly of scientists moving into government as both administrators and advisers. While we are more familiar with the famous warning against the industrial-military complex in Eisenhower's farewell address, we should also note the next sentence in which he warned of the influence of scientists and academicians. Within a matter of months the Kennedy administration appeared to obliterate the distinction entirely as academicians took over the management of programs. The group that later critics would come to label "the best and the brightest" had taken over.

    From the historical perspective of the present, it seems clear that the United States was developing its own version of that cadre of trained officialdom designated by European theorists as "bureaucrats," yet the refusal to label them as such and the continuing use of the term as a pejorative continued. In the years before World War II, academicians interested in public administration carried on the American tradition of British disdain of bureaucracy. Leonard White's article on Public Administration for the 1930 edition of the *Encyclopedia of the Social Sciences* was both the high point of the Anglo-American establishment of concepts of democratic administration and the watershed moment in what even White was prepared to see as a momentous transition. White acknowledged responsibility to Wilson, as well as to German methodological influences and those of American industrial management; but his references to the emergence of fascism in Italy—Hitler was still a year away and Mussolini was still viewed as an interesting experiment—indicated that even with all of its efficiency, it was still "at the opposite pole from the American," and he went on to spell out the differences.

"On the one hand are centralized systems in which administrative authority is concentrated in the hands of national officials, in whom is vested the responsibility for all administrative action, central or local, who appoint, supervise, and at will remove local agents to execute orders issuing from above. . . . On the other hand are decentralized systems, inherent in the structure of federal states and characteristic of Anglo-Saxon civilization, in which local autonomy prevails over the demands of central control, yielding in the face of modern economic problems but retaining a powerful vitality well displayed in the home rule movement for cities in the American commonwealths." Also, White made the basic and traditional distinction between "[T]he centralized type of administration which is related to the bureaucratic (i.e., the professional), and the decentralized type to the self-governmental (i.e., the amateur)." "Fascist Italy," he explained, "has eliminated the amateur from her administrative system in favor of a politico-professional bureaucracy; the United States, in spite of the technical nature of many aspects of administration, is still powerfully influenced by preference for amateur self-governmental forms."[18]

It is important to remember that White was writing while Hoover was still President. Both were still committed—as Franklin Roosevelt would continue to be—to Wilson's faith in the compromise between methods and ideology. White's identification of bureaucracy with non-democratic forms of government is precisely the sort of argument Hoover would make when he began his public criticisms of the New Deal.[19] Part of White's argument was made for him, too, by the editors' selection of Harold Laski to write the article on Bureaucracy for the *Encyclopedia.* Laski's brief essay goes not one step beyond the tone of the 11th edition of the *Britannica* two decades earlier, uses the same pejorative quotes, and assures us that the bureaucratic state is just as anti-democratic as it always was.

The editors also suggest another important distinction for us, one that relates importantly to their grudging confirmation of the role of industrial management theory. Public Administration as an entry is alphabetized under A, not under P, while the entry for Business Administration is under B. Misguided searchers who look for it under A are referred to the next letter in the alphabet, conveniently just above the reference to "Administration, Public," which gives them the correct reference. The distinction between business administration and public administration was one which the post-Progressive generation wanted to make clear, although in other parts of the world, including the admired Great Britain, the distinction provoked less disturbance. Like White's assertion of the difference between "professionals" and "amateurs," it was one to which Americans were peculiarly sensitive. White's generation of reformers was promoting professionalism in government, training experts, and trying to create a science of politics, even while they were agreeing that the replacement of their democratic amateurs by the new professionals might—just might, mind you—suggest that some important changes were underway.

They protected their faith in democracy by assuming that the values which held them together as a reforming community of scholars were values shared by all Americans, regardless of their professional interests. They assumed, too, that administrative skills and procedures, like social values, were common, more or less, to all professions, not specific to professions. The possibility that their commitment to neutrality and objectivity might contain some threatening flaws appears not to have occurred to them, at least as a serious issue, until well after World War II.

The closest they came to understanding the possibility of real conflict had always been in their relation to the business community. Whether administration designed to produce services differed significantly from administration designed to produce profits became a question that generations of Americans answered differently just as political-pendulum swings alternately defined business and industry as the model of innovation and opportunity which the rest of the world would do well to imitate and the chief stumbling block on the road to prosperity. Samuel Insull was the hero of the Twenties and the villain of the Thirties. Henry Ford was the focus of similar ambivalence. Ida Tarbell could censure John D. Rockefeller and Standard Oil in the Progressive era and idolize Owen D. Young and RCA a decade-and-a-half later. Thorstein Veblen could castigate and caricature the business leaders of the turn of the century and call upon the industrial engineers of the 1920s to take responsibility for reforming the nation's industrial system. Historians now tend to view Herbert Hoover as the era's victim, the man trapped by the paradoxes of the American view of management in an industrial society committed to preserving capitalism and free enterprise yet free to blame it for its inabilities to realize the American dream every time for everyone.

In the decades that followed the New Deal both its defenders and its critics distorted the picture by claiming either that it was an era of effective reform to which one could return by finding an attractive and compassionate leader or that it was a threatening period of dictatorial centralization or national management in Washington. It was, in fact, neither one. Both of the pictures have at their center conceptions of bureaucracy which, for better or for worse, bear little relation to the actual role of bureaucracies in American history.

The good New Deal bureaucrat is a trained and benevolent public servant dutifully carrying out the programs of a popularly elected American philanthropist. The bad New Deal bureaucrat is a tyrannical ideologue attempting to impose a narrow intellectual elite's standard of well-being on a complex, pluralist society. The real New Deal bureaucrat was, by and large, something quite different. "He," and the surprising number of "shes" among them, were administering politically designed programs with the expressed intention of maintaining intact the political system that had designed them.[20] While their distaste for partisan politics matched that of their Progressive forebears, their commitment to the two-party political debate was profound. While they were aware of the academic distinction between politics and administration, they were never fooled by it. The civil servant called for by their civil service reforms was a servant of political interests backed by the voters, not an administrative neuter fulfilling

scientific objectives rationally defined. The protection of
civil service was a protection from the mindless victimi-
zation produced by partisan politics, not a protection from
the responsibility of serving the political aims signified by
such changes. It was certainly never intended to certify
scientifically defined policies believed by adherents to be
above political judgment and control.

Bureaucratic agencies established by the New Deal took
it from both sides. They were, on the one hand, evidence
of the radical takeover of authority by a suspect elite.
They were, on the other hand, partisan boondoggles writ
large. Critics and supporters alike would, for half a century
after the New Deal, continue to enjoy the parks, roadways,
waterways, and public buildings built by the New Deal
without ever associating them with the work of a federal
bureaucracy.

Both labels stuck. Bureaucracy was radical and
wasteful, revolutionary, tyrannical, and dishonest.
Abolishing it would remain the most attractive and popular
remedy, while making it more efficient and effective would
gradually drift toward a private professional preserve where
political scientists, teachers of public administration, and, by
the 1950s a new group of sociologically oriented social
scientists interested in bureaucratic theory would debate a
curious historical reality only they seemed able to
understand.

Modern technology, post-industrialism, and the ideas of
Max Weber and Talcott Parsons were now ways of
describing the consciousness that had emerged. When by
1962 the *New International Encyclopedia of the Social
Sciences* appeared, its article on bureaucracy marked the
essential transformation. Reinhard Bendix quickly swept
past the pejoratives of the Anglo-American tradition and
presented his readers with a brilliant panoramic view of the
new Euro-American social thought. The American bureaucrat had come of age, or so it seemed.

The fact that by 1976 the Democratic Party could
support a winning candidate whose campaign could be
directed against the bureaucracy in Washington was certainly
not envisaged by the proud academicians of the
Encyclopedia. Nor was the fact that the argument would be
sustained successfully by the Republicans as well, to become
by the 1980s a major movement that could be defined not
only as bipartisan but as a return to democracy, the

recapture of a lost heritage. Sweeping aside a century of regulatory idealism built on the dream of a federal government, that would protect its citizens from predatory interests, leaders in both parties extolled a new freedom, the freedom from bureaucratic dictation. Even the Supreme Court in its recent attack on Gramm-Rudman could call on the tradition by criticizing the power of an appointed bureaucrat, the Comptroller General, rather than raising the issue of separation of powers.

Bureaucracy, the Threat to Democracy: The Real Battle

Americans make no distinction, in political terms, between public needs and popular desires. Their refusal to accept such a distinction and to agree to an objective standard of public need defined by rationally determined considerations may distinguish Americans from members of societies where the state defines needs and debates only the degree and the timing of their fulfillment. Americans charge their government with the responsibility of meeting their individual needs in accordance with the shifting moods and perceptions that determine exactly what those needs are. The public will accept decisions that seem plausible if they are defended as expansions of democratic opportunity. But as the consequences of those decisions unfold, the American public will assume no responsibility for its own role in the process. The mood swings are precipitous and the penalties severe. Americans who elect leaders who reflect a current consensus on their attitudes toward political issues of the day will turn against those same leaders if and when that consensus changes.

Men who are elected for their administrative skills rather than their presence as popular public figures may find themselves sorely taxed by an unexpected public need for drama and charismatic leadership. The public wanted what Herbert Hoover represented in 1928. By 1931 it was clear that they sensed a need for something else, qualities which Hoover himself considered objectionable. He was never forgiven for his inability, in fact his refusal, to transform himself into the new, and needed, public image.

In an important sense the problem is not a new one. The debates that began in the Progressive Era used the

terms "politics" and "administration" as the way of defining
what has variously been viewed as a Manichaean opposition,
a pair of correlative terms, or a necessary, if not altogether
happy, partnership in the management of the democratic
state. What seems clear, however, is that the dynamics of
the relationship are and have continued to be historically
volatile, moreso, perhaps, than in any of the familiar
cultures of western society where the growth of the
administrative state and its relation to the social order are
traced by students of administrative history. It might be
useful to try to suggest some reasons for that volatility.

First, as Tocqueville suggested, Americans may be more
committed believers in the essential politics of self-
government than any other people on earth. As he pointed
out, the belief that the passage of a law will solve every
problem tends to be at the root of the American reform
impulse. Even the most popular presidents have been forced
to subject their administrative judgment to Congress and the
courts. The Supreme Court has been pressed to respond to
political judgments, at times to forestall legislative
punishment.

Secondly, Americans have tended to look on
government, and the federal government in particular, as the
distributor of resources and the opportunities for
advancement which such resources represent. Such
distribution has always been subjected to the rule that
benefits must be available to all, not just to the needy, and
that there be as little administrative intervention as possible
in what is essentially a process of democratic redistribution.
That was as true of public lands in the nineteenth century
as it is of educational opportunities, social security, medical
benefits, and jobs today. Americans do not want to think
of themselves as dependent upon state managers whose jobs
they cannot threaten by the casting of a ballot or the
rewriting of a law. The attractiveness of the short ballot
and the growth of appointed rather than elected officialdom
in American government has always been limited by the
public's sense that it could find substitute controls and the
legislature's sense that its threatened rebellions would elicit
appropriate responses. Control over jobs and resources
remains the basic of the cry of corruption, whether the
target be a lowly ward heeler whose living depends on the
voters he drags to the polls on election day or the

management of a high level technology industry supplying the armed services with absurdly expensive screwdrivers.

Thirdly, Americans hold their elected administrators responsible for serving them and accept patronage as part of the process. The justice meted out to political and administrative decision-makers has no equivalent of the legal distinction between involuntary manslaughter and premeditated murder. This ruthlessness of public judgment leads politicians and administrators alike to at least two sources. They can try to please every one a little, thereby lessening the impact of criticism even though the end result may be the equivalent of doing nothing at all; or they can set up an opponent, one enemy who is preventing the action they really want to take, thereby directing attention away from themselves.

Nothing has done more to strengthen the role of administrative courts and the battles over the use of the legislative veto than the confusion of the political and administrative processes and the resulting conflicts among administrators charged with managing the programs. Frustrated president resort to the invention of new methods, the questionable use of old ones, and the inevitable force of public exhortation, which in itself may become a highly a highly questionable theater in the world of public affairs. Presidential candidates running against incumbents, presidents seeking reelection, second-term presidents fighting unresponsive congresses, and vice presidents hoping to succeed to candidacy, if not to office, all face the problem of attempting to turn administrative problems into political theater. The situation is an open invitation to irresponsibility, if not, under certain circumstances, a guarantee of it. Suggestions that there be a single term for presidents are all built on the belief that such a restriction would separate the office from the politics of reelection; but that, in a way, is too close to the logic that dictated the mischievous twenty-second amendment in the first place. A president without political clout ceases to be a political leader. From a historical point of view, the only real answer to the problem of maintaining administrative power in the presidency would be to remove the limitation on reelection entirely, thereby giving the political public the only kind of leader it feels it can control.

The dream of removing partisanship from American politics is essentially an elite dream that has no place in

the American public's most profound conception of its own
political power. Part of the hostility to bureaucracy stems
from the fact that Americans see it as an inhibiting force,
blocking their access to political power. Part of the
inherent inefficiency of bureaucracy in the American
administrative tradition is a result of that hostility, a
consciousness on the part of even the most committed
administrator that meeting the public's perception of need is
the bottom line.

John Kennedy's *Profiles in Courage* may be the clearest
expression of the paradox. Each of his courageous figures
sacrifices a political career in the interest of some
principle. They do not stay in Congress, or win the
presidency, or succeed in gaining whatever career prize they
set out to win. Most of them are martyrs; and while
martyrs may be useful models for developing certain kinds
of character, losing, as our Kennedys were raised to
understand, is not the name of the game.

The threat of some kind of administrative tyranny is
the oldest threat to democracy in our 200 years of
independent history. It is the menace in twentieth century
communism, just as it was in nineteenth century monarchy.
The inefficiency, irrationality, and corruption we are willing
to sustain in order to protect ourselves from it have
succeeded, perhaps, in creating bureaucratic forms that are
uniquely ours. We demand a bureaucracy we can control, by
our votes, our bribes, our capacity for public wrath, and, if
necessary, by the price we are willing to pay for
inefficiency.

This is not to argue the impossibility of adminis-
tratively efficient democracy, only its fragility. For our
commitment to individual autonomy, to self-interest, and to
material well-being as the touchstones of American
democracy places limits on the definitions of efficiency that
are acceptable to us, particularly in times of economic
stringency. Politics remains our method of requiring the
state to serve us.

The growth of the bureaucratic state may be the single
most unintended consequence of the Constitution of 1787, in
a sense, perhaps, the heart of the partisanship the framers
thought they could avoid. What may be the most consistent
with their intention, however, is the hostility to bureaucracy
we inherited from them, and that we have continued to
preserve. It is a reality with which we have learned to

live, albeit somewhat uncomfortably; but it is a reality that should give pause to those who believe that there is in the intentions of the framers of the Constitution of 1787 a world to which we can return. All of the current interest in deregulation cannot obliterate the existence of the bureaucratic state or relieve us of the responsibility of adjusting our democracy to it. The battle between bureaucracy and democracy is written into our history. So is the fact that democracy must win. All we have left to debate is the cost.

ENDNOTES

1. Ralph Ketcham, *Presidents Above Party: The First American Presidency, 1789 to 1829* (Chapel Hill: University of North Carolina Press, 1984).

2. Matthew A. Crenson, *The Federal Machine: Beginnings of Bureaucracy in Jacksonian America* (Baltimore: Johns Hopkins University Press, 1975).

3. The reference is used by the author of the article on Bureaucracy in the famous 11th edition of the *Encyclopedia Britannica* and is dutifully repeated even today in the *Oxford English Dictionary*. When Harold Laski covered the topic for the *Encyclopedia of the Social Sciences*, he again repeated it.

4. Arthur S. Link, ed., *The Papers of Woodrow Wilson*, vol. 5 (Princeton: NJ: Princeton University Press, 1968).

5. *Ibid.*, p. 366.

6. *Ibid.*, p. 367.

7. *Ibid.*, pp. 367-68.

8. William Graham Sumner, *Andrew Jackson*, in the American Statesman series, edited by J.T. Morse (New York: AMS Press, Inc., repr. of 1899 ed.).

9. The late Joseph Ben David was being particularly acute in his efforts to mark the distinction between the development of American educational institutions and those in other parts of the world. He, however, has concentrated on the issue of intellectual development rather than political power. *Fundamental Research and the Universities* (Paris: OECD, 1968).

10. Although the essay was not published until 1954 (Princeton University Press), it was apparently delivered on several occasions as a graduate address.

11. Woodrow Wilson, *Leaders of Men* (Princeton, NJ: Princeton University Press, 1954); Walter Lippmann, *Public Opinion* (New York: Harcourt, Brace and Co., 1922); Graham Wallas, *Human Nature in Politics* (London: A Constable and Co., Ltd., 1908); John Dewey, *The Public and Its Problems* (Denver: A. Swallow, c 1927, 1954, 3d ed.).

12. Stephen Skowronek, *Building a New American State: The Expansion of National Administrative Capacities, 1877-1920* (Cambridge: Cambridge University Press, 1982).

13. Charles Maier, "Between Taylorism and Technology: European Ideologies and the Vision of Industrial Productivity in the 1920's," *Journal of Contemporary History*, vol. 5 (No. 2, 1969), pp. 27-61.

14. Judith A. Merkle, *Management and Ideology: The Legacy of the International Scientific Management Movement* (Berkeley: University of California Press, 1980).

15. Max Weber, *General Economic History*, translated by Frank H. Knight (New York: Greenberg, 1927). Hans H. Gerth and C. Wright Mills, *From Max Weber: Essays in Sociology* (New York: Oxford University Press, 1946); and Talcott Parsons' translation of *The Theory*

of Social and Economic Organization (New York: Free Press, 1947).

16. Edward Shils, in Daniel Lerner and Harold D. Lasswell, eds., *The Policy Sciences* (Stanford, CA: Stanford University Press, 1951). The volume is a kind of monument to the emergence of a distinction between policy science and behavioral scientific research.

17. Guy Alchon, *The Invisible Hand of Planning: Capitalism, Social Science, and the State of the 1920's* (Princeton, NJ: Princeton University Press, 1985).

18. Leonard White, "Public Administration," *Encyclopedia of the Social Sciences*, vol. 1 (New York: MacMillan Company, January 1930), p. 444.

19. Herbert Hoover, *The Challenge to Liberty* (New York and London: C. Scribner's Sons, 1934).

20. The presence of women is traceable not to any premonitions of the liberation movement that followed the era but to the fact that women were represented in such overwhelming numbers among the managers and providers of social services at the state and local levels, services now being transferred to the federal government.

CHAPTER FOUR

Operationalizing the Constitution Via Administrative Reorganization: Oilcans, Trends, and Proverbs

JAMES L. GARNETT[*]

Campaigns to reorganize administrative structures of federal, state, and local governments have been the battlegrounds over which much of American public administrative theory has been spawned, advocated, and criticized.[1] These reorganization battles over structure, power, process, and doctrine have often been so pitched that opponents or advocates of reorganization have accused the opposition of insanity, tyranny, godlessness, naivete, backwardness, and questionable ancestry. Despite such controversy, government reorganizing has played a vital role in making the constitutional system work.

Administrative reorganizations have been characterized as *garbage cans*, "highly contextual combinations of people, choice opportunities, problems, and solutions."[2] This essay views reorganizations as *oilcans*, lubricating constitutional

---

[*] **James L. Garnett** is Associate Professor of Business and Public Management at the West Virginia College of Graduate Studies. He has worked in state government and consulted for national and local government agencies. He is author of *Reorganizing State Government: The Executive Branch* and author or coauthor of several articles and chapters on administrative organization and reorganization. His MPA and Ph.D. are from the Maxwell School, Syracuse University.

machinery so it can function.   More specifically, reorganizing has been an extra-constitutional means of reducing
friction and conflict stemming from constitutional issues
surrounding the proper balance and separation of powers.[3]
Reorganizing within the existing constitutional framework to
flesh out and operationalize it has dominated over efforts to
overhaul the constitution itself into a parliamentary or other
system.[4]

Instead of junking the 1787 model for a different
constitutional system, Americans, using their spirit for
tinkering and inventiveness, have relied on repairing and
lubricating the old model to keep it running. Reorganizing
to repair and improve the system of government has largely
been an adaptive process combining *ideology* and *pragmatism*
to meet changing needs.   As with many machinery lubri-
cants, reorganizations have rarely been neutral interventions
but have often been terrifically heated while doing their
job.   Reorganizations typically create as well as reduce
political and administrative friction. But reorganizing has
also avoided tackling constitutional issues head-on, instead
confronting issues of governance at a relatively less volatile
and more manageable level.

This essay first addresses reorganization's facilitating,
lubricating role, observing the different emphases and trends
taken to keep constitutional machinery running to achieve
system goals of *accountability* and *competence*.   This essay
concludes by examining some proverbs of reorganization and
by drawing implications for future reorganization practice
and research.

Reorganization as Lubricant for the Constitutional System

The U.S. Constitution is conspicuously mute about
administrative structure. Article 1, Section 8 sets forth the
powers of Congress, but the Constitution is conspicuously
silent about how Congress or the president should exercise
these powers.   The Constitution makes no mention of
"administration" or "management" and refers sparingly to
"executing the laws."   Article 2, Section 2 makes the
president ". . . Commander in Chief of the Army and Navy
of the United States, and of the militia of the several
states . . .," but no equally clear designation of the

president as Commander in Chief of the Executive Branch exists. Article 2, Section 2 mentions "Heads" and "principal Officers" of "executive Departments." But the Constitution avoids specifying which executive departments should exist, how many are needed, and how these departments should be organized. The only mention of "organizing" appears in Article 1, Section 8, giving Congress power "to provide for organizing, arming, and disciplining the Militia. . . ." Here, "organizing" more accurately means "mobilizing" than "structuring." Because administrative organization gets no real attention in the Constitution, no express provision is made for reorganizing. By implication rather than through express provision, the U.S. Constitution allows structural and other changes through enacting laws or amending the Constitution itself.

The constitutional upper hand given Congress, fragmentation of powers, and the void about administrative organization and management have been criticized as weak foundations for achieving efficient administration.[5] The U.S. Constitution places more emphasis on governmental *accountability*, ability to control those in power and hold them responsible for their actions, than on *competence*, ability of government to do its business. The constitutional Framers were not necessarily against strong, efficient management, although suspicion of British executive excesses still ran strong. The role of administration was perceived differently at a time when members of Congress outnumbered the entire executive branch workforce in Washington.[6] Constitutional machinery was designed for its time, before the onslaught of modernizing and bureaucratizing forces.

The U.S. Constitution says even less about state organization and nothing about local government. Article IV requires the United States to guarantee states a "Republican Form of Government." Article VI binds state legislators and "all executive and judicial Officers" by oath to support the Constitution, implying that states will also have three branches. The Constitution embodies the Framers' distrust of cities and their evils by ignoring cities, giving them no constitutional stature whatsoever and giving states no guidance or restrictions for treating local governments. Over the years, state constitutions and municipal charters have provided their own detail about organizing. Like municipal charters, many state constitutions specify departments and administrative officials, and a growing number even specify the maximum number of cabinet departments. Despite greater constitutional detail about organization and despite looser adherence to separation of powers in local government, for example with council-manager systems, state and local governments have substantially followed the national pattern of three branches, constitutional separation of powers, and checks and balances. Thus state and local governments have also had to find ways to make constitutional systems work.

Much reorganizing during the twentieth century at all levels of government has been an attempt either to carry out the logic inherent in separation of powers or to reduce the friction and ambiguity created by it. Reorganizations have essentially served to lubricate and preserve constitutional machinery by emphasizing popular representation, neutral expertise, and executive leadership.[7] Each of these three thrusts has affected government's *accountability* and *competence*.

Reorganizing to Govern by Popular Representation

Formal government structure following independence emphasized legislative supremacy, long ballot, and primarily figure head executives on the state and local level, and after Jackson, at the national level.[8] Even though the structure they created was ambiguous about administration, the actions of founders who later became President—Washington, Adams, and Madison—showed administrative decisiveness. Through strength of character and the momentum of a young republic, they were strong administrators despite uncertain constitutional machinery.[9]

Stressing elected representation hardly meant true social representativeness. The administrations of Presidents until Jackson were dominated by men from economically and socially prominent families. These "gentlemen" managed government departments based on personal style much as they would run a bank or a company.[10] If the U.S. Constitution established a government by law rather than men, government by men still dominated administration in the Federalist and Republican eras.

Jacksonian Democrats rebuked such government by aristocracy, instead promoting government by commoners. Astute Jacksonians, however, recognized that even in the

1820s and 1830s many government jobs required more ability and honesty than all commoners possessed. Jacksonians coped with this problem via administrative reorganization rather than constitutional revision. Department reorganizations under Jackson both limited administrative authority and imposed internal audits and controls to foster honesty. Emphasizing rules and regulations, division of labor, job simplification, office rather than officeholder, and other bureaucratic traits facilitated personnel interchange. By reorganizing toward a more bureaucratic, less personal system, Jacksonian Democrats achieved more of a government by laws as well as a government by men—different men. The Jacksonian era led to greater popular representation through (1) longer ballot, (2) wider circle of political appointments, (3) more direct citizen participation, and (4) legal and bureaucratic limits on administrative authority. Expanded voting and bureaucracy increased accountability in some directions, but lessened accountability in others. The issue of accountability got emphasized; government competence still suffered.

It became evident after the Civil War that excessive emphasis on popular representation led to fragmentation and was the wrong way to run the constitutional system. The long ballot and lack of government cohesion provided the opportunity for political machines to achieve power. These machines did achieve some cohesion, but corruption often resulted and decision-making was hardly representative.

Despite the Jacksonian reorganizations at the national level and creation of new departments at all governmental levels, reorganizing government got relatively little conscious attention during this first hundred years after the U.S. Constitution was adopted. The size and scope of government at all levels was small. A less-complex social and economic life made fewer demands on governments. Those governments were often preoccupied with issues other than reshaping themselves, many related to opening and developing new states and territories. Most growth in the national government, for example, expansion of the Post Office, resulted from serving expanded population and territory rather than taking on new tasks.[11] But magnified social and economic complexity brought about by further urbanizing and modernizing—and increased corruption—heightened the appeal for reorganizing government.

Reorganizing to Govern by Neutral Expertise

One body of reorganization doctrine arising after the Civil War aimed at operationalizing the Constitution by correcting the excesses of unbridled representation. "Everyman" had proven unable to govern honestly and effectively. It was time to call in the experts! One place where governments looked for examples of how to manage increasing size and complexity was business. The growth of business companies since the Civil War in terms of number, size, and managerial capacity provided one model for government administration. Much of the reform movement beginning in municipal government and spreading to state and federal government sought to emulate the apolitical business model emphasizing professional, nonpartisan administration.[12]

The central mechanisms for achieving neutral expertise in government included: (1) installing and strengthening merit systems, (2) relying on nonpartisan experts, (3) using boards and commissions for conducting government business, and (4) staggering terms of appointment to insulate against political influence. Municipal reorganizations to adopt a council-manager plan stressing nonpartisan, professional government expertise were common by World War I. At all levels of government, reorganizations to create independent or semi-independent agencies, boards, or commissions such as the Tennessee Valley Authority, Farm Credit Board, Port Authority of New York and New Jersey, state boards of higher education, and state and local professional licensing boards are examples of using neutral expertise to manage the constitutional system.

Bipartisan and staggered appointment was intended to make these bodies more resistant to partisan or corrupt influence. But these precautions also limited the chief executive's control over these agencies, resulting in fragmented power, diffused direction, and virtual capture of such "islands of decision-making" by special interests.[13] Other problems surfaced. What kinds of expertise were needed and who could provide that expertise was often unclear. In addition, who was to decide when experts disagreed, an increasingly common problem as governing became more technical? While fewer experts were partisans for political party than their governing predecessors, many experts were hardly neutral, exerting partisanship for their agency, program, or profession. This thrust stressed the goal of competence but underemphasized the need for accountability.

Reorganizing to Govern by Executive Leadership

Other scholars and reorganizers eventually perceived that emphasizing neutral expertise with its resulting fragmentation was the wrong prescription for the weakness inherent in separation of powers. The reorganization oilcan had been used to keep government machinery operating, but too much lubrication in the wrong places caused malfunction.

About the turn of the twentieth century, this perceived system of "diffusion of powers" stimulated a preoccupation with *integration* and *coordination* that has since dominated reorganization doctrine. For example, leading statements on federal, state, and local reorganization voice the "canons of integration" calling for: (1) concentrating authority and responsibility primarily through a strengthened chief executive, (2) integrating related functions by department, (3) reducing the number and administrative power of independent boards and commissions, (4) reducing the number of officials directly elected or appointed by others than the chief executive, and (5) strengthening audit, budget, and other fiscal controls.[14] Executive leadership, like popular representation, again emphasizes accountability over competence, although government's general competence has increased over time.

Examples of Reorganizations Pursuing These Thrusts

Reorganizations representing each thrust, sometimes several combined, have abounded since the Civil War, most since 1900. The federal Reorganization Act of 1939 gets credit for strengthening presidential leadership. But the trend toward a more managerial presidency began years earlier with the Taft Commission's (1910-13) efforts and has generally continued since Roosevelt's 1939 reorganization.[15] Federal reorganization efforts from the Taft Commission through President Carter's reorganization project adhered to the orthodoxy of executive leadership.

State and local governments have likewise often reorganized to consolidate control in the executive. About

46 percent of the state administrative branch reorganizations adopted or attempted between 1910 and 1985 were characterized by consolidating agencies along functional lines, decreasing the governor's span of control and increasing gubernatorial appointment power, and decreasing use of boards and commissions for administrative work.[16] Fealty to the canons of integration remained strong among governors and state organizers into the 1970s. South Dakota's then Governor Richard Kneip captured his influence by claiming, "The [1973] plan of reorganization in South Dakota contains many of the fundamental principles of classical organization propounded by such theorists as A. E. Buck and Luther Gulick."[17]

County government, long the bastion of the plural executive and long ballot, has joined the trend toward reliance on executive leadership. For example, use of council-executive structures with an independently elected county executive increased from 8 counties in 1950 to 142 counties in 1977. County governance by elected commissioners still predominates in counties under 50,000 population, but the majority of counties over 100,000 population rely on a structure using a professional administrator.[18] The traditional county formulation for minimizing fragmentation has been to combine legislative, executive, and sometimes judicial powers in an elected county commission. But this plural executive-legislative has often lacked internal decisiveness and has typically had to share administrative responsibility with other independently elected officials like a county clerk, auditor, assessor, and sheriff—vestiges of emphasizing representation. This fragmentation has led to more reorganizations creating strong county executives.

The long-range trend in city government has also been toward centralizing control in the executive, whether the strong mayor or city manager. By the end of the nineteenth century, municipal reform turned decisively toward concentrating power in the mayor. After Staunton, Virginia's intervention of the council-manager plan in 1908, that plan spread widely through the efforts of reformers in universities, the National Municipal League, Short Ballot Organization, and even the United States Chamber of Commerce who favored the businesslike division of policymaking and administration ala a board of directors and chief executive. By 1917 council-manager plans were "fast becoming *de riguer* among reformers."[19] Today, use of the council-manager structure is greater in white collar suburbs, the South and West, and small and medium-sized cities.

Reorganizations emphasizing neutral expertise for making constitutional machinery function have occurred before and during the push for executive leadership. For example, 54 percent of state reorganizations adopted or attempted from 1910-1985 were most like the neutral expertise approach because they left more administrative boards and had less consolidation than other types of reorganization.[20] In addition, the many new special districts, public authorities, and public benefit corporations created at all levels of government exemplify neutral expertise. Their structure—central staff and operating divisions reporting to a general manager or executive director who reports to a board of directors and bondholders among others—captures the corporate model. From 1962 to 1982, nonschool special districts increased 56 percent while the number of other forms of local government changed little.[21]

Current Trends in Reorganizing

President Carter's political setbacks, coincident in time with his comprehensive reorganization program, have cooled the ardor for traditional federal reorganization. President Reagan has avoided the traditional approach taken by previous presidents. He does not so much reject reorganization orthodoxy as avoid it by changing policies and management procedures more than *structures*.[22] Although macro structure has less emphasis in the Reagan administration, observers note a trend toward centralization within federal agencies. A smaller number of politically appointed managers are setting policies for career employees to implement, sometimes creating flatter hierarchies and increasing spans of control.[23] Political and managerial strategy now dictates organizational structure rather than following it.

While emphasizing privation and management strategies, President Reagan has not ignored the prospect of traditional structural reorganization. A 1982 plan to eliminate the Department of Energy by merging it into the Department of Commerce got a cool reception from Congress. Later, in 1984-85, President Reagan requested a study on the feasibility of folding the Department of Energy into the Interior Department. Also, the President's Commission on Industrial Competitiveness has recommended adding new federal cabinet level departments for trade and science and technology, and the Packard Commission has likewise recommended restructuring the Department of Defense.

A similar trend toward emphasizing procedural reform exists in state government, where management improvement task forces promoted procedural changes in Kentucky (1980), Louisiana (1981), and West Virginia (1986). While most state reorganizations have combined structural and procedural changes, the relative emphasis appears to be shifting from structural to procedural. One example of recent state procedural reorganization is New Mexico's General Service Department, which now uses the Professional Office System (PROFS) to provide electronic mail, messaging, scheduling, and text processing services.

Local governments have joined the orientation toward revising management systems, but structurally-oriented reorganizations are also evident. Some cities have converted from the council-manager plan to the strong mayor plan because of perceived political needs to change structure to cope with changing conditions. As some cities have outgrown the usual 10,000-250,000 population range for council-manager plans and have become more urbanized and pluralistic, some have converted to a strong-mayor system to manage conflict which greater pluralism typically brings. Rochester, New York, made this conversion, officially returning to a strong mayor form in 1985. San Diego retains the council-manager plan in its charter, but the mayor has become a stronger official, not through charter revision but through actual practice.[24] Other cities, like Dallas and San Antonio, and many urban counties, like Fairfax, Virginia, and Sacramento, California, have continued to embrace council-manager government. Even within those governments, recent local structural reorganizations generally stress executive leadership.

Most administrative reorganizations in this century, except for Great Society programs of the 1960s, have accented neutral expertise and executive leadership rather than popular representation since these emphases were intended to correct the excessive representativeness flourishing before the reform movement. Yet traits of representativeness exist in state and local government structures having multiple elected executives or having elected legislators administering departments much like under the Articles of Confederation.

Thus, the popular representation, neutral expertise, and executive leadership strains are all evident in federal, state, and local administrative reorganizations in the second hundred years following the Constitution's ratification. Some reorganizations change trifles; others drastically transform who governs and how. But even the most drastic reorganizations have involved lubricating and tinkering with the basic three branch, separation-of-powers machinery rather than scrapping it for another system. Other forms, particularly the parliamentary system, have attracted much attention from constitutional reformers but have never been adopted at the national level.[25]

Why Extra-Constitutional Reform Through Reorganization?

Why have Americans relied on reorganizing the 1787 model rather than make fundamental constitutional changes? Reverence for the Constitution's sanctity has not prevented important amendments on other issues. Has difficulty amending the Constitution discouraged that option? Since no amendment to reorganize administration has been tried except for limiting presidents to two consecutive terms, the federal level offers little direct experience, although other amendments have faced tough hurdles. But at least 31 of the state reorganizations attempted since 1900 used constitutional amendment. The record shows that the all-or-nothing nature of constitutional revision makes it the riskier strategy. All three of the total reorganization defeats from 1947-1985 came via constitutional amendment.[26] Reorganizing by statute has dominated in the states, although reorganization in the 1960s and 1970s utilized a greater range of legal mechanisms. Municipalities typically change structures via charter revision rather than ordinance, but like states have primarily kept the basic tripartite separation of powers system. For those states and localities which have revamped their structures via constitution or charter, the reorganization oilcan has served to lubricate administrative machinery between major overhauls of the same basic model.

Another explanation for foregoing profound constitutional change involves tactics. Some reformers felt they could repair constitutional inadequacies better through periodic, partial adjustments than by attempting to overhaul the entire system. For example, reformers advocating executive leadership calculated that strengthening the executive under the guise of more businesslike, more scientific administration deflected much opposition that would likely have arisen from a more threatening direct assault on the Constitution. In the words of Luther Gulick: "We could sell it [administrative orthodoxy] . . . because both the conservatives and the liberals believed in science and believed in rationality. . . . We were not trying to develop a systematic, logical, comprehensive philosophy of the political or administrative system of our government."[27]

Gulick's admission provides another reason for relying on periodic lubrications and tuneups to modify government organization: reformulating a comprehensive administrative and political system is exceedingly difficult to conceptualize and an even harder object of consensus. Explaining another case of "nonconstitutional management of a constitutional problem," Edward Hamilton observes: " . . . a student of the Constitution might remind us, the straightforward remedy would seem obvious. The document contains an orderly procedure for amendment, or even for total revision. But few would maintain that the present strength of the American political consensus is sufficiently impressive to warrant confidence that a wholesale revision would yield more improvements than new defects."[28]

Thus, for reasons of legal and political tactics and a lack of consensus about what would replace the 1787 model, Americans have chosen to reorganize periodically, adapting governmental machinery to changing conditions and needs.

Proverbs of Reorganization

Just as orthodox administrative theory produced what later critics termed as "proverbs of administration,"[29] some "proverbs of reorganization" have evolved. This bicentennial period is an appropriate occasion to reexamine these proverbs since they address key aspects of the relationship between the Constitution and administrative reorganization. The first two proverbs question how well the reorganization oilcan has served to improve government's competence. The third proverb emphasizes politics, power, and control—

accountability issues. The fourth proverb stresses the role of administrative ideology in organizing and reorganizing government. As often happens, earlier principles or proverbs of reorganization have been "debunked" and replaced with newer conventional wisdoms. This section examines both the former and current proverbs.

Reorganization as Economy

Former Proverb: *Administrative reorganizations promote government economy.* **Current Proverb:** *Reorganizations fail to save governments money.* Economy has been a standard rationale for federal, state, and local reorganizations. Early, congressionally initiated efforts at federal reorganization, like the Cockrell Committee (1887-89) and Dockery-Cockrell Committee (1893-95), set the tone with a preoccupation on administrative detail and economy. Major federal reorganizations since then have generally paid lip service to the proverb of economy, but conventional wisdom about federal reorganization refutes these claims.[30] One analyst summarizes this conventional wisdom this way: "Of all the forms of reorganization . . . reorganization for efficiency and economy is clearly the most discredited."[31]

At the state level, claims by A. E. Buck and others for economies via reorganization have been countered by other researchers noting higher expenditures or lack of substantiated savings.[32] More recent and more systematic efforts to assess reorganization's effect on state expenditures also show mixed results. Kenneth Meier's study of 16 states that adopted executive branch reorganizations between 1965 and 1975 found that five states showed short-term reductions in expenditure growth (not actual decreases in expenditures), but these reductions lacked statistical significance. Of the 16 states, only California experienced a long-term decrease in spending growth rate following reorganization.[33] Another study by James Conant on reorganization's effects on expenditures in five New Jersey state departments showed overall budget totals increased after a 1982 reorganization, but that tangible savings were achieved through discrete changes reorganization made in these departments.[34]

Measuring the economic effects of reorganization is difficult. Many factors affect government expenditures before, during, and after reorganization. Such historical factors as economic health, inflation, greater population, changes in a government's role, mandates from higher level governments, and higher demands on entitlement programs affect government spending regardless of reorganization. The difficulty of measuring savings, even those that actually exist, has reinforced the notion that no economies exist.

The conventional wisdom that reorganization produces little economy has also been fed by the types of reorganizations adopted. Most major federal, state, and local reorganizations have combined changing the organization chart *and* revising management procedures. Reorganizations in the first half of this century tended to emphasize changes in organization charts—changes in grouping and reporting relationships. But more recent reorganizations emphasize revised management procedures. Reorganizations, primarily geared to modernizing management procedures, privatizing service delivery, revamping priorities, or retrenching government may well reduce spending. Most reorganizations thus far studied have been growth-oriented in a generally expanding government sector. Reorganizations in the face of budget shortages, like the 1981 reorganization in Tennessee to cut transportation department costs, will likely do more than pay lip service to economy.

To summarize, savings via reorganization are likely to be modest rather than drastic,[35] long-term rather than short-term,[36] on a departmental or program level rather than systemwide,[37] result more from tangible workforce reductions and management systems improvements,[38] and be less likely to reduce the overall bottom line than to offset other expenses or be targeted for new priorities. Without more incisive analysis, existing conventional wisdom that reorganization in general is antithetical to economizing is just as untested and proverbial as blanket claims for economy.

Reorganization as Management Reform

Former Proverb: *Reorganizing government to achieve the correct structure produces more effective and efficient administration.*[39] **Current Proverb:** *Governmental structure has little influence on performance.* Classical reformers believed strongly that "correct" structures adhering to the canons of integration would produce good outcomes.[40] More recently President Nixon echoed this belief, "Just as inadequate organization can frustrate good men and women, so it can dissipate good money . . . the major cause of the ineffectiveness of government is not a matter of men or of money. It is principally a matter of machinery."[41] Belief that structure is central to administrative performance pervaded classical organization theory and also dominated federal, state, and local governments for the first half of the twentieth century.

Claims that reorganization produces government efficiency and effectiveness received heavy criticism from skeptics in the first decades of the twentieth century, yet remained largely unscathed. Rigorous intellectual criticism in the 1940s exposed the shaky premises underpinning administrative orthodoxy without stopping its use by government practitioners.[42] But findings of several policy scientists in the 1960s and 1970s that socioeconomic characteristics of a state or community explained policy outcomes better than any political or organizational "black box" deflated the importance of structure.[43] This emphasis on socioeconomic determinants exposed the proverb of structuralism and itself became a "new orthodoxy." But this attack on structural orthodoxy prompted a counterattack from other forces who criticized the atheoretical nature of this research, the bias of using expenditures to measure policy outcomes, and the paucity of administrative variables used.[44]

Despite criticism of determinants research, the idea that structure counts little remains conventional wisdom.[45] Instead of demonstrating the irrelevance of structure, critics turned the tables, challenging believers to prove that structure *does* make a difference. Some scholars have continued to suspect that structure matters more than the "new orthodoxy" admits. Also, public officials have continued to mouth the importance of structure before reorganizing. But without evidence that organizational structure indeed affects administrative and service performance, advocates of structural reorganization have "kept a low profile."

But evidence that structural arrangements do make a difference continues to be found in business and is reported again in government. In business, where effectiveness and efficiency are usually easier to measure, structure's contribution has been demonstrated better.[46] In addition, public sector research on service delivery in transportation,[47] sanitation,[48] and police[49] among others shows that organizational structure does effect service efficiency and effectiveness. Some of these researchers cautiously and rightfully call for further research on the relationship between structure and performance before making sweeping conclusions. Criteria for evaluating reorganizations need to be tailored to the specific situation and organization rather than relying on global measures, but the conventional wisdom that structure makes little or no difference to government performance needs reassessment.

Reorganization as Politics

Former Proverb: *Reorganization is a businesslike, scientific, apolitical process.* **Current Proverb:** *Reorganization is nothing more than the continuation of politics by other means.* Some reformers who preached the canons of integration de-emphasized the role of politics in reorganizing. Since they viewed reorganizations as apolitical, businesslike applications of scientific principles, politics was considered irrelevant or a necessary evil which might undermine scientific principles.[50] After World War II, scholars brought politics back into the reorganization process or, more accurately, better articulated the politics always present.[51] Perhaps because politics was so obviously salient yet overlooked, analysts overcompensated with a new conventional wisdom that reorganization is virtually all politics. Lester Salamon articulates this thinking: "'War,' Karl von Clausewitz once wrote, 'is nothing more than the continuation of politics by other means.' The same, it can now safely be asserted, is also true of that peculiar form of warfare known as government reorganization."[52]

Few practitioners or observers would deny the presence and sometimes pervasiveness of politics in reorganizing. Even authorities associated with orthodoxy, like Gulick, appreciated reorganization's political nature. Yet reorganization is more than just politics, often embodying management science, cultural values, human psychology, and other elements.[53] Preoccupation with reorganization's political aspects is as great a proverb as neglecting or denying its political nature.

Roosevelt and Brownlow as Zenith of Reorganization

Former Proverb: *The reorganization movement reached its zenith with the Brownlow Committee and the federal Reorganization Act of 1939.* **Current Proverb:** *The FDR-Brownlow impact on governmental organization has been vastly inflated.* Efforts by President Franklin Roosevelt and his Committee on Administrative Management (Brownlow Committee) perhaps have received more scrutiny than any other reorganization. Some have hailed this effort as a watershed or highpoint in the reorganization movement.[54]

Skeptics emphasize the weak act itself. The Reorganization Act of 1939, which finally passed after backlash to Roosevelt's court-packing and other factors led to initial defeat in 1938, was a political document watered down by compromise. The compromise Act of 1939 omitted extending the Civil Service Merit system, modernizing accounting procedures, overhauling 100 independent agencies, authorities, boards, and commissions and consolidating them into existing and new cabinet departments, and other Brownlow recommendations. Conventional wisdom on the Reorganization Act of 1939 views it as a product of political compromise much in keeping with other reorganization efforts like those following the Taft Commission and Hoover Commissions which accomplished less than they set out to achieve.[55]

But Roosevelt, Brownlow, Merriam, and Gulick have had the last laugh. Though the 1939 Act accomplished little directly, President Roosevelt soon after used reorganization plans authorized by the Act to transfer budgeting, research, and planning capabilities to the Executive Office of the President. This strengthening of presidential managerial capacity laid groundwork for the extensive managerial control exercised by the Office of Management and Budget during President Reagan's administration.[56] In addition, the orthodox doctrine exemplified in the *Papers on the Science of Administration*, first assembled as staff working papers for the Brownlow Committee, still permeates government administration in the United States today.[57] Hierarchy, specialization, grouping by function, unity of command, and other orthodox precepts so shape organizational life despite their being debunked in academic circles that practitioners and scholars have difficulty thinking in different terms.

Even when actions depart from orthodox theory, orthodoxy remains a frame of reference. The current proverb depreciating the result of Roosevelt's reorganizing efforts is just as much a proverb as the one sanctifying these efforts.

Implications

Barring crisis, Americans have repeatedly preferred to seek partial, satisfying solutions to governmental problems. This also holds for the underlying system of governance. Administrative reorganization has been one device for accomplishing what Don K. Price has termed "adjustment without amendment."[58]   Given the lack of consensus about what fundamental constitutional amendments are necessary, reorganizations will continue to make needed and unneeded adjustments.   Reorganizations will occur at all governmental levels, reflecting new or altered priorities,[59] power shifts,[60] changes in governmental role,[61] or need to modernize.[62]

As controversy over the proverbs shows, the record of reorganizing has rarely achieved the glowing promises claimed.   Americans must not only become more realistic in their expectations for reorganizing—oilcans and tuneups can only accomplish so much.   They must also become more selective and creative when reorganizing, or they will continue to misuse or underutilize this tool.   Government's approach to organizing and reorganizing has predominantly emphasized *tradition* ("we have always organized this way") and *ideology* ("doctrine tells us to organize this way").   The prevailing mindset limits use of generic organization theory in government, including applying organizational design to create organizations for contingent tasks, technologies, employees, and conditions.[63]

A design dilemma must be faced in future organizing and reorganizing.   Americans' allegiance to doctrine, whether embodied in popular representation, neutral expertise, or executive leadership, and their preference for ad hoc structural tinkering run against the concept of organizational design—intentionally tailoring structure to fit with political and management strategy, technology, and other factors.   But some consider reorganizing more like gardening than engineering or architecture.   "Like gardening, reorganization is not an act, but a process, a continuing job.   And like gardening, reorganization is work whose benefits may largely accrue to one's successors."[64] Even if the organic view of reorganizing is more appropriate than the mechanistic, greater intentionality promises to yield more benefits to future successors. Gardens need not grow like topsy. Perhaps reorganizers should be emulating genetic engineering to produce new hybrids designed for special tasks and needs.

Also as the proverbs show, the subject of reorganization tends to produce more heat than light. Both former and current proverbs tend to the extremes toward particular perspectives. What is needed is more practice and research based on broader, more balanced views of reorganization, its limitations, and possibilities.

ENDNOTES

1.   The flavor of this theory is captured in Charles S. Hyneman, "Administrative Reorganization: An Adventure into Science and Theology," *Journal of Politics*, vol. 1 (1939), pp. 62-75; Dwight Waldo, *The Administrative State: A Study of the Political Theory of American Public Administration*, 2d. ed. (New York: Holmes & Meier Publishers, 1984); James L. Garnett, *Reorganizing State Government: The Executive Branch* (Boulder: Westview Press, 1980); Peri E. Arnold, *Making the Managerial Presidency: Comprehensive Reorganization Planning, 1905-1980* (Princeton: Princeton University Press, 1986).

2.   James G. March and Johan P. Olsen, "Organizing Political Life: What Administrative Reorganization Tells Us About Government," *American Political Science Review*, vol. 77 (March 1983), p. 286.

3.   A similar thesis is taken by Peri E. Arnold, "Executive Reorganization & the Origins of the Managerial Presidency," *Polity*, vol. 8 (Summer 1981), pp. 565-599.

4.   See Waldo, *The Administrative State*, and Donald L. Robinson, ed., *Reforming American Government: The Bicentennial Papers of the Committee on the Constitutional System* (Boulder: Westview Press, 1985).

5.   See Waldo, *The Administrative State*, and Arnold, *Making the Managerial Presidency*.

6.   Arnold, *Making the Managerial Presidency*, p. 8.

7.   This discussion inevitably draws from Herbert Kaufman, "Emerging Conflicts in the Doctrines of American Public Administration," *American Political Science Review*, vol. 50 (December 1956), pp. 1057-1073.

8.   Herbert Kaufman, *Politics and Policies in State and Local Government* (Englewood Cliffs: Prentice-Hall, 1963), pp. 35-36.

9.   See Leonard White, *The Republican Era* (New York: Macmillan, 1958); and Arnold, *Making the Managerial Presidency*. According to a thesis advanced by Skowronek, the underlying fragmentation established by the Constitution created an environment for weak administration that surfaced after President Jackson under presidents with a weaker conception of management and faced with a larger, more complex society to govern. See Stephen Skowronek, *Building a New American State: The Expansion of National Administrative Capacities, 1877-1920* (Cambridge, England: Cambridge University Press, 1982), and Arnold, *Making the Managerial Presidency*.

10.   Michael Nelson, "A Short, Ironic History of American National Bureaucracy," *Journal of Politics*, vol. 44 (August 1982), pp. 747-778.

11.   See Nelson, "A Short, Ironic History."

12.   Herbert Kaufman, "Emerging Conflicts in the Doctrines of American Public Administration," *American Political Science Review*, vol. 50 (December 1956), p. 1063;

Waldo, *The Administrative State*, pp. 30-39; and Richard J. Stillman, II, *The Rise of the City Manager* (Albuquerque: University of New Mexico Press, 1974).

13. Kaufman, "Emerging Conflicts," p. 1063.

14. The basic canons of integration are voiced in the President's [Franklin Roosevelt] Committee on Administrative Management, *Report with Special Studies* (Washington: Government Printing Office, 1937); Commission on Organization of the Executive Branch of Government (first Hoover Commission), *Report to Congress* (Washington: Government Printing Office, 1949); and President Nixon's Message to Congress on his Departmental Reorganization Program, March 25, 1971. At the state level, the best statement of administrative orthodoxy is found in A. E. Buck, *The Reorganization of State Governments in the United States* (New York: Columbia University Press, 1938); and at the local level, the New York Bureau of Municipal Research, *New York State Constitution and Government: An Appraisal* (New York: New York Bureau of Municipal Research, 1915).

15. Arnold, "Executive Reorganization & the Origins of the Managerial Presidency."

16. Garnett, *Reorganizing State Government*, and Garnett, "Organizing and Reorganizing State and Local Government," in Jack L. Rabin and Don Dodd, eds., *State and Local Government Administration* (New York: Marcel Dekker, Inc., 1985), updated by author.

17. Richard F. Kneip, "Reorganizing the Executive Branch," in *Innovations in State Government: Messages from the Governors* (Washington: National Governors' Conference, 1974), p. 37.

18. National Association of Counties and International City Management Association, *The County Yearbook, 1978* (Washington: National Association of Counties and International City Management Association, 1978).

19. Waldo, *The Administrative State*, p. 33.

20. Garnett, *Reorganizing State Government*, and "Organizing and Reorganizing State and Local Government," updated by author.

21. U.S. Bureau of the Census, *1982 Census of Governments, vol. I: Governmental Organization* (Washington: Government Printing Office, 1983).

22. See James D. Carroll, A. Lee Fritschler, and Bruce L. R. Smith, "Supply-Side Management in the Reagan Administration," *Public Administration Review*, vol. 45 (November/December 1985), pp. 805-814; Michael G. Hansen, "Management Improvement Initiatives in the Reagan Administration: Round Two," *Public Administration Review*, vol. 45 (March/April 1985), pp. 441-446; Harold Seidman and Robert Gilmour, *Politics, Position, and Power: From the Positive to the Regulatory State* (New York: Oxford University Press, 1986).

23. Carroll, Fritschler, and Smith, "Supply-Side Management."

24. Glen Sparrow, "The Emerging Chief Executive: The San Diego Experience," *National Civic Review* (December 1985), pp. 328-547.

25. For recent essays debating the need for constitutional change, see Robinson, *Reforming American Government*.

26. Garnett, *Reorganizing State Government*, updated by author.

27. Luther H. Gulick, interview with James L. Garnett (30 November 1976).

28. Edward K. Hamilton, "On Nonconstitutional Management of a Constitutional Problem," in Charles H. Levine, ed., *Managing Fiscal Stress: The Crisis in the Public Sector* (Chatham, NJ: Chatham House, 1980), p. 53.

29. Herbert A. Simon, "The Proverbs of Administration," *Public Administration Review*, vol. 6 (Winter 1946), pp. 53-67.

30. The prevailing proverb is best expressed in Harold Seidman, *Politics, Position, and Power: The Dynamics of Federal Organization* (New York: Oxford University Press, 1970); and Lester Salamon, "The Question of Goals," in Peter Szanton, ed., *Federal Reorganization: What Have We Learned?* (Chatham, NJ: Chatham House, 1981).

31. Salamon, "The Question of Goals," p. 66.

32. See, e.g., Buck, *The Reorganization of State Governments*, and G. Ross Stephens, "Monetary Savings from State Reorganization in Missouri or You'll Wonder Where the Money Went," *Midwest Review of Public Administration*, vol. 7 (January 1973), pp. 32-35.

33. Kenneth J. Meier, "Executive Reorganization of Government: Impact on Employment and Expenditures," *American Journal of Political Science*, vol. 24 (August 1980), pp. 396-412.

34. James Conant, "Reorganization and the Bottom Line," *Public Administration Review*, vol. 46 (January/February 1986), pp. 48-56.

35. Conant, "Reorganization and the Bottom Line."

36. Meier, "Executive Reorganization of Government," and Salamon, "The Question of Goals."

37. Conant, "Reorganization and the Bottom Line."

38. *Ibid.*

39. Even though many reorganization studies use the terms interchangeably, efficiency and effectiveness are different concepts. *Efficiency* is the ratio of service or product inputs to outputs. *Effectiveness* is the degree to which an agency or program achieves its objectives.

40. See, for example, J. M. Mathews, "State Administrative Reorganization," *American Political Science Review*, vol. 16 (August 1922), pp. 387-98; Buck, *Reorganization of State Governments*; and Gulick, interview.

41. Nixon, "President's Message," p. 3.

42. Herbert A. Simon, "The Proverbs of Administration," *Public Administration Review*, vol. 6 (Winter 1946), pp. 53-67; Herbert Simon, *Administrative Behavior: A study of the Decision Making Processes in Administrative Organization* (New York: Free Press, Macmillan, 1947); and Waldo, *The Administrative State*.

43. See Richard E. Dawson and James A. Robinson, "Interparty Competition, Economic Variables and Welfare Policies in the American States,"*Journal of Politics*, vol. 25 (1963), pp. 265-289; Thomas R. Dye, *Politics, Economics, and the Public: Policy Outcomes in the American States* (Chicago: Rand McNally, 1966).

44. The most perceptive critiques of determinants research include Herbert Jacob and Michael Lipsky, "Outputs, Structure, and Power: An Assessment of Changes in the Study of State and Local Politics," *The Journal of Politics*, vol. 30 (1968), pp. 510-538; Phillip M. Gregg, "Units and Levels of Analysis," *Publius*, vol. 4 (Fall 1974), pp. 59-86.

45. Leading the prevailing proverb that structure counts little and influencing many others through their significant work are: Herbert A. Simon, *Administrative Behavior*; James G. March and Herbert A. Simon, *Organizations* (New York: John Wiley & Sons, 1958); Herbert Kaufman, "Reflections on "Administrative Reorganization," in Joseph Pechman, ed., *Setting National Priorities: The 1978 Budget* (Washington: The Brookings Institution, 1977).

46. Demonstrating the salience of structure for business performance are: Joan Woodward, *Management and Technology* (London: Her Majesty's Stationery Office, 1958); Alfred D. Chandler, Jr., *Strategy and Structure: Chapters in the History of the American Industrial*

Enterprise (Cambridge: The MIT Press, 1973); and James W. Frederickson, "The Strategic Decision Process and Organizational Structure," *The Academy of Management Review*, vol. 11 (April 1986), p. 297.

47. James L. Perry and Timlynn T. Babitsky, "Comparative Performance in Urban Bus Transit: Assessing Privatization Strategies," *Public Administration Review*, vol. 46 (January/February 1986), pp. 57-66.

48. James M. Hartman assisted by Linda M. Mitchell, "Sanitation," in Charles Brecher and Raymond D. Hortons, eds., *Setting Municipal Priorities: American Cities and the New York Experience* (New York: New York University Press, 1984), pp. 415-445.

49. Dennis C. Smith, "Police," in Brecher and Horton, *Setting Municipal Priorities*, pp. 380-414.

50. See, for example, Buck, *The Reorganization of State Governments*, p. 28.

51. Many scholars stress the political nature of reorganization, especially Harold Seidman, *Politics, Position, and Power*; and Salmon, "A Question of Goals."

52. Salamon, "A Question of Goals," p. 58.

53. Cultural and communications aspects of reorganization have recently been explored by Steven Maynard-Moody, Donald D. Stull, and Jerry Mitchell, "Reorganization as Status Drama: Building, Maintaining, and Displacing Dominant Subcultures," *Public Administration Review*, vol. 46 (July/August 1986), pp. 301-310.

54. See Barry D. Karl, *Executive Reorganization and Reform in the New Deal* (Cambridge: Harvard University Press, 1970); and Herbert Emmerich, *Federal Organization and Administrative Management* (University: University of Alabama Press, 1971).

55. Richard Polenberg, *Reorganizing Roosevelt's Government* (Cambridge: Harvard University Press, 1966); and Harvey C. Mansfield, "Federal Executive Reorganization: Thirty Years of Experience," *Public Administration Review*, vol. 29 (July/August 1969), pp. 332-345.

56. "Budget Office Evolves Into Key Policy Maker," *Congressional Quarterly* (14 September 1985), pp. 1809 and 1815.

57. Luther H. Gulick and Lyndall Urwick, eds., *Papers on the Science of Administration* (New York: Institute of Public Administration, 1937).

58. Don K. Price, "Words of Caution About Structural Change," in Robinson, ed., *Reforming American Government*, p. 47.

59. Rufus E. Miles, Jr., "Considerations for a President Bent on Reorganization," *Public Administration Review*, vol. 37 (March/April 1977), pp. 155-162.

60. Garnett, *Reorganizing State Government*; and Seidman and Gilmour, *Politics, Position, and Power.*

61. Samuel Beer, "The Modernization of American Federalism," *Publius*, vol. 3 (Fall 1973), pp. 50-95.

62. Frederick C. Mosher, ed., *Governmental Reorganization: Cases and Commentary* (Indianapolis: Bobbs-Merrill, 1967).

63. Barry Bozeman and Michael Crow, "Organization Theory and State Government Structure: Are There Lessons Worth Learning?" *State Government*, vol. 58 (1986), pp. 144-151.

64. Peter Szanton, "So You Want to Reorganize the Government?" in Peter Szanton, ed., *Federal Reorganization: What Have We Learned?* (Chatham, NJ: Chatham House, 1981), p. 24.

CHAPTER FIVE

Public Executives: Imperium, Sacerdotium, Collegium? Bicentennial Leadership Challenges

CHESTER A. NEWLAND[*]

Challenges surrounding public executive leadership as America enters the third century of the Constitution are examined here. The focus is chiefly the presidency but with some comparisons and contrasts with professional local government managers. Since the beginnings of formal study of public administration, these two quite different executive levels have been principal concerns. Space limits prevent dealing with other executives here, and these two levels best highlight bicentennial era developments.

Three crucial dimensions of the present environment of presidential and other public executive performance are discussed initially. *First*, big national expenditures fund many public activities which are performed by private interests and state and local governments; except for such direct entitlements as Social Security, relatively less is spent on functions performed directly by the national government. *Second*, American political parties—never disciplined in a European parliamentary sense—declined for

---

[*] **Chester A. Newland** is Professor of Public Administration with the University of Southern California in Sacramento and Washington. He is a past president of the American Society for Public Administration and is a member of the National Academy of Public Administration.

nearly three decades before the 1980s as vehicles of sustained, national coalition building; special interest groups and political action committees have grown enormously in numbers, expenditures, and influence. *Third*, mass media largely dominate communication of political and governmental affairs; political image makers encourage a media focus on personality and contrived situations more than on substantive achievement. Factors two and three combine to produce a common result: BIG money is required to finance today's politics. That has major consequences for public administration.

Big money in politics is significantly related to the first of two functions of chief executives which are discussed in part two of this assessment: executive staffing and increased reliance by presidents and other partisanly elected chief executives on transient political appointees for positions formerly filled by long-term professional experts. Besides executive staffing, a cluster of substantive functions of the chief executive is discussed in part two: policy leadership, implementation, and institutional/organizational maintenance and development. One thesis here is that achievement by the president and other elected political executives in these substantive responsibilities has been substantially diminished by a combination of high-level spoils and imperial/sacerdotal imagery.

The final part of this chapter focuses briefly on needed reforms. One thesis is that shared legislative/ executive systems and bipartisan, informed, and professional performance of public service are required to meet America's needs but that both the political environment and some public administration developments in the last 25 to 30 years have moved in opposite directions. A related proposition is that imperatives of political financing are seriously undermining public administration and that American politics must be a priority concern of the field, as it was in the reform era 100 years before when America celebrated its constitutional centennial.

The Governmental, Political, and Media Environment

American constitutional history since 1933 has been a record of national and presidential aggrandizement. But during the first half of this period of governmental growth, expansion was associated with reform values of public administration's "Golden Era": civic duty and public service; clearly defined channels of responsibility and accountability; economy and efficiency; and professional expertise and merit staffing. During the past 25 to 30 years, the conditions and values associated with continued growth of the national government have dramatically changed. By the start of the 1960s and continuing to the mid-1970s, effectiveness became a larger consideration than efficiency and economy, as governments entered a new policy era. By the start of the 1970s, professional experts were being increasingly displaced at the top of the national government by politically partisan appointees, and by the 1980s, a new era of high-level spoils had emerged. The images of the presidency in these two periods, 1930s-1950s and 1960s-1980s, are likewise studies in contrasts, as the media and other forces have increasingly shifted focus from coherent substance to personality and dramatic events.

Private and State/Local Performance of Nationally-Funded Functions

Before the New Deal and the beginnings of changes that resulted in big national government, American faith was deeply rooted in self help and self governance; private enterprise and competition; and popularly controlled, local, and limited government. The New Deal went far in changing the limits on the national government, and it went a considerable way in modifying conditions of the capitalist economy. But Roosevelt did not ask the nation to break with the deeper social and economic culture. Despite contrary hopes by some supporters and fears of more critics, the daring innovations of the New Deal were more actions to preserve personal liberties, individualism, and private property than to alter these deep currents of the American heritage. Pluralism and pragmatism were then developing in political currency, not waning, and they supported diversity and involvement in programs of the expanding national government, with efforts aimed at getting varied private interests and state and local governments engaged in myriad recovery activities. Support, not displacement, was a dominant theme. In short, while the New Deal built foundations for big national government, it also formed them to accommodate maximization of personal choice and performance of many federally funded activities by state and local governments and private interests. War soon followed, dramatically expanding traditional reliance on private business for mobilization. Atomic energy, interstate highway, and space science developments later furthered this pattern.

This mode of big government spending and performance of public functions in large part by private proxy linked support for expansion of the national government to powerful economic forces. Lyndon Johnson's Great Society was constructed on like ideas of bureaucratic clientelism learned in his New Deal youth and from his leadership in Congress and in space programs: create and coopt special interests and get them "to come reason together" as a coalition. Theodore Lowi's analysis of "interest-group liberalism" is a familiar explanation of some dimensions of these developments.[1]

By 1980, the growth of big national government by proxied performance had reached the following dimensions, as assessed by Frederick C. Mosher:

> . . . this suggests that only between 15 and 20 percent of federal spending is directed to activities that the federal government performs itself (other than making and superintending payments to others). More than half of that amount is applied to the operations, maintenance, and personnel compensation of the armed forces. The corollary is that considerably less than one-tenth of the federal budget is alloted to domestic activities that the federal government performs itself. My guess is that the percentage of federal expenditures so allotted amounts to between 5 and 7 percent of the budget.[2]

One consequence of big government by proxied performance is that profit-oriented private interests and state and local governments and their employees are coopted as proxy votes for more of the same. This is a contrary variation of the Niskanen thesis[3] that budget-maximizing bureaucrats are the cause of expanded governmental spending. Even some heirs to the public choice heritage now see the causes of governmental growth in more complex terms[4] and are skeptical of contracting out of public functions. Stuart Butler of the American Heritage Foundation, for example, has forcefully argued this position,[5] and Ted Kolderie effectively digested that perspective in 1986 in the *Public Administration Review*.[6] From a related but more mixed and self-contradictory perspective, David A. Stockman attributed the failure of the Reagan administration to reduce overall governmental spending to the *Triumph of Politics*. He filled his book with candid descriptions of ideological warfare about funding of such special interests as Jesse Helm's tobacco constituents, the dairy lobby, Medicare recipients, and defense contractors.[7]

While causes of governmental expansion are too complex for single explanations, increased spending is a reality. The national government budget amounted to only $4.7 billion (7.4 percent of GNP) when Franklin Roosevelt was elected in 1932. By 1936 when the Brownlow study (the President's Committee on Administrative Management) was started, the budget had increased to $8.4 billion (11.1 percent of GNP). Just before the War, the 1940 budget totaled $9.4 billion, still just over 11 percent of GNP. By 1950, the budget had increased to $42.5 billion (15 percent of GNP); in 1960 it was $92.5 billion (18.5 percent of GNP); in 1970 it was $196.6 billion (20.3 percent of GNP); and in 1980 it had climbed to $576 billion (22.5 percent of GNP). Under Reagan, the budget increased to $948.3 billion in FY 1985 (24.5 percent of GNP); and for FY 1987 the President's budget proposal, rejected by the Senate, called for expenditures of nearly $1 trillion.

Besides the political support for sustained or enlarged governmental spending which profitable proxied performance, grants, and income support programs may induce, this approach to government has major implications for public management. Frederick Mosher stated the case succinctly: ". . . the changes since the beginnings of the New Deal and since World War II have been of such magnitude as to alter fundamentally the nature of federal responsibilities and modes of operating, calling for a quite different approach to the role of federal management in American society."[8] Some of the management changes which in fact have occurred are touched on later in this analysis. First, two other key aspects of the public executive environment warrant discussion.

Declining Parties; Powerful Special Interests

Coalitions to promote broad, long-term, and reasonable compromises in the general civic interest are difficult to form and sustain today. Political party performance of that function started fading nationally in the late 1950s, and that decline continued into the 1980s. David Broder described this development in 1972 in his book, *The Party's Over.*[9] Today transient coalitions to win diverse objectives of special interests are formed with relative ease, in contrast with the period from the 1930s to the 1960s. Today's political developments might well be titled *The Parties' Takeover*, as special interest groups have vastly increased in number, financial resources, and political activities.

Declining political party capacity to sustain community-oriented rather than special interest coalitions is most evident nationally, although it appears present at all levels. Decline was first greatly felt throughout American society in the drum beat of 1960s' extremism: "you've got to be left or right!" Starting with John Kennedy, every presidential candidate and incumbent since has had to devise means of continuous and shifting coalition formation. Dorothy James, reviewing recent books on the subject in 1986, observed that "the authors agree that political parties are continuing to decline, leaving them open to transitory electoral combinations." She concluded that the emergence of any new party coalition is "highly improbable in the foreseeable future."[10] However, glimmers of a peculiar party renaissance, in loose league with Political Action Committees (PACs), could be discerned in work by the 1984 and 1986 congressional campaign committees.[11] President Reagan's fixed adherence to an agenda has also enhanced identification with his party, although at costs of an ideological orientation and strong Political Action Committee (PAC) influence. In 1984, only $612,247 of "independent" PAC spending was on behalf of Mondale; $15.3 million promoted Reagan's reelection.[12]

Special interest groups have flourished since the 1960s, and PACs have grown from 608 in 1974 to 4,009 at the outset of 1985. In the period, 1974-1980, PAC spending increased by 500 percent, and average contributions to congressional candidates tripled. While some research shows limited direct PAC influence on congressional roll call votes,[13] Federal Election Commission reports show that some 75 percent of PAC contributions go to incumbents whose records are known.[14] In the 1983-84 election cycle, nearly $105 million was spent by some 3,000 PACs in House and Senate races. In presidential elections, all independent PACs combined spent only $1.6 million in 1976, whereas the National Conservative Political Action Committee (NCPAC) alone spent $9.8 million promoting President Reagan's 1984 reelection.[15] On March 18, 1985, in *Federal Election Commission (FEC) v. NCPAC*,[16] the U.S. Supreme Court ruled in an opinion by Mr. Justice Rehnquist that Congress cannot limit such independent spending by PACs on behalf of presidential candidates.

The condition behind the decline of the parties before the emergence of PACs lies deep in American society. Richard Hofstadter observed some roots of the problem in 1948: "Bereft of a coherent and plausible body of belief—for the New Deal, if it did little more, went far to undermine old ways of thought—Americans have become more receptive than ever to dynamic personal leadership as a substitute."[17] Regional bases of party stability which remained strong through the 1950s have since been diminished and only partially replaced by new regional affinities.

The ephemeral but beguiling appeal of personality foreseen by Hofstadter was particularly evident in the 1980 election. Analysis shows that the one clear mandate was for an *image* of strong national leadership.[18] The vote demonstrated little sympathy for Reagan's later positions, except for support for some modest enhancement of defense. The principal chronicler of presidential elections from Eisenhower to Reagan, Theodore H. White, summarized the entire period from 1956 through 1980 in his poignant book title, *America in Search of Itself*. Of 1980, he wrote: " . . . there was questioning but not only of control but of national purpose itself. Somehow, public affairs had gone off track, almost as if the country had lost its way into the future. There was no sense of coherence in government; it did not respond; it could not manage."[19]

Evidence is that in presidential elections from 1952 through 1980, except for the vote for Reagan, Americans were concerned with issues of policy and performance. Reporting their findings in 1985, Arthur H. Miller and Martin P. Wattenberg noted that ". . . incumbents have been judged primarily on the basis of retrospective performance, challengers on prospective policy, and candidates running in nonincumbent races on prospective performance."[20] Although policy and performance concerns were clearly present before 1980, the focus was on the candidates personally, and they carried much of the burden of coalition formation without consistent party composition and coherence.

The political reality for presidential leadership—the necessity of direct, coordinated, White House relationships with a broad spectrum of special interest groups—gained institutional recognition in the Ford Administration by creation in the Executive Office of the President (EOP) of the Office of Public Liaison (OPL).[21] That new EOP office successfully served to link the unelected Ford administration with important interests.   However, during the first two Carter years OPL degenerated.   Carter had won election with a coalition of often-contradictory groups and without Democratic party alignment.   Pollster Pat Cadell exercised enormous influence over both President and Mrs. Carter, exacerbating discontinuities and conflicts in policies and their implementation. It was an administration which would not jell.   A more direct linkage between policy priorities and interest groups was sought after the second year by Anne Wexler, who clearly saw the OPL function as coalition building.   However, it remained obvious that needed coordination could not be achieved in the Carter White House.

By contrast, the Reagan administration's sophisticated public opinion polling, deliberately-managed communications, and professionally projected presidential image would require books to report, and too many such volumes have been produced to labor the point here.[22]   The Reagan victory in 1980 was crafted through sustained attention to coalition building, relying heavily on opinion polls and position assessments to create support.   Once in office, the polling and cultivation of PACs and other special interests continued as if the presidency were a continuous referendum focusing strategically on personality and image and on perceptions of issues by coalition forces.   In an era of declining political parties, this is the fate of many politicians: incessant coalition building and/or capture by powerful interest groups.   That has clearly become the fate of the American presidency.

Mass Media and the Sacerdotal Chief Executive

George Reedy wrote in 1970 of *The Twilight of the Presidency*,[23] based on perceptions of excessive cultivation of Lyndon Johnson's ego (which, like those of most presidents, needed no nourishment) and isolation of the presidency from ordinary public realities which are of extraordinary importance for executive leadership in a constitutional democracy. As a professional journalist and long-time LBJ associate, Reedy was aware of contradictory impacts of the media on the President—and vice versa. Television and print media both captured Johnson's attention and isolated him as he simultaneously watched three television monitors (while following the adjacent press ticker tape), falling more and more out of touch with political reality while eagerly following the media's incessantly repeated versions of it. The images of LBJ conveyed by the media were as unreal as the other messages which helped to lead him and the presidency into tragic isolation from the political world in which he had earlier functioned effectively as an exceptionally informed leader. The tragedy of Lyndon Johnson was, as much as anything else, one of mutually-indulged fascination between the media and the President.

In constitutional terms, problems of the 1960s paled against Richard Nixon's Watergate and related abuses of presidential power. The excesses led Arthur Schlesinger, Jr., to characterize the office in 1973 as the *Imperial Presidency*,[24] with power nurtured to the point of crisis. While the media and especially television contributed greatly to the aggrandizement of presidential power and the growing Imperial character of the office under presidents from Eisenhower through Nixon, the working press and related media deserve credit for discovering, reporting, and contributing to correction of many abuses. But the focus on the presidency intensified even more after Watergate, nurturing further aggrandizement.

Within the decade following Schlesinger's characterization of the presidency as Imperial, it took on yet another media-oriented image. With apologies to the fifth century's Gelasius and other important contributors to Western political thought, the American presidency today may be termed Sacerdotal.

Both Henry Fairlie in 1985[25] and Herbert Schmertz of the Mobil Oil Corporation in 1986 characterized the situation in such terms. Schmertz observed that the presidency has become a "shamanistic position—one in which the President, rather than execute the laws of the nation and perform the public will, becomes instead a figure who presides over the nation's public ceremony."[26] Schmertz attributed the change to interaction between the media and the presidency: "The result of this inordinate media focus on the White House is that presidential personality has become more important than presidential achievement. A president who charms and fascinates and entertains us becomes more precious than one who advances the nation's goals."[27]

This situation is not one created simply by the media. Political image making commonly starts from two perspectives: qualities projected by an official (or candidate) and predispositions of voters which are projected on the official. Pollsters and other professional image makers since the contest between Eisenhower and Stevenson have adapted mass communication techniques to politics and government as they have to other aspects of society.

Big money is required to participate in today's political environment of big special interests, PACs, and big media. This is associated with reliance on private interests and state and local governments to perform national government functions. Resulting impacts on leadership in public administration are large. Some of these are discussed next.

Executive Staffing and Substantive Performance

Two clusters of chief executive functions are discussed here. The first is executive staffing which thrusts the president and many other partisanly elected public executives into political spoils activities. The other cluster is substantive: (a) policy/program leadership and implementation and (b) institutional/organizational maintenance and development.

Staffing: More Politicians; Fewer Professionals

The greatest civil service issues today are old ones in new guise: To what extent are appointed officials and career civil servants responsible to the chief executive and/or to the legislature and/or the law? To what extent should the bureaucracy be staffed by partisan political appointees and/or merit-based, career civil servants? To what extent should careerists be involved in policy deliberations; and to what extent should partisan appointees be involved in program implementation and administrative management?

As policy choices have become increasingly complex and controversial since the early 1960s, and as regulations, transfer payments, grants, and contracting out of functions have increased in the past 25 to 30 years, answers to those questions have shifted in practice to greatly increased exercise of partisan presidential power over the bureaucracy at some expense of congressional authority; substantially increased staffing by partisan, presidential loyalists and coalitionists who represent special interests; reduced reliance on careerists in policy deliberations; and increased utilization of presidential partisans in administrative management and program implementation, including field-level positions.

The high financial stakes involved in government today account significantly for these changes. The three environmental factors discussed in part one largely explain the big money required to finance elections and other political activities, leading to the new spoils. *Illegal* corruption is not extensively evident, although reports of problems with contractors in defense, space, commodities, and other publicly-funded activities have increased dramatically since the late 1970s.[28] Also, the relatively small compensation of public office is seldom the objective in today's spoils; more often public compensation may be a disincentive for high income individuals to accept appointments. An incentive instead may be anticipated future income from connections established and information gained while briefly in politically-appointed office. Trading of political access for financial gain is hardly new, of course; Thomas G. Corcoran, President Roosevelt's "fixer," became conspicuous for dealings as a lobbyist after leaving the White House. Today, the fixers are legion, and hawking of access is too routine to be conspicuous. Michael K. Deaver's remunerative brokerage of connections made headlines in 1986 only due to his current-style boldness and President Reagan's continued personal support of his friend's official White House access. Edward J. Rollins, Lyn Nofziger, and many other first-term Reagan officials have engaged in political brokerage with little notice, as much smaller numbers did earlier in the Carter, Nixon, and Johnson administrations.[29]

To deal with politically changed conditions, the Nixon administration took the first dramatic steps to staff with presidential loyalists many positions formerly filled by career experts. Some of those efforts were reported by Richard P. Nathan in *The Plot That Failed*.[30] Much later, supporting partisan control of the bureaucracy, Nathan summarized the most moderate and informed views behind both the Nixon and Reagan efforts: "I think it is appropriate and, in fact, desirable in our governmental system for political appointees to be involved in administrative processes. I believe, furthermore, that when the wheel of government rotates again to the liberal side on domestic issues, this is precisely what social policy liberals must do in their turn."[31] This viewpoint embraces disruptions and discontinuity as the most effective way to accomplish desired governmental changes. This perspective reflects what may now be a dominant view of political scientists, but it contrasts with practices which dominated public administration before the late 1960s. For example, Don K. Price, in a 1944 *Public Administration Review* exchange with Harold J. Laski, was able to say with confidence: "Partisan appointments have become nearly obsolete in the United States government."[32] By 1986, notions of the Nixon, Carter, and Reagan administrations had made Don Price's observation obsolete.

Carter's Civil Service Reform Act (CSRA) of 1978 did more to legitimate civil service deinstitutionalization and politicization than any other single development. During the preceding two decades, however, collective bargaining and related pressures had already given civil service some image of "just another self-interest group." Also, long before that, linkages of career bureaucracies with special interests served by them were common. But the CSRA provided centralized means of presidential politicization; it made legal some personnel flexibilities which the Malek/May Manual of the Nixon years sought to accomplish indirectly. Interestingly when the Act abolished the bipartisan Civil Service Commission and placed the new Office of Personnel Management under a single partisan appointee of the president, the change was justified in part from experience of professionally-managed local governments *in which such partisan domination of civil services is not allowed.*

Although the distinctions were lost in Carter's 1978 change, the differences are enormous between the increasingly partisan and powerful presidency, characterized by incessant conflicts with Congress, and local governmental institutions which focus authority in the legislative body, with subordinate, professionally-managed administration. Also, with respect to staffing, practices in professionally-managed governments have little resemblance to national developments under the CSRA. While alternatives to bipartisan civil service commissions and narrowly protectionist "merit" systems are common, including appointment of the personnel officer by the professional chief executive and managerial authority to hire, fire, develop, and discipline employees, high standards of professional expertise are required and practiced in professionally-managed local governments. By contrast, U.S. OPM directors have been clear partisans in background and conduct. Reagan's first OPM director filled top positions with factional partisans, most of whom lacked job-related expertise, and he frequently demonstrated disdain for Congress. President Reagan renominated him for factionally partisan reasons, although he lacked sufficient support even in the Republican-controlled Senate to survive the hearing process.[33] Unlike such special-interest-oriented, presidentially-dominated practice, council-manager government commonly focuses on collaboration for responsible public service.

Presidential staffing is clearly political and for partisan advantage, however, and those who accept that difference from professionally-oriented government have unsuccessfully attempted to improve it. Two related sets of problems have plagued the presidential political appointment system since the Nixon years: deficient quality and continuity of appointees and the necessity of legally enforced ethical standards for these nonprofessionals.

The National Academy of Public Administration (NAPA) has studied both of these issues, stressing needs for improved recruiting of qualified political appointees, enhanced executive compensation, and "clarification" (easing) of rules on conduct and conflicts of interest.[34] One past effort to deal with these issues has added a dilemma: requirements of the Ethics Act of 1978 have discouraged acceptance of subcabinet-level political appointments by experienced experts, increasing reliance on junior-level political operatives to fill such positions as those of assistant secretaries. Thus, the result has sometimes been opposite to the Act's purpose. Several prescriptions for political appointee problems have been written, two by former Nixon administration officials, Frederick V. Malek and Laurence E. Lynn, Jr.[35] Neither appeared to have an impact on the political system. Lynn later completed research on five Reagan appointees, published in 1985 by the Urban Institute. He summarized 1981 presidential staffing as follows: ". . . the Reagan administration appeared from the outset to embrace the notion that faithful supporters in key executive positions could be a potent tool of administrative leadership. The primary qualification for appointment—overshadowing managerial competence and experience or familiarity with issues—appeared to be the extent to which an appointee shared the president's values. . . ."[36]

Studies like those of by NAPA, Malek, and Lynn are based on assumptions that presidential staffing is or should be, in the words of one Academy book, "to improve management in the rough and tumble of power politics" and "to appoint men and women whose competence, integrity, creativity, and political sensitivity will serve the nation well."[37] Experience since the late 1960s suggests that those concerns for governmental excellence are a lower priority of the contemporary presidency than are the prizes of high-level spoils. In contrast with spoils practices of the earlier era, today's appointees generally lack long-standing ties to Congress (which formerly enhanced shared powers); they owe their loyalties and access to the special interests which comprise the president's coalition and which fund elections. Playing this new form of spoils may be required of a president to sustain support in this era of weak political parties, powerful but fluid interest groups, and image projection through mass media. All are expensive practices. National incapacity and corruption are two increasingly evident costs which are noted below.

Policy Leadership, Implementation, and Institutional Maintenance

Policies and their implementation are the big prizes in America's trillion-dollar national government, with its dependence on proxied performance by private interests and state and local governments. At all governmental levels, policy complexity reached new highs by the 1960s, resulting in new challenges for public executives and a proliferation of policy studies programs in universities. Pressures were first felt and acted upon mostly at local levels where dramatic conflicts and changes were directly experienced. Major structural changes to deal with new policy complexities were not formally made in the Executive Office of the President until the Nixon administration, although new patterns of policy choice started under Kennedy and became highly significant under Johnson. Contrasts between these local and national government developments are instructive for this bicentennial era.

Local Government Leadership. Local government councils and their appointed professional managers provided much of the initial public administration leadership in the 1950s and 1960s as policy/program effectiveness issues became greater than the traditional reform era concerns for economy and efficiency. In 1958, the *Public Administration Review* published a symposium which focused on city managers' policy responsibilities.[38] Later, when Norton Long wrote in 1965 in *PAR* about challenges of educating public administrators for policy leadership, he focused on city managers, not national or state government executives, as chief examples of those fulfilling such responsibilities.[39] Following conflicts of the late 1960s, Keith Mulrooney edited a *PAR* symposium which captured much of the orientation of socially-activist local management at that time.[40]

In 1978-79, the International City Management Association (ICMA) worked through a Committee on Future Horizons of the Profession to probe responsibilities for leadership to the year 2000. George Schrader, then Dallas City Manager and chair of the committee, summarized dominant perspectives: "Greater day-to-day involvement in concerns of elected officials," and "more emphasis on brokering among interests in the community, negotiating among conflicting interests."[41] Throughout its deliberations, the ICMA Committee stressed what members called "Buy Back Federalism." Members urged reduction of both national government funding and restrictions on local government affairs. These managers preferred higher professional standards and less partisanly directed practices than are associated with nationally-funded, proxied performance of public functions. In the group's later 20-year projection for the profession, four public service ideals were stressed:

- The prime ideal of the profession must be that of excellence in management. . . .

- We must be the strongest believers in democracy. . . .

- The concept of equity is also one of our ideals for the future. . . .

- Our commitment to ethical conduct should remain high.[42]

In short, professional local managers examined 25 years of practical policy leadership experience, explored probable future trends and needs, and embraced public service and civic idealism as realistic means to reconcile challenging requirements of politics and administration. *That reflective process and the resulting choice contrast with directions taken in the national government in the same period.*

The Policy Era and the Presidency. In the 1960 presidential campaign, a policy backlog was an issue against Eisenhower and Nixon. Acting even before his narrow victory on pledges to interest groups in his coalition, Kennedy appointed partisan task forces to develop policy agendas. By the end of 1960, eleven groups were working on foreign policy and eight in domestic affairs. This practice continued after Kennedy took office, as in the development of Executive Order 10988, which introduced collective bargaining into the federal service over strong protests of an overwhelming majority of career service organizations, keeping a campaign pledge to AFL-CIO supporters.

Under Truman and Eisenhower, reform era orthodoxy had more often prevailed in policy development. Congress set policy, subject to increasing executive branch leadership from Roosevelt forward; institutionalized professional expertise in the agencies and in the EOP, particularly in the Bureau of the Budget (BOB), guided presidential policy involvement; and EOP remained small, relying on cabinet departments and agencies to implement programs, subject to close congressional oversight and liaison with long-term career executives. The "iron triangle" of Congress, interest groups, and specialized bureaucracies served political interests of the time, but with some public service orientation to general interests.   Under both Truman and Eisenhower, BOB functioned as a nonpartisan, professionally-staffed agency.   Kennedy did not alter BOB's budget role, but policy influence was shifted to the President's coalition groups and personal aides.

Lyndon Johnson moved much further to establish policy leadership in the White House Office, relying on his own congressional experience and assigning Joseph Califano responsibility for coordination of Great Society programs. BOB's traditional policy role and capacity declined drastically.   In his memoirs, Johnson stated the reason for his actions: "I had watched this [policy] process for years, and I was convinced that it did not encourage enough fresh or creative ideas.   The bureaucracy of the government is too preoccupied with day-to-day operations, and there is a strong bureaucratic inertia dedicated to preserving the status quo."[43] While Johnson fully entrusted implementation to careerists, he and his aides personally brokered the policy process with Congress and with coalition groups in such fields as civil rights, health research, the arts, transportation, communications, and defense.   It was a diverse political coalition which helped Johnson win by a landslide in 1964, but it fell apart under pressures of the Vietnam War.

Developments of the presidential policy apparatus from Nixon through Reagan are too extensive for summary here. Detailed analyses elsewhere[44] support some clear conclusions.   The first relates to achievement of a workable balance in policy activities between Congress, the EOP, and cabinet departments and agencies.   Congressional efforts to limit the size of the policy apparatus have only obscured EOP expansion, and restrictions on its partisan character have entirely failed.   When BOB was reorganized into the Office of Management and Budget (OMB), the newly created Domestic Council was required by law to be staffed by personnel subject to the Hatch Act.   From the start under John Ehrlichman, however, it developed into a policy agency composed of presidential loyalists.   Contrary to congressional intentions, Nixon's policy apparatus and its interagency task forces became instruments for isolating cabinet officers from the President and for EOP control of subordinates in the departments, bypassing responsible Cabinet officers and agency heads.   Under President Ford, the most active part of the domestic policy machinery, the

Economic Policy Board (EPB), effectively linked the EOP, cabinet officers, and operating agencies, correcting the Nixon era circumvention of cabinet officials. The Reagan administration, drawing in part on Ford's EPB history, managed a cabinet council arrangement which also went far in linking key levels of political policy officials in the administration. Careerists were mostly excluded, however, particularly during Reagan's first five years. Also, the budget and OMB's Stockman determined policy more than the Office of Policy Development did. With the OMB appointment of James Miller in 1985, officials expressed hope that the change, along with the earlier appointments of Donald Regan as chief of staff, would reverse that relationship. In fact, Cabinet Council reorganization in Reagan's second term did enhance forceful leadership by key Cabinet officials.[45]   With respect to the larger issue—collaborative congressional/executive policy development—the Reagan administration in its first year almost entirely won over Congress for the Economic Recovery Act of 1981 and related changes. That was because Congress went along with the President. But thereafter, the administration showed virtually no disposition during the first term to collaborate with Congress, not even the Republican-controlled Senate. Thus, policy processes became deadlocked as a result of increasing concentration of power in the presidency and a failure to share responsibility with Congress to deal with such problems as the deficit.

A second cluster of issues concerns achievement of an optimum balance in the EOP policy apparatus and in the executive branch generally between institutionalized professional expertise and presidential loyalists and partisans. The deinstitutionalization of BOB as a professionally oriented policy shop, which started modestly under Kennedy and Johnson, was culminated under Nixon. Partisan politicization of the separate EOP policy apparatus (the Domestic Council) at its creation started a sustained practice. Later, the CSRA of 1978 provided a vehicle for deinstitutionalization and politicization of upper reaches of civil service, and the Reagan administration vigorously used it for that purpose. Also, in the first transition following adoption of the Inspectors General Act of 1978, Reagan summarily fired all of the Inspectors General to assert presidential (rather than shared congressional) control over them, violating the clear spirit of the law.

In 1986, the Iranian arms/Contra money laundering operation in the Reagan White House was but one more example of disastrous consequences of these two failures of the American presidential system. That scandal reflected both deliberate, sustained presidential rejection of shared legislative-executive authority and failure to rely on professional expertise within legally institutionalized channels.

Underlying these two sets of issues is the greatest challenge for a successful presidency: *achievement, in collaboration with Congress, of a reasonable measure of strategic, deliberate, presidential policy leadership in behalf of general public interests* in today's environment of declining political party capacity to sustain a coalition devoted to civic responsibility; powerful, fluid special interests which often have single purposes which they will not compromise; and mass media in which image making is an incessant reality. *The first half of that equation has been lost in American national government to the second half.*

Similar contests between conflicting interests are being waged in many state and local governments also, but space constraints limit this assessment. It may be sufficient to note that political pressures on council-manager governments—those which still contrast most with the presidential system in resisting special-interest politicization and deinstitutionalization of expertise—have increased dramatically since the mid-1970s. These pressures—largely for partisan, mayoral systems—derive significantly from efforts of contractors, regulated interests, PACs, and party activists to forge local bases for political activities which bridge the varied levels of American government.

Bicentennial Challenges: Special-Interest Brokerage versus Transformational Leadership

Descriptions and prescriptions of roles of presidents and of professional public executives are nearly impossible to combine in a brief analysis. Even to highlight contrasts between them is difficult, but the effort is instructive about leadership challenges in this bicentennial era. One crucial issue is the relationship of high cost politics and public administration—also a problem of the reform era when

America celebrated the centennial. Today's variation on the issue focuses most clearly on the presidency, where special-interest brokerage dominates despite sophisticated projection of an image of transformational leadership.

Collegial/Transformational Leadership Challenges

This descriptive essay has ignored most important prescriptions for successful executive leadership which are based on futures projections and historical and other research on effective performance of presidents and professional executives. For example, Harlan Cleveland's 1985 book, *The Knowledge Executive*, and his Dimock award-winning essay in *PAR* analyzed many relevant issues of "an information-rich polity" in which "the very definition of 'control' changes."[46] Dealing with presidential leadership in 1986, Cleveland further developed his analysis in the difficult area of foreign policy as "people's policy." He explained that "the President's task is not 'to make policy.' It is *to cohere* and *to consult*: to formulate in an understandable strategy the many things the U.S. government is trying to do at any one time to carry the people's policy into action."[47]

The sort of interaction between leaders and followers which was called for by Cleveland was earlier described by James MacGregor Burns as more than merely transactional or a progress of exchange. In his landmark study, *Leadership*, Burns in 1978 provided an assessment which still fits the American presidency: "True leadership is not merely symbolic or ceremonial, nor are 'great men' simply the medium or mechanism through which social forces operate."[48] In American national government today, both the presidency and Congress generally have become largely mechanisms through which special interests operate in a process of exchange. By contrast, the historical leaders termed great by Burns engaged in transformational leadership for "the achievement of real change in the direction of 'higher' values."[49]

Looking in 1980 toward the year 2000, professional local managers portrayed their executive leadership challenge in transformational terms, like Burns's. They stressed brokerage of community-oriented policies which are sustained by informed, popular consent, maintaining *The Essential Community*.[50] They stressed the symbiotic character of effective citizenship (civic duty) and professional expertise (responsible public service) in constitutional democracy. As the linking pin, these professionals focused on the popularly elected legislature. Like America's constitutional founders, they envisioned legislative policy dominance and shared legislative-executive responsibility as crucial to constitutional government in a society of popular self governance. This local system of governance goes even farther, however, in rejection of the separation of powers than does the constitutional system of checks and balances. Council-manager government is closer to a parliamentary form in the legislature's authority to dismiss the executive at any time; *and* it is not a *cabinet*-parliamentary form, in which the executive is nonetheless superior to the legislature.

This focus on a popularly responsible legislature as crucial to excellence in public administration was fundamental to the reform movement which started 100 years ago. Related was a concern with the degeneration of politics due to control by proliferating special interests in the then-new technological-engineering era. Those years had parallels to the information era and politics of this bicentennial period. But these contrasts were also important: the new emphasis on the executive in the reform era focused at the national level on shared legislative-executive responsibility and initially on bipartisan structures for regulatory control, both of new technologically-based policy fields and of developing internal governmental institutions, like civil service.

Stress of shared powers as the American public executive became increasingly important from the 1880s through the 1930s was based on the heritage from the first century under the Constitution. As Louis Fisher has documented, the doctrine of separation of powers had largely given away in practice by the 1790s to the practical workings of checks and balances.[51] Thus, shared powers dominated legislative-executive relationships almost from the inception of the Constitution into the 1960s. However, political changes from the 1960s into the 1980s significantly undermined conditions which formerly encouraged legislative-executive collaboration while bolstering others which contribute to conflicts (which were often high already). Two such factors associated with the presidency have been stressed throughout this analysis.

First, politicization and deinstitutionalization of professional expertise in the leadership of EOP and the executive branch generally have contributed to a shift from shared legislative-executive authority to a growing separation of powers. In the period of aggrandizement of the presidency from the 1930s through the 1950s, the presidency and the expanding executive branch were increasingly associated with such lofty administrative ideals as cutting-edge expertise, professional commitment to public service, economy and efficiency, and accountability. While members of Congress could never easily contradict their district and state interests, it was increasingly possible to compromise many of them in support of shared national priorities which were crafted with advice of trusted professional experts with substantial, long-established reputations which were linked not only to specialized interests but to more broadly authoritative communities nationwide. *Those career experts were generally as subject to congressional oversight as to presidential control.* But those conditions changed starting in the 1960s, accelerating under Nixon, and culminating with Carter and Reagan. Ties between professionally expert civil servants and members of Congress were increasingly cut off by a jealously powerful executive branch, and single-interest oriented groups eagerly moved into the void. Today, the upper reaches of the executive branch are largely staffed by highly transient representatives of the particularistic interests and personal loyalists who comprise the President's political coalition. Relatively few have long-established ties to Congress and to public service values. Their principal links with Congress are often through special interests and PACs which have become principal bridges between the branches and levels of government.

A second, related factor which undermined collaborative legislative-executive relations in the 1960s and 1970s (and which has changed slightly in character in the 1980s) is the growing dependence of presidential and congressional incumbents and other candidates on particularistic interest groups to form transient coalitions. These forces exacerbated declining capacities in the 1960s-1970s to join Congress and the President in a system of shared responsibility. Two U.S. Supreme Court decisions, *INS v. Chadha* (1983)[52] and *Bowsher v. Snyar* (1986),[53] ignored most of the nation's history to add further to the growing separation between the branches. By the mid-1980s, PACs and other interest groups had become the most powerful links between legislative and executive branches, resulting in a new form of shared powers system in service to special interests.

Major factors behind these developments include the growing sums of money involved in government and politics. As national government expenditures have expanded to one quarter of GNP, the stakes in government contracts, transfer payments, grants, and regulations have become enormous. Pressures to fill positions which administer these activities with interest group partisans who support the president are large for substantive reason alone, and increased costs of politics appear to be associated with them. In short, executive branch offices have again become expected rewards for expensive political support.

Consequences for public administration have already become large. Most clearly, professional experts have been displaced increasingly by transient political appointees. Expert liaison between Congress and the executive branch has suffered greatly as a result, and multitudes of lobbyists have surged into the gap. Contract management has grown in importance and become increasingly subject to erratic partisan control. Cost overruns, excessive prices, performance failures, and corruption in space, defense, and other national government contracts have become routine, increasing as deinstitutionalization and politicization have advanced.

Examples are common. Contrast performance of the National Aeronautics and Space Administration under Administrator James Webb, a professional public executive who led in the 1960s in placing Americans on the moon, with later developments under James M. Beggs, an example of a private industry contractor appointed to lead the agency in the 1980s when the United States nearly became dependent on other nations to launch some essential space satellites. Or out of hundreds of major Defense Department scandals of the 1980s, note pressure exerted by the Navy Secretary's office in 1986 which led a defense contractor to fire Lawrence J. Korb, who was linked to a report suggesting reordering of military priorities to deal with budget deficit problems. Navy Secretary Lehman was quoted as saying, "I certainly said things like, 'How the hell can Raytheon get away with going up, speaking out against the president's bill like that?'. . . . I applaud the fact that my two secretaries and others complained to Raytheon about that kind of behavior."[54]   Or consider the Postal Service, reorganized in the 1970s to escape the old-type spoils and permit business-type practices; board member Peter Voss admitted in 1986 to "receiving bribes for trying to swing contracts to one of the vendors."[55]

State and local governments which function under political-brokerage executive systems and special interest dominated legislatures also provide examples of the new politics and the new spoils.   In California, for example, campaign expenditures for election to the state legislature have increased by 3,000 percent since 1958, with incumbents outspending challengers 105 to 1.

"During the 1983-84 election cycle, over $50 million in campaign contributions was raised by both incumbents and challengers.   Much of this came in the form of PAC contributions."[56]   When William G. Hamm resigned as California's Legislative Analyst in 1986, he called this campaign financing problem the "most debilitating source of pressure," and described it as symptomatic of "a highly damaging sense of values that makes it difficult for public service to be as effective as it potentially can be in state capitals."[57]   Four major strong-mayor cities (Chicago, New York, Philadelphia, and Washington) were centers of corruption scandals in 1986 centering around public-private relationships—the current form of spoils: "easy campaign money and cozy relationships."[58]

Bicentennial and Third Century Reform?

Actions are needed in this bicentennial era as they were 100 years ago to reform America's political institutions.   Fortunately, two different developments since the nation's centennial limit the scope of changes needed now.   First, local council-manager governments in which a majority of Americans now live have generally reconciled the needs for both popular control and professional expertise.   While many local and most state governments are experiencing problems like those which now impinge on the presidency, integrity and performance at many local and state levels remain high and are resources for national reform.   Second, the United States has learned much since the 1940s about successful reliance on private interests and state and local governments to accomplish national public purposes. That dispersed performance system suits America's traditions. Although increasingly tarnished by growing reports of shoddy products and shabby deals, American private enterprise still enjoys some reputation for general integrity and capacity on which to build more constructive public-private relationships to serve public interests.

Major reforms are urgently required in three areas: (1) financing of elections and other political activities at all governmental levels; (2) top executive branch staffing in the national government; and (3) management of proxied performance of public functions at all levels. Changes needed in these areas require more joint legislative-executive responsibility and elimination of the imperial/sacerdotal qualities which have become attached to the American presidency.

Actions at several levels are needed. As an early step, political financing and its connections to (mostly legal) corruption of public policy and implementation processes urgently need to be researched, highlighted, and changed, although the NCPAC decision noted above found consti-tutional obstacles to some needed reforms. Public administrators for over 50 years have excluded such political matters from their concerns. Many business leaders have also. By contrast, reformers from the centennial era for the next 50 years focused on the correction of such civic problems as prerequisite to responsible public administration and private enterprise.

Those earlier reformers also understood another dimension of constitutional self governance which now needs to be reapplied. Public administration in its developing years drew on a wide range of talented people: private sector civic workers, business leaders, responsible politicians, professionally expert public practitioners, and academicians. They formed a community devoted to values of civic duty and public service; public administration was, thus, not isolated from the currents of the times. That came later. (The politics-administration dichotomy, combined with even more unrealistic efforts to expunge it, had the impact of a lobotomy: public administration detachment.) The field remains largely in a time warp of 1930s-1940s formulations, but with little of the Golden Era's public service idealism; and political science generally remains caught up in 1950s-1960s devotion to partisan politicization of administration, but also with an absence of higher civic purpose.

Public-private partnerships have dominated the practice of American public administration for decades. Changes in research, management practices, ethical expectations, and teaching have been slow in catching up with this reality. Meanwhile, problems in the relationships—and their consequences—have grown with the expansion of the national government to a trillion dollar level and its capture by exchange politics. To straighten out these problems, which go to the heart of today's constitutional government, the values underlying present relationships require major changes. As a first priority, today's public and private providers of public services need to join with others to clean up their acts and the systems of political financing and high level spoils which are entangled with them. Related bicentennial challenges of the constitutional system must also be dealt with: (1) elimination of the imperial and sacerdotal trappings which have come to characterize the presidency and restoration of conditions required for a government of shared legislative-executive authority and (2) leadership to help Americans lift the nation out of a politics of mere exchange in pursuit of self interests into a practice of civic responsibility. Public administration can no longer afford to set itself apart from these challenges.

ENDNOTES

1.   Theodore J. Lowi, *The End of Liberalism* (New York: W. W. Norton & Co., 2d ed., 1979). Also, Lowi, "Ronald Reagan—Revolutionary?" in Lester M. Salamon and Michael S. Lund, *The Reagan Presidency and the Governing of America* (Washington: The Urban Institute, 1985), pp. 29-56.

2. Frederick C. Mosher, "The Changing Responsibilities and Tactics of the Federal Government," *Public Administration Review*, vol. 40 (November/December 1980), pp. 541-548.

3. William A. Niskanen, Jr., *Bureaucracy and Representative Government* (Chicago: Aldine Publishing Co., 1971).

4. For a critique of the Niskanen thesis, see: Gary J. Miller and Terry M. Moe, "Bureaucrats, Legislators, and the Size of Government," *American Political Science Review*, vol. 77 (June 1983), pp. 297-322. For an assessment of various theories of causes of governmental growth, see David Lowery and William Berry, "The Growth of Government in the United States: An Empirical Assessment of Competing Explanations," *American Journal of Political Science*, vol. 27 (November 1983), pp. 665-694.

5. Stuart Butler, *Privatizing Federal Spending: A Strategy to Eliminate the Deficit* (Washington: The Heritage Foundation, 1985).

6. Ted Kolderie, "The Two Different Concepts of Privatization," *Public Administration Review*, vol. 46 (July/August 1986), pp. 285-291.

7. David A. Stockman, *The Triumph of Politics* (New York: Harper and Row, 1986), pp. 394-395.

8. Mosher, *supra*, p. 541.

9. David S. Broder, *The Party's Over; The Failure of Politics in America* (New York: Harper, 1972).

10. Dorothy B. James, "Book Reviews" (of eleven recent books), *Presidential Studies Quarterly*, vol. 16 (Winter 1986), pp. 118-119.

11. Alan Ehrenhalt, "Political Parties: A Renaissance of Power?" *Congressional Quarterly*, vol. 43 (26 October 1985), p. 2187.

12. Elder Witt and Jeremy Gaunt, "Court Strikes Down Limits on Independent PAC Outlays," *Congressional Quarterly*, vol. 43 (March 23, 1985), p. 532.

13. John R. Wright, "PACs, Contributions, and Roll Calls: An Organizational Perspective," *American Political Science Review*, vol. 79 (June 1985), pp. 400-414.

14. Federal Election Commission (FEC), *Annual Report 1985* (Washington: FEC, June 1, 1986).

15. Witt and Faunt, *op. cit., supra.*

16. *Federal Election Commission v. National Conservative Political Action Committee, et al.*, 105 S. Ct. 1459 (March 18, 1985).

17. Richard Hofstadter, *The American Political Tradition* (New York: Alfred Knopf, 1948; Vintage Books, 1955), p. vii.

18. Gregory B. Markus, "Political Attitudes During an Election Year: A Report on the 1980 NES Panel Study," *American Political Science Review*, vol. 76 (September 1982), pp. 538-560.

19. Theodore H. White, *America in Search of Itself, The Making of the President, 1956-1980* (New York: Harper & Row, 1982), p. 1.

20. Arthur H. Miller and Martin P. Wattenberg, "Throwing the Rascals Out: Policy and Performance Evaluations of Presidential Candidates, 1952-1980," *American Political Science Review*, vol. 79 (June 1985), p. 359. "Statistics of the Week," *National Journal* (October 19, 1985), p. 2388.

21. Martha Joynt Kumar and Michael Baruch Grossman, "Political Communications from the White House: The Interest Group Connection," *Presidential Studies Quarterly*, vol. 16 (Winter 1986), pp. 96-97.

22. A series on the Reagan administration by the Urban Institute includes numerous sources. For a review, see Guthrie S. Birkhead, "Reagan's First Term," *Public Administration Review*, vol. 45 (November/December 1985), pp. 869-875.

23. George E. Reedy, *The Twilight of the Presidency* (New York: World Publishing Co., 1970).

24. Arthur M. Schlesinger, Jr., *The Imperial Presidency* (Boston: Houghton Mifflin, 1973).

25. Henry Fairlie, "Political Ailments: King Ron and His Royal Polyps," *The New Republic* (August 12, 1985), pp. 8-10.

26. Herbert Schmertz, "The Media and the Presidency," *Presidential Studies Quarterly*, vol. 16 (Winter 1986), pp. 11-21, 15.

27. *Ibid.*, p. 15.

28. David C. Morrison, "On the Defensive," *National Journal* (26 April 1986), pp. 984-988; "Trying Times for Weapons Tester," *National Journal* (19 April 1986), pp. 946-947.

29. Dick Kirschten, "OMB's Miller Says Deaver Visit Was No Shock to White House," *National Journal* (12 April 1986), pp. 894-895. Burt Solomon, "Hawking Access," *National Journal* (May 3, 1986), pp. 1048-1953.

30. Richard P. Nathan, *The Plot That Failed: Nixon and the Administrative Presidency* (New York: Wiley, 1975).

31. Richard P. Nathan, "Political Administration is Legitimate," in Lester M. Salamon and Michael S. Lund, eds., *The Reagan Presidency and the Governing of America* (Washington: The Urban Institute, 1985), pp. 375-379, 376.

32. Don K. Price, "A Response to Mr. Laski," *Public Administration Review*, vol. 4 (Autumn 1944), pp. 360-363, 362.

33. Bernard Rosen, "Crises in the U.S. Civil Service," *Public Administration Review*, vol. 46 (May/June 1986), pp. 207-214.

34. John W. Macy, Bruce Adams, and J. Jackson Walter, eds., *America's Unelected Government* (Cambridge, MA: Ballinger Publishing Co., 1983).

35. Frederick V. Malek, *Washington's Hidden Tragedy* (New York: Free Press, 1978); Laurence E. Lynn, Jr., *Managing the Public's Business: The Job of the Government Executive* (New York: Basic Books, 1981).

36. Laurence E. Lynn, Jr., "The Reagan Administration and the Renitent Bureaucracy," in Salamon and Lund, *op. cit.*, pp. 339-374, 340.

37. Macy, *et al., supra*, p. xii.

38. Charles R. Adrian, *et al.*, "Leadership and Decision-Making in Manager Cities," *Public Administration Review*, vol. 18 (Summer 1958), pp. 208-222.

39. Norton E. Long, "Politicians for Hire—The Dilemma of Education and the Task of Research," *Public Administration Review*, vol. 25 (June 1965), pp. 115-125.

40. Keith F. Mulrooney, "Can City Managers Deal Effectively with Major Social Problems?" *Public Administration Review*, vol. 31 (January/February 1971), pp. 6-14, 12.

41. George R. Schrader, "A Glimpse into the Future," a progress report to the ICMA Executive Board (Quebec City: ICMA, July 17, 1979), pp. 4-5.

42. ICMA Committee on Future Horizons, *New Worlds of Service* (Washington: ICMA, October 1979), pp. 14-15.

43. Lyndon Baines Johnson, *The Vantage Point* (New York: Holt, Rinehart & Winston, 1971), p. 327.

44. Chester A. Newland, "Executive Office Policy Apparatus: Enforcing the Reagan Agenda," in Salamon and Lund, *op. cit.*, pp. 135-168. See extensive sources cited.

45. Ronald Brownstein and Dick Kirschten, "Cabinet Power," *National Journal* (28 June 1986), pp. 1582-1583 and 1588-1589.

46. Harlan Cleveland, "The Twilight of Hierarchy: Speculations on the Global Information Society," *Public Administration Review*, vol. 45 (January/February 1985), pp. 185-195, 188. Also, *The Knowledge Executive* (New York: Dutton, 1985).

47. Harlan Cleveland, "Coherence and Consultation: The President as Manager of American Foreign Policy," *Public Administration Review*, vol. 46 (March/April 1986), pp. 97-104, 97.

48. James MacGregor Burns, *Leadership* (New York: Harper & Row, 1978), p. 454.

49. *Ibid.*, p. 434.

50. Laurence Rutter, *The Essential Community, Local Government in the Year 2000* (Washington: International City Management Association, 1980).

51. Louis Fisher, *The Politics of Shared Power* (Washington: Congressional Quarterly, Inc., 1981).

52. 462 U.S. 919 (1983).

53. 54 U.S.L.W. 5064 (1986).

54. Molly Moore, "Lehman Calls Korb's Stand 'Personal Affront,'" *The Washington Post* (17 July 1986), p. A-5. Also see Fred Hiatt, "Pentagon Pressure Forces Out Company Official," *The Washington Post* (12 July 1986), pp. A-1 and A-7.

55. Editorial, "Scandal," *Government Computer News* (4 July 1986), p. 30.   Also Judith A. Sullivan, "USPS Board Pressed for Some Explanation," *Government Computer News* (1 August 1986), p. 16.

56. Bill Hall, "Executive Summary, Campaign Reform, the Failings of Limited Campaign Reform" (Los Angeles: mimeographed paper by Bill Hall, 17 April 1986).

57. William G. Hamm, "The State of the States and Public Service," in Chester A. Newland, ed., *The State of American Public Service* (Washington: NAPA, 1986).

58. Neal R. Peirce, "City Corruption Scandals Dominate in 1986," *National Journal* (10 May 1986), p. 1130.

CHAPTER SIX

Political Appointees and Career Executives:
The Democracy-Bureaucracy Nexus
in the Third Century

JAMES P. PFIFFNER[*]

The balance between presidential appointees and career executives in governing the United States is a fundamental question of who shall rule.[1]   But it is also a question of governmental and organizational mechanics. The democratic principle that the president along with political appointees ought to direct policy in the executive branch is not in question, but judgments about the most effective way to organize that political control have been changing.   In recent years the balance has shifted toward using more political appointees to assure tighter White House control of administration.

The western European democracies of France, Britain, and Germany allow only 100 or so new political appointees to each new administration to establish its control of the government.[2]   In contrast, a new administration in the

---

[*]   **James P. Pfiffner** is Associate Professor of Public Affairs at George Mason University.   His books include *The President, the Budget, and Congress: Impoundment and the 1974 Budget Act* (Westview, 1979); *The President and Economic Policy* (ISHI, 1986); and *The Strategic Presidency: Hitting the Ground Running* (Dorsey, forthcoming).   He was Senior Research Associate with the Presidential Appointee Project of the National Academy of Public Administration.

United States fills thousands of political positions with its own appointees.   Major reasons account for this.   The United States has a separation of powers rather than a parliamentary form of government, and it does not have the party discipline in Congress that parliamentary systems often enjoy.   Neither does it have the same governmental and administrative traditions that matured in Europe over the centuries.

In the United States the spoils system developed to assure that a new president's programs were implemented by those sympathetic to his policies.   This was done with the Jacksonian assumption that government jobs were so simple that virtually anybody could handle them.   The legacy of the reform movement removed most federal government jobs from the spoilsmen by expanding appointment by merit (often by "blanketing in") but still left the top tier of positions to presidential discretion.[3]   After the high water mark of the merit system was reached in the 1940s, the pendulum reversed directions, and the proportion of political appointees began to increase again, particularly in the 1970s and 1980s.

Though little danger exists that the scale of personnel spoils will be approached again, this article argues that the balance in the United States has shifted too far toward a greater number of political appointees.   It argues that recent presidents have come to office with distrust and hostility toward the career bureaucracy and that this attitude has been reflected initially in their political appointees.   Evidence is offered that this distrust of career executives is misplaced and that most administrations experience a "cycle of accommodation" with the career bureaucracy.   The conclusion will be that the "in and outer" system is a good one that has served this country well, but that the balance should be shifted back toward fewer presidential appointees.   The number of political appointees can be reduced without reducing the responsiveness of the permanent government to legitimate political leadership.

Presidential Mistrust and Increasing Control

Presidential candidates in the United States have increasingly come to office distrusting the career bureaucracy.   They suspect it to be salted with holdovers from the previous administration and to be unsympathetic to their priorities. They believe this will lead to foot dragging, if not outright sabotage. Running against the Washington bureaucracy also has potent political appeal to the voters. It is inevitable that the appointees recruited to join an administration are affected by this rhetoric, particularly those with no prior experience in the federal government.

This attitude is certainly not a new phenomenon, but it has been increasing in recent years. When President Eisenhower came to office after 20 years of Democratic rule, Schedule C positions were created to allow the Republicans to place their own appointees at lower levels in the bureaucracy, GS-15 and below. President Kennedy felt that the career bureaucracy tended to be too stodgy and would not be able to move vigorously enough to "get the country moving again." He used temporary task forces rather than relying exclusively on traditional bureaucratic structures.[4] He also began the centralization of policy-making in the White House instead of relying heavily on his cabinet secretaries as had Eisenhower. Lyndon Johnson was an exception to the trend of distrust toward the bureaucracy, but not to the trend of centralizing control in the White House.

President Nixon had a legendary distrust and hostility toward the bureaucracy which he called, "dug-in establish-mentarians fighting for the status quo."[5] His administration began with the attitude that there would be, in John Ehrlichman's words, "guerilla warfare" with the bureaucracy. This distrust led that administration to establish a White House "counter-bureaucracy" in the Domestic Council, to propose a major reorganization of the executive branch, to place White House political appointees as "spies" in the departments and agencies, and to attempt illegal political placements through the career merit system.[6]

Jimmy Carter ran as an outsider against the establishment. He asserted that "Our government in Washington now is a horrible bureaucratic mess. . . . We must give top priority to a drastic and thorough reorganization of the federal bureaucracy. . . ."[7] Carter and many of his appointees adopted an attitude of moral superiority toward Congress and the bureaucracy.[8]

The Reagan administration has probably been more distrustful of the bureaucracy than any previous one.

Reagan also ran as an outsider against Washington, declaring that government is part of the problem, not part of the solution and promised there would be no more business as usual. In office, the Reagan administration forced severe cutbacks on the domestic side of the government and reduced nonmilitary employment by reductions in force, leaving about 92,000 fewer employees in domestic agencies in 1983 than in 1981.[9]. Reagan appointees began their terms by systematically excluding career executives from policy-making deliberations based on the fear that they would try to undercut the administration's policies if they were included.[10]

More Appointees

This trend of increasing distrust of the bureaucracy was accompanied by an increasing centralization of control of personnel and policy in the White House. This includes greater numbers of political appointees available to an administration and tighter control of appointments by the White House. At the upper levels the number of executive branch presidential appointments requiring Senate confirmation has increased. In 1933 there were 71 such positions; by 1965 there were 152; and President Johnson made 237 appointments to these top positions.[11] By 1984 there were 523 of these PAS appointments.[12]

In addition to these presidential appointments, department and agency heads can also make numerous political appointments. Each administration can appoint up to 10 percent of the Senior Executive Service (SES) at the top management level (GS-16 to Executive Level IV). This amounts to about 700 of 7,000 total SES positions. The SES regulations also increased political control of the bureaucracy by allowing agency heads to transfer executives throughout the agency and to place political appointees in any position which is not "career-reserved." In addition, "limited-term" and "limited-emergency" appointments can be appointed for terms up to three years.

Schedule C positions are reserved for confidential or policy related functions at the GS-15 level and below. Schedule C positions have steadily increased in number since their creation in the 1950s, with the Reagan administration increasing their numbers significantly over the number used by the Carter administration.[13] In 1985 there were 1,665

Schedule C positions governmentwide, up from 911 in 1976.[14] In addition, immediately after a transition a new administration can appoint up to 25 percent more Schedule C's to assist with the transition for the first 120 days of an administration. In 1981 this time period was extended for an additional 120 days by OPM Director Donald Devine.[15]

The total number of allocated, noncareer employees in the executive branch increased from 2,794 in 1979 to 2,951 in 1984 (excluding White House staff, military, Coast Guard, Foreign Service, and Public Health Service).[16] The number of appointees is not fixed and varies depending on who does the counting and how positions are defined. The specific numbers are not important; what is important is the *trend* toward more political appointees for each presidential administration. The direction of this trend is not in dispute.

Increasing Control

The increasing number of political appointees available to presidents over the past several decades has been accompanied by increasingly tighter control of these appointments by the White House. While subcabinet appointments (associate and assistant secretaries) are presidential appointments, Schedule C and SES appointments are made by agency heads and departmental secretaries. Since the 1950s, presidents have usually allowed agency heads to appoint their own teams below the subcabinet level, and even at the subcabinet level generally gave them wide discretion. A Brookings Institution study in 1965 concluded that the selection of assistant secretaries was "a highly decentralized and personalized process revolving around the respective department and agency heads," with the president generally delegating selection to his cabinet secretaries. "Where the secretary and White House staff conflicted over an appointment, the secretary generally won."[17]

This practice has been reversed since the 1950s with increasing control of all political appointments being drawn into the White House.[18] The Reagan administration took this trend to the extreme by insisting on White House control or clearance of each noncareer appointment in the government. According to Pendleton James, the director of Reagan's Presidential Personnel Office, "We handled all the

appointments: boards,   commissions,   Schedule   C's,
ambassadorships,   judgeships. . . .   if   you   are   going   to   run
the government, you've got to control the people that come
into it."[19]   Edwin Meese argued: "The president has to
decide   right   off   the   bat   that   there   will   be   one   central
control point.   And that while you encourage department
heads to develop names, the ultimate approval is that of the
president."[20]

Politicization

The tight White House control of political appointees
by   the   Reagan   administration   was   accompanied   by   an
attitude of tight control of career executives by the White
House appointees.   This approach entailed an attempt
strictly to separate policy issues from administrative ones
and to exclude career executives from policy deliberations.

The   most   extreme   defense   of   this   approach   to
governing has been put forth by Michael Sanera of the
Heritage Foundation, a conservative think tank that had
high level access to the Reagan administration.[21]   Sanera
argues that big government is "inefficient" and "destructive"
and that career bureaucrats will actively try to sabotage any
administration that is trying to achieve significant change.

To counter this type of subversion Sanera recommends
several tactics for political appointees.   One of these is
"jigsaw puzzle management" in which

> Career staff will supply information, but they
> should never become involved in the formulation
> of   agenda   related   policy   objectives. . . .   once
> controversial policy goals are formulated, they
> should   not   be   released   in   total   to   the   career
> staff.   Thus   the   political   executive   and   his
> political staff become "jigsaw puzzle" managers.
> Other staff see and work on the individual pieces,
> but never have enough of the pieces to be able to
> learn the entire picture.[22]

Sanera also encourages political appointees to promote
conflict and uncertainty among their subordinates in order
to ensure a rich flow of information.   These precepts flow
directly against accepted management theory and practice in
the private sector.   But Sanera feels that what is lost in

efficiency will be made up by greater political control.[23] Another analysis of political control of the bureaucracy, or "politicization," is made by Terry Moe.[24] Moe argues that the incongruence between public expectations for presidential performance and the actual resources available to presidents drives presidents to embrace politicization and centralization in order to gain as much control as they can in order to implement their priorities.

Arguments by reformers and public administration scholars in favor of treating the bureaucracy as neutral experts are beside the point, according to Moe, because they do not address the underlying systemic pressures on presidents. He argues that these reformers will inevitably fail and that it would not be a good thing if they succeeded.

> Reagan did much more than continue a historical trend. In moving ambitiously down the paths of politicization and centralization, he built a set of administrative arrangements that by past standards proved coherent, well integrated, and eminently workable. . . . future presidents . . . will have every reason to learn from and build upon the Reagan example in seeking to enhance their own institutional capacities for leadership.[25]

Once an area of administration has been politicized it is virtually impossible to reverse the process. Each new administration feels it is entitled to the same political controls as its predecessor, and members of Congress and political parties resist any reduction in their opportunities for influence. In the nineteenth century this dynamic of political control through the spoils system did not abate until the Pendleton Act began a period of major reform.

The Politics/Administration Dichotomy

In its simple form the politics/administration dichotomy holds that a distinction exists between policy and administration. Political leaders make decisions about what policy should be and those in the bureaucracy merely carry out policy and follow orders from their political superiors. Those who have argued for the strict separation of politics from administration have based their reasoning on Woodrow Wilson and Max Weber.

Wilson argued: "Administration lies outside the proper sphere of politics. Administrative questions are not political questions. . . ."[26] Weber characterized the contrasting roles of the politician and the bureaucrat: "To take a stand, to be passionate . . . is the politician's element. . . . indeed, exactly the opposite, principle of responsibility from that of the civil servant. The honor of the civil servant is vested in his ability to execute conscientiously the order of the superior authorities. . . . Without this moral discipline and self-denial, in the highest sense, the whole apparatus would fall to pieces."[27]

But in the modern, industrialized, technocratic state these simple distinctions break down. Just as a legislature cannot specify all of the details of complex programs, neither can political appointees give precise and complete orders about how their policy decisions must be implemented. They cannot because they do not have the time, but more importantly they do not have the expertise. Career civil servants have made their careers managing the details of programs and may even have helped write the legislation that established them. They have the information upon which programmatic decisions must be made. In addition, they are experts at applying bureaucratic rules and regulations to particular programs: oiling the budget, personnel, and paper flow parts of the machine.[28] The simple version of the politics/administration dichotomy "assumes a degree of hierarchy of authority, of simplicity of decision, and of effective political supremacy that now seems unrealistic to students of modern government."[29] As a practical matter this type of division of labor is impossible.

Because of this many social scientists have declared the politics/administration dichotomy to be hopelessly naive. According to Moe, ". . . the politics-administration dichotomy has been firmly rejected as a naive misunderstanding of the inherently political context and nature of the administrative process."[30] But despite the impossibility of a simplistic dichotomy between politics and administration, it remains a highly important normative ideal. It is from Weber's normative sense, rather than from Wilson's empirical claim that we should derive the contemporary meaning of the politics/administration dichotomy.

"Modern critics have scored points by mistaking social science theory for what was actually a normative political doctrine," Hugh Heclo argues.[31] This normative doctrine stresses that the legitimate authority for administration policy-making derives from the president and is delegated to his appointees in the government. Despite the fact that career bureaucrats are, of necessity, involved in policy decisions, they ought not to lose sight of the democratic imperative that presidential appointees are the legitimate locus of decision-making in the executive branch. The appropriate posture of the civil servant is to carry out faithfully legitimate policy decisions, despite personal preferences. Without this chain of legitimacy the democratic linkage between the electorate and the government would become unacceptably attenuated.[32]

In addition to these normative distinctions, differences of background and style distinguish bureaucrats and politicians, each set of officials making different contributions to the formulation of public policy. Appointees' political skills are needed to identify goals and to mobilize support for them. The strength of civil servants, on the other hand, lies in designing programs to implement those goals.[33] These differences reflect contrasting roles and are rooted in institutional positions. Political appointees are in-and-outers. That is, they are recruited to serve a particular president and rarely stay longer than a president, usually much less. The average tenure of a political appointee in a position is about two years. This rapid turnover is often motivated by the desire of presidential appointees to make their mark quickly and to move on, either to a higher position in the government or back to the private sector to make more money. Much of the appointees' agendas are driven by the mandate to reelect a president or to leave a good record to run on for the partisan heir-apparent.

Career executives, in contrast, have a longer-term perspective. They will still be operating programs and administering agencies after the political birds of passage have left. This causes them to pay attention to the health of institutions and to the integrity of the processes that assure nonpartisan implementation of the laws. The rules and regulations designed to do this can also be used to insulate and protect civil servants from either legitimate or illegitimate political controls. This longer-term perspective makes them less willing to upset long established practices quickly. But "bureaucratic inertia" is not a sufficiently subtle description of this type of behavior. Hugh Heclo describes the elements of bureaucratic dispositions as gradualism, indirection, political caution, and a concern for maintaining relationships.[34] Bureaucrats are concerned about the institutions they manage as well as the current policies of those institutions. Politicians tend to see organizations as convenient tools to achieve their policy objectives.[35]

The basic dilemma that underlies government in the United States is that the permanent bureaucracy must be responsive to the current president, yet it must maintain the necessary professionalism in its career managers to be able to accomplish missions effectively and efficiently. The different strengths of political appointees and career bureaucrats must thus be merged in an appropriate balance if government is to be both responsive and effective.

The Cycle of Accommodation

Despite initial distrust of career executives, political appointees usually develop over time a trust for the career executives who report to them. This is a predictable cycle that has operated in all recent presidential administrations, even if not in all political appointees. The cycle is characterized by initial suspicion and hostility which is followed by two or three years of learning to work together. This results in a more sophisticated appreciation of the contribution of the career service and a mutual respect and trust.

To take an extreme case, John Ehrlichman, who had characterized relations with the bureaucracy as "guerilla warfare," later felt that it was a "big mistake" for the Nixon administration to exclude career executives from policy deliberations, both because of their expertise and because of their ability to develop support for the administration's programs. "I did not encounter devastating problems with the bureaucracy." You have to remember that the career service is not a "faceless, formless enemy."[36]

Other high-level White House officials have come to similar conclusions about the career service. Theodore Sorensen recalled his White House experience with the bureaucracy: "The career services are a vastly under-used resource, particularly by new presidents who come in suspicious of the career services and confident that they can run everything themselves with their political hired hands. That's a mistake. I don't think that a president needs to have a vast number of political appointees going well down into the agencies. I believe the career services will respond to a president who has some confidence and trust in them, and who knows how to tap their expertise."[37]

After serving in the Carter White House for four years, Jack Watson had strong feelings about the career bureaucracy. "I honestly believe that the career bureaucracy for the most part are professionals, civil servants in the positive sense, who want to serve the new administration. . . . I never experienced some sinister counter force out there seeking to undermine and sabotage our administration. A president should go into office with an operating assumption, a rebuttable presumption, that the people of the government are there to serve him and to help him succeed."[38] "One good careerist is worth ten campaigners," declared Harrison Wellford, Carter's top management person at OMB.[39]

Craig Fuller of the Reagan White House said, "My experience in the four years that I've been here is that . . . the relationship between the political appointee and the career people in the departments is very much a partnership. . . . I don't come at this with some notion that we have some norm of behavior among the career staff that is totally at odds or variance with the ideals of the political appointee. . . ."[40]

These attitudes of White House aides are shared by the vast majority of presidential appointees in recent administrations. In a survey sent by the National Academy of Public Administration (NAPA) to all presidential appointees between 1964 and 1984, each appointee was asked to characterize how *responsive* and *competent* the career employees of their agencies were. Those who responded that career employees were "responsive" or "very responsive" (four or five on a five-point scale) are reported in Table 1.

Thus the evidence is overwhelming that experienced political appointees, regardless of administration, party, or ideology, believe that career executives are both competent and responsive.

More personal reflections of presidential appointees from different administrations reinforce these statistical data.[41]

The Johnson Administration—John Gardner, Secretary of Health, Education and Welfare:

> I would strongly urge any incoming top official to come in with the recognition that he has a lot of potential allies around him. . . . People who would be glad to help if they got the chance. One of the great mistakes people make in coming in is developing a we/they attitude toward their own staff. . . . Big mistake.   There are a lot of potential teammates out there, and you have to find them.   And the faster you do the better. . . .I fairly soon found the people who could keep me out of the beartraps and could advise me. . . . I found that immensely helpful, and I think any newcomer will.

TABLE 1

Presidential Appointees' Perceptions of Career Employees' Competence and Responsiveness

Administration	Competence	Responsiveness
Johnson	92%	89%
Nixon	88%	84%
Ford	80%	82%
Carter	81%	86%
Reagan	77%	78%

Source: National Academy of Public Administration, Presidential Appointees' Project, *Leadership in Jeopardy: The Fraying of the Presidential Appointments System* (Washington: NAPA, 1985). All presidential appointees who were still alive and whose addresses could be verified were polled. The response rate was 56 percent.

The Nixon Administration—Elliot Richardson, Secretary of Commerce, Defense, HEW, and Attorney General:

> I did find them easy to work with. I did find them competent. . . . they saw their own roles in a manner that virtually required political leadership. They didn't want to have to make the choices on competing claims that are the function of the political process. . . . People who had devoted a lifetime or significant part of it to expertise in their field are entitled to be listened to with respect. . . . many presidential appointees make the gross mistake of not sufficiently respecting the people they are dealing with . . . and get themselves into trouble as a result.

The Carter Administration—Walter McDonald, Assistant Secretary of Treasury:

> Without exception I never found an administration as it was leaving office that had anything but praise for the career service in general, and respect. . . . I think a learning process takes place. I think politicals learn after they're burned a few times that careerists are really there to serve them. They're not wedded to any party. . . . And it's very hard for the politicals to understand that. . . . and it takes four years to convince them of this. How you do this, god, I don't know.

The Reagan Administration—Richard Lyng, Secretary of Agriculture:

> In every case, I found career people that were absolutely splendid. Their experience was absolutely invaluable. I needed them, it was essential. The career people kept me from shooting myself in the foot. . . . The way you get them (career bureaucrats) with you is to treat them like equals, point out I need you to help me. These people want the job done right. I

never cared if a fellow was a Democrat or a Republican, because ... all of them are nonpartisan. ... A presidential appointee who doesn't work with the career people will not make it.

Career Executives and Political Management

The ways in which career executives are critical to the success of their political superiors are many. They are highly educated and they know the intricacies of the laws and regulations governing programs they implement. They are the repositories of organizational memory. They remember who were allies and enemies in past turf battles. They know whom to go to for help in central management agencies or in Congress. Their personal intelligence and communications networks have been built up over many years dealing with the same organizations, people, and issues.

One political appointee described the importance of the memory of career executives. "Those same people keep you out of trouble. You get a decision, someone recommends this, and some special interest group comes in and says 'do this,' or some agency in the government or the White House. You bring in the staff and say, what if we do this? They'll say well, if you do that, this is what will happen, and these guys will get mad. Or they'll say, yeah, that was tried in 1931 and again in 1938 and here's what happened. You've got to have those guys with you."[42] To ignore this source of advice and expertise is shortsighted and self defeating.

Not only are career executives responsive, but they perform functions that are essential to the proper operation of the government and to the success of the political appointees for whom they work. While we expect career executives to be responsive to political leadership, at the same time we expect them to resist illegal or unethical direction from above. For instance, we would expect career bureaucrats to resist orders to allocate grants based on illegal or political criteria at variance with the established laws and regulations governing the grant process. We would also expect them to blow the whistle rather than to cover up illegal activities by their colleagues or political superiors.

One example of appropriate bureaucratic resistance was the refusal of the Internal Revenue Service (IRS) to audit George McGovern's campaign aides' tax returns at the order of the Nixon White House.[43] Thus we expect bureaucrats to be responsive, but not *too* responsive.

In legitimate matters career executives should be expected to do more than passively carry out orders. A "yes boss" attitude is not merely inadequate, it may be downright dangerous. One career executive remembers warning his newly appointed political boss that a sole source contract granted to the boss's former colleagues "would not pass the smell test" in Washington. His boss did not grant the contract and later thanked him for the warning.[44] In contrast, one "responsive" bureaucrat followed orders without questions and "left my ass in one of the biggest slings in town by letting me redecorate the office," according to one political appointee.[45] These contrasting examples illustrate the types of responsiveness that may make or break a new political appointee.

True neutral competence is "loyalty that argues back," according to Hugh Heclo.[46] One appointee of President Reagan described his relations with career civil servants: "They were responsive to clear, rational guidance. They wouldn't always agree, I would have been concerned had they always agreed with me; but I was always the boss, that was never in doubt."[47] Having "my own person" in the job is not enough; that person must have the requisite knowledge and skills to make the bureaucratic machine work and the good judgment to warn the boss about impending trouble.

That the responsiveness of career employees will not prevent turf battles or the frustration of presidential initiatives must be stressed. Bureaucratic warfare and turf battles always plague presidents, but the cleavages run along agency and programmatic lines, with political appointees and bureaucrats on the same sides of the barricades. Incidents like end runs to Congress and leaks to the press surface in every administration, but as likely as not they are instigated by a president's own political appointees.

Resistance to presidential directives is inevitable, but it is important to keep in mind that this resistance stems from members of Congress, interest groups, and the leadership of executive branch agencies. Career bureaucrats may be a part of these opposing forces, but they are seldom the instigators or even the most influential participants. Using the career service as a scapegoat for all resistance to presidential desires may be comforting, but it does not represent an accurate analysis of power in Washington.

The Trade-Off Between Responsiveness and Effectiveness

The United States' system of executive branch leadership was designed to maximize responsiveness to the electorate by ensuring that many top positions throughout the government are filled by supporters of the president. But there is a trade-off in efficiency and effectiveness for responsiveness. Just as the separation of powers system undercuts efficiency, the political appointee system often results in inefficiencies, with rapid turnover of positions and reversals of policy direction. But this is a small price to pay for a system that brings with it the ability to respond rapidly to the wishes of the electorate.

In addition to providing this democratic link, the "in-and-outer" system has other virtues. It brings into the bureaucracy fresh ideas and "new blood" to try them out. It brings in people who have not been worn down by the system and who can afford to work at full speed for the president's program for several years and return to their previous careers when they approach the burnout stage. It brings in people who are working on the cutting edge of new technologies or management practice, people who can transfer new ways of doing things to the government.

But the increasing number of political appointees and the increasingly deep penetration of them into the bureaucratic machinery may have reached the point of diminishing returns. Is there a point at which increasing political control no longer enhances the effective implementation of presidential priorities? Some would suggest that this point has been passed in the United States in the 1980s. Patricia Ingraham has concluded: "The end result is *not* enhanced presidential direction or control but a political management void."[48]   In comparing the United States to western European democracies, Hugh Heclo has observed: ". . . the foreign studies suggest that accountable political control of the bureaucracy is not necessarily a function of the number of political appointees in the bureaucracy. In fact the relationship may be inverse."[49]

Drawbacks of this shift of balance toward a larger number of political appointees are several. First, it is difficult to recruit high quality political appointees for some of the lower subcabinet positions. Elliot Richardson observed in 1985:

> I think this Administration has tried to cut too deep into the system by turning jobs traditionally held by career people over to appointees. The price paid is I think significant . . . the lower level the job, the less attractive it may appear to one coming from the outside. The consequence of this is that a lot of people recruited as political appointees for that sort of job have not had outstanding competence. This Administration is full of turkeys who have undercut the quality of public service in their areas.[50]

Filling high level appointive positions is not a major problem, but the lower levels of the subcabinet (for instance deputy assistant secretaries) are increasingly filled with those who are relatively young and inexperienced. While these people may be talented, they may not have the maturity or experience needed in positions of great responsibility. They may be merely "ticket punchers" looking for experience to allow them to get good jobs when they leave the government.

Second, the skills and motivation of the career service are undermined. According to John Gardner, "There are far more political appointees, and the political tests of those appointees are narrower and sharper, certainly more deeply partisan over the past 15 years. Also, the degree to which they subordinate the career people under them, diminishing the integrity and dignity of the career people, is increasing. You can't have an effective government with people who are cowed and dumped on."[51]

Another problem with layering too many political appointees over career bureaucrats is that it closes off career options to career executives. According to Elliot Richardson, "you reduce the opportunities for career people to rise to positions of responsibility. You have amputated the career level and thus reduced the attractiveness of the career service."[52] Shutting off career paths too soon may let the career service "go to seed. . . . And so it is that by not being consulted, senior careerists over time become less worth consulting, less worth appointing to the more responsible departmental positions."[53]

Third, the short tenure in office of political appointees aggravates the problem. It takes a considerable amount of time to master the operations of high level positions in huge organizations. And it is only after the job itself has been mastered that the incumbent can work at maximum effectiveness. But the tenure of political appointees in office has fallen to about two years.[54] The short terms of many appointees encourages them to think in terms of their own careers rather than the interests of the organization they are running. They may be tempted to sacrifice "long-term working relations and procedural norms for immediate policy objectives." They have enough time to make mistakes, but not enough time to learn from them.[55]

Finally, layering political appointees, particularly in staff positions, diffuses legitimate political authority and attenuates the link between the responsible political official and the career implementors of policy. Frederic Malek, who had broad experience as an appointee of President Nixon and who headed the White House Personnel Office, makes a convincing argument for fewer political appointees:

> The solution to problems of rigidity and resistance to change in the government is *not* to increase the number of appointive positions at the top, as so many politicians are wont to do. . . . this task is difficult for an administration and is seldom done effectively. . . . In many cases, the effectiveness of an agency would be improved and political appointments would be reduced by roughly 25 percent if line positions beneath the assistant secretary level were reserved for career officials.[56]

These observations are even more relevant in the late 1980s than they were in the late 1970s when fewer political appointees were available to presidents.

Conclusion

Recent presidents have tried to increase control of the executive branch by increasing the number of political appointees and by tightening White House control over political appointments and career executives. This article has argued that career executives are responsive to legitimate political control and that increasing politicization is counterproductive to effective government. The trend toward more political appointees should be reversed for the following reasons.

1. A democratic government needs the capacity to change directions when a new president and Congress are elected. The ability to change means that the institutional capacity to do so must be available to a new administration. The bureaucratic machine must be there and ready to respond. This capacity is impaired if the bureaucracy is completely decapitated with each change of administration. Thus, career executives must be able to operate at the upper levels of the government and gain experience with "the big picture." But along with this power comes the duty to embrace the normative ideal of the politics/administration dichotomy, even as they are involved in policy formulation and high level decision-making.

2. Each president needs a capable and effective governmental apparatus to carry out the administration's policy priorities. It is particularly important for new presidents to "hit the ground running" with their policy initiatives in order to take advantage of the election mandate and the honeymoon with Congress.[57] They will be able to do this only if the bureaucracy is ready to move. But the longer it takes new political appointees to establish working relationships with the career bureaucracy, the longer it is before the bureaucracy can work effectively for a president. The more political appointees there are and the more layers which separate the agency head and career executives, the longer it will take to establish effective control.

3. The present large number of political appointees strains the capacity of the White House to do effective recruitment and selection. According to Frederic Malek, President Nixon's presidential personnel assistant, "If you try to do

everything, I'm not so sure you can succeed.   It's an awfully difficult job just to handle the *presidential* appointees.   I'm concerned that if you try to do too much, you may be diluted to the point where you're not as effective."[58]

The argument here is not to discard the in-and-outer system that has served government well.   The argument is that the capacity of the White House is being strained and the effectiveness of the government is being undermined by the present trend toward increasing numbers of political appointees.   Reversing this direction would increase the capacity of the government to function efficiently and effectively without sacrificing political accountability or responsiveness.

ENDNOTES

1.   The author would like to thank the following colleagues for comments on an earlier draft: Edie Goldenberg, University of Michigan; Michael Hansen, American University; Charles Levine, Congressional Research Service; Nancy Lind, Illinois State University; Terry Moe, Stanford University; Alana Northrop, California State University; Lester Salamon, the Urban Institute; and Richard Stillman, George Mason University.

2.   See James W. Fesler, "The Higher Civil Service in Europe and the United States," in *The Higher Civil Service in Europe and Canada*, edited by Bruce L. R. Smith (Washington: Brookings, 1984). In France the total number is 500, but most of these come from the career civil service.

3.   On the development of public personnel policy in the United States, see Frederick C. Mosher, *Democracy and the Public Service* (New York: Oxford University Press, 1984).

4.   For an argument that this undermined bureaucratic capacity, see Gary Wills, *The Kennedy Imprisonment* (New York: Atlantic/Little Brown, 1982).

5.   *Public Papers of the Presidents, 1971*, pp. 448-465.

6.   See *Violations and Abuses of Merit Principles in Federal Employment*, Hearings before the Subcommittee on Manpower and Civil Service of the House Committee on Post Office and Civil Service, 94th Congress, 1st Session (April 10, 1975).

7.   Quoted in James Sundquist, "Jimmy Carter as Public Administrator," *Public Administration Review*, vol. 39 (January/February 1979), p. 8.

8.   See Charles Jones, "Keeping Faith and Losing Congress: The Carter Experience in Washington," *Presidential Studies Quarterly*, vol. 14 (Summer 1984), p. 437; and James Sundquist, "Jimmy Carter as Public Administrator," *Public Administration Review*, vol. 39 (January/February 1979), p. 3.

9.   Edie N. Goldenberg, "The Permanent Government in an Era of Retrenchment and Redirection," in Lester Salamon and Michael Lund, eds., *The Reagan Presidency and the Governing of America* (Washington: Urban Institute, 1985), p. 390. The number of full-time equivalent positions eliminated came to about 75,000.

10. See James D. Carroll, A. Lee Fritschler, and Bruce L. R. Smith, "Supply-Side Management in the Reagan Administration," *Public Administration Review*, vol. 45 (November/December 1985), p. 805.

11. David Stanley, Dean Mann, Jameson Doig, *Men Who Govern* (Washington: Brookings Institution, 1967), p. 4; and Linda Fisher, "Fifty Years of Presidential Appointments," in G. Calvin Mackenzie, ed., *The In and Outers* (Baltimore: Johns Hopkins University Press, 1987).

12. Patricia W. Ingraham, "Political Direction, Control and Abuse: The Administrative Presidency and the Significance of the Fine Line." Paper presented at the 1986 American Political Science Convention, p. 21.

13. See Bernard Rosen, "Effective Continuity of U.S. Government Operations in Jeopardy," *Public Administration Review*, vol. 43 (September/October 1983), p. 383.

14. Ingraham, "Political Direction, Control and Abuse," p. 22.

15. *Federal Register*, vol. 46, No. 115 (June 16, 1981), p. 31405; Federal Personnel Manual Bulletin 213-32 (April 24, 1980), "Temporary Schedule C Appointing Authority").

16. *Ibid.*, p. 21.

17. Dean Mann with Jameson Doig, *The Assistant Secretaries* (Washington: Brookings Institution, 1965), pp. 99, 265.

18. For an analysis of this trend see James P. Pfiffner, "Nine Enemies and One Ingrate: Presidential Appointments During Transition," in G. Calvin Mackenzie, ed., *The In and Outers* (Baltimore: Johns Hopkins University Press, 1987).

19. National Academy of Public Administration, "Recruiting Presidential Appointees," Conference of Presidential Personnel Assistants (December 1984), p. 10.

20. Interview with Edwin Meese, Attorney General's Office (July 2, 1985).

21. Michael Sanera, "Implementing the Agenda," in *Mandate for Leadership II*, edited by Stuart M. Butler, Michael Sanera, and W. Bruce Weinrod (Washington: The Heritage Foundation, 1984).

22. "Implementing the Agenda," pp. 514-515.

23. For a detailed critique of Sanera's position, see James P. Pfiffner, "Political Public Administration," *Public Administration Review*, vol. 45 (March/April 1985), p. 352.

24. "The Politicized Presidency," in John E. Chubb and Paul E. Peterson, eds., *The New Direction in American Politics* (Washington: Brookings Institution, 1985).

25. "The Politicized Presidency," p. 271.

26. "The Study of Administration," *Political Science Quarterly*, vol. 2 (June 1887), pp. 197-222, reprinted in Frederick C. Mosher, ed., *Basic Literature of American Public Administration, 1787-1950* (New York: Holmes and Meier, 1981).

27. "Politics as a Vocation," in H. H. Gerth and C. W. Mills, eds., *From Max Weber* (New York: Oxford University Press, 1946), p. 95.

28. See Edie Goldenberg, "The Permanent Government in a Time of Retrenchment and Redirection," in Lester Salamon and Michael Lund, eds., *The Reagan Presidency and the Governing of America* (Washington: Urban Institute, 1985), pp. 384-385.

29. Joel D. Aberbach, Robert D. Putnam, and Bert Rockman, *Bureaucrats and Politicians in Western Democracies* (Cambridge: Harvard University Press, 1981), p. 6.

30. Terry M. Moe, "The Politicized Presidency," in John E. Chubb and Paul E. Peterson, *The New Direction in American Politics* (Washington: Brookings Institution, 1985), p. 265.

31. "The In and Outer System: A Critical Assessment," in G. Calvin Mackenzie, ed., *The In and Outers* (Baltimore: Johns Hopkins University Press, 1987).

32. For a discussion of several different interpretations of the role of civil servants, see Edie N. Goldenberg, "The Permanent Government in a Time of Retrenchment and Redirection," in Salamon and Lund, eds., *The Reagan Presidency and the Governing of America.* See also Paul Light, "When Worlds Collide: The Political/Career Nexus," in G. Calvin Mackenzie, *The In and Outers* (Baltimore: Johns Hopkins University Press, 1987).

33. See Richard Rose, "Steering the Ship of State: One Tiller But Two Pairs of Hands," Centre for the Study of Public Policy, University of Strathclyde (1966), p. 8.

34. Hugh Heclo, *A Government of Strangers* (Washington: Brookings Institution, 1977), Chapter 4.

35. See Hugh Heclo, "Executive Budget Making," in Gregory Mills and John Palmer, eds., *Federal Budget Policy in the 1980s* (Washington: Urban Institute, 1984).

36. Interview with John Ehrlichman, Santa Fe (June 3, 1983).

37. Interview with Theodore Sorensen, New York City (March 25, 1985).

38. Interview with Jack Watson (June 17, 1983).

39. Interview with Harrison Wellford (July 7, 1983).

40. Quoted in *P A Times* (January 1, 1985).

41. Each of these quotations is taken from the transcripts of interviews of the NAPA Presidential Appointees Project. The interviews were conducted by Jeremy Plant and Michael Hansen.

42. NAPA, Presidential Appointees Project, interview with Richard Lyng, assistant secretary of agriculture for President Nixon and secretary of agriculture for President Reagan.

43. See Richard Nixon, *RN* (New York: Grosset and Dunlap, 1978), p. 676; and H. R. Haldeman, *The Ends of Power* (New York: Times Books, 1978), p. 150.

44. Interview with Al Zuck, Washington (1983).

45. Quoted by Hugh Heclo, *A Government of Strangers* (Washington: Brookings Institution, 1977), p. 177.

46. Hugh Heclo, "OMB and the Presidency—The Problem of Neutral Competence," *The Public Interest*, No. 38 (Winter 1975), pp. 80-82.

47. NAPA, Presidential Appointees Project, interview with Erich Evered, administrator, Energy Information Administration, 1981-84.

48. Ingraham, "Political Direction, Control, and Abuse," p. 16.

49. "A Comment on the Future of the U.S. Civil Service," in Bruce L. R. Smith, ed., *The Higher Civil Service in Europe and Canada* (Washington: Brookings Institution, 1984).

50. NAPA, Presidential Appointees Project, interview with Elliot Richardson.

51. *New York Times* (July 4, 1985), p. A14.

52. NAPA, Presidential Appointees Project, interview with Elliot Richardson.

53. Hugh Heclo, "The In and Outer System: A Critical Assessment," in G. Calvin Mackenzie, ed., *The In and Outers* (Baltimore: Johns Hopkins University Press, 1987).

54. See Linda Fisher, "Fifty Years of Presidential Appointees," in G. Calvin Mackenzie, ed., *The In and Outers* (Baltimore: Johns Hopkins University Press, 1987).

55. Hugh Heclo, "The In and Outer System: A Critical Assessment," in G. Calvin Mackenzie, ed., *The In and Outers* (Baltimore: Johns Hopkins University Press, 1987).

56. Frederic V. Malek, *Washington's Hidden Tragedy* (New York: The Free Press, 1978), pp. 102-103.

57. For an analysis of the need for presidents to move quickly upon taking office, see James P. Pfiffner, *The Strategic Presidency: Hitting the Ground Running* (Chicago: Dorsey, forthcoming).

58. NAPA, "Recruiting Presidential Appointees: A Conference of Former Presidential Personnel Assistants" (December 13, 1984). Emphasis added.

CHAPTER SEVEN

American Federalism: Madison's Middle Ground in the 1980s

MARTHA DERTHICK*

"Let it be tried . . . whether any middle ground can be taken, which will at once support a due supremacy of the national authority, and leave in force the local authorities so far as they can be subordinately useful."

So wrote James Madison to Edmund Randolph not long before the constitutional convention.[1] Much of American constitutional experience has consisted, as did much of Madison's work in Philadelphia, of a search for that middle ground.

At the convention, even partisans of the states conceded that there must be a stronger central government than the Articles of Confederation provided. And even supporters of national supremacy conceded that the states

---

* **Martha Derthick** has been the Julia Allen Cooper Professor of Government and Foreign Affairs at the University of Virginia since 1983. Before that, she was on the staff of the Brookings Institution for 12 years, five of them as director of Brookings' Governmental Studies program. She teaches courses on intergovernmental relations and is the author of several books on that subject. In 1983 she received the Donald C. Stone award of the American Society for Public Administration Section on Intergovernmental Administration and Management for contributing significantly to intergovernmental management through research.

should not be abolished.[2]   So the convention settled on a
"composition" or "compound republic," as Madison termed it
in *The Federalist*.[3]   That is, the new government combined
features of federal and purely national forms, most obviously
in the structure of its legislature, wherein the states were
represented, equally, in one house, and the people directly,
in proportion to their numbers, in the other.

Eventually, this creation came to be widely regarded as
the prototype of federal government, or at least as the most
important and successful example of it.   K. C. Wheare,
writing a basic text on federal government in 1953, began
by looking to the Constitution of the United States for his
definition.   The basic principle, he concluded, "is that of
the division of powers between distinct and co-ordinate
governments."[4]   In certain matters, for example the coining
of money and the making of treaties, the general
government was independent of the state governments,
whereas the states, in turn, were independent of the general
government in other matters.

One wonders if the Founders believed that their
"composition" would be stable.   Some evidently doubted it.
At the outset of the convention, after explaining the
distinction between a federal government as it was then
understood ("a mere compact resting on the good faith of
the parties") and a national one ("having a complete and
compulsive operation"), Gouverneur Morris seemed to say
that the convention must choose one or the other: "He
contended that in all communities there must be one
supreme power, and one only."[5]   "A National Government
must soon of necessity swallow [the states] all up," George
Read of Delaware predicted.[6]   "Mr. Bedford [also of
Delaware] contended, that there was no middle way between
a perfect consolidation, and a mere confederacy of the
States."[7]   In 1828, when the composition was nearly 40
years old and under severe strain, Madison seemed uncertain
about its prospects but still hopeful.   "It will be fortunate if
the struggle [between the nation and states] should end in a
permanent equilibrium of powers," he wrote.[8]

As the "composition" approaches 200 years of age, it is
still not easy to render a simple, indisputable judgment on
the outcome.   Surely the national government has proved
supreme.   It got the better of the states in the original
contest, as well as in the major tests of subsequent
centuries.   The nineteenth century, embracing the great

debates over nullification and secession and culminating in the Civil War, virtually disposed of the doctrine that the states have the right to decide disputes over the distribution of governmental power. The twentieth century then proceeded to dispose of the original precept that the powers of the national government are confined to those enumerated in a written constitution—a development that was far enough advanced by the end of World War II to cast doubt even then on Wheare's definition.[9]

On the other hand, even now the national government does not operate alone. State governments survive, not as hollow shells (as their detractors often charge and their defenders always fear), but as functioning entities, with their own constitutions, laws, elected officials and independently-raised revenues. Though Congress has pervasively invaded domains once thought exclusively those of the states and though it very much constrains their conduct with commerce clause regulations applying directly to them and with grant-in-aid conditions, on the whole it has refrained from displacing them—apart, that is, from piecemeal preemptions of regulatory functions under the commerce clause, a practice that is well within the bounds of constitutional tradition and indubitably sanctioned by the supremacy clause. As a general rule, when Congress essays new domestic responsibilities it relies on cooperation of the states, with the result that the two levels of government in our federal system are today massively and pervasively intertwined—a fact that is of utmost importance for the conduct of public administration.

As it happens, quite apart from the impending bicentennial of the Constitution, the 1980s are an eminently suitable time for taking stock of the federal system for two reasons. First, because the Reagan era has provided surcease from the passage of expansive new federal legislation, we can pause to appraise the changes that took place between 1965 and 1980, a period marked by numerous innovations in intergovernmental relations. Second, within the Supreme Court and between the Court and the Reagan administration's second attorney general, a rather heated debate has developed over the importance of federalism and the judicial behavior required to preserve it.

The Practice of Intergovernmental Relations:
Shared Programs

For a student of federalism to make sense of the events of 1965-1980 is no easy task. A great deal happened. Grant-in-aid programs proliferated in the customary categorical pattern and then were revised by the introduction of general revenue-sharing and three broad-based grants—two (for community development and employment and training) which the Nixon administration designed and a third (social services) that developed unintentionally when several powerful, populous states successfully exploited a loophole in the federal law providing for public assistance grants.[10]   As of 1984, following attempts by the Reagan administration to expand block grants and reduce general revenue-sharing, 20 percent of federal grants were classified as broad-based or general-purpose.

Against the decentralization embodied in less-conditioned grants, however, must be set numerous centralizing acts of Congress that occurred in the same period.   Congress replaced several public assistance grant programs with a direct federal program of income support (Supplemental Security Income or SSI) and displayed a heightened willingness to try to make national policy for the remaining category of public assistance, Aid to Families with Dependent Children.   It experimented boldly and sometimes irresponsibly with a new grant-in-aid technique, what the Advisory Commission on Intergovernmental Relations has called the "cross-cutting requirement."[11] Employed mainly to prevent discrimination in the use of grants, this technique encompasses in one statutory stroke *all* grant programs or some large class of them, in contrast to Congress's earlier practice of attaching conditions specifically to particular categorical programs.[12]

Related to the "cross-cutting requirement," yet clearly distinguishable from it, is another new and bold grant technique, that which ACIR calls the "cross-over sanction."[13]   Historically, Congress has confined the sanction of withholding grant funds quite narrowly within grant categories.   Withholding would apply only to activity wherein the recipient's transgression of federal requirements was alleged, but in the 1970s Congress began to threaten sanctions that crossed the boundaries of particular programs. Thus, for example, if states do not meet the pollution control standards of the Clean Air Act, they may be penalized by the withholding of highway aid funds. To assure that the states supplemented federal payments under SSI to the extent that Congress wished, it threatened them with loss of Medicaid grants. Numerous other examples exist. In general, categorical grant-in-aid programs of the 1970s, whether newly enacted or only amended, displayed a much enlarged willingness to intrude in state and local affairs. Statements of federal objectives were often as expansive as grant-in-aid techniques were inventive.

Nor was Congress's inventiveness confined to grant-in-aid programs. In the process of enacting dozens of laws in the 1970s for the regulation of environmental, work-place, and product hazards, Congress repeatedly applied a new technique of intergovernmental relations that has become known as "partial preemption."[14] Very roughly, it is to regulatory programs what the conditioned, categorical grant-in-aid is to spending programs—that is, a way of propounding national objectives and inducing the states to cooperate in pursuing them; the two are often used in tandem. Partial preemption entails the setting of federal regulatory standards but gives the states the option of various forms of participation in the regulatory regime. More often than not, the federal government relies heavily on them for enforcement.

Under the Clear Air Act, for example, Congress sets standards for permissible levels of common pollutants and deadlines for meeting them. States are instructed to adopt implementation plans designed to attain the standards, and the federal Environmental Protection Agency (EPA) reviews the state plans.[15] If a state fails to act or fails to secure EPA's approval of its plan, EPA can develop its own plan for the state. Both the state and federal governments may take action against polluters.

The Surface Mining Control and Reclamation Act uses a similar technique. The act sets forth numerous, detailed performance standards that coal-mining operations must meet. States wishing to assume regulatory responsibility must admit plans for approval by the Office of Surface Mining (OSM) of the Department of the Interior. State laws, regulations, and administrative performance must meet the requirements of the federal act. If a state chooses not to regulate, fails to gain approval of its plan, or fails to implement the plan satisfactorily, OSM is required to take charge.[16]

As a third example, under the Occupational Safety and Health Act of 1970 the Secretary of Labor is required to promulgate standards, but states may regulate those matters that federal regulations fail to address, and they may also assume responsibility in areas where the federal government has acted if their own standards are "at least effective" as the federal standards.[17]

The Persistence of State Discretion

From the perspective of the mid-1980s, one can hardly say that the results of this outburst of congressional activity are clear, but it is perhaps not too soon to say that they are clearly ambiguous.   Even where the urge to centralize was strongest—in income support and environmental protection programs—state governments retain a great deal of discretion in policy-making and freedom from federal administrative supervision.   Despite fears of some partisans of the states that they were being turned into mere administrative agents of an overbearing central government, federalism lives.   It is manifest in the persistence of interstate differences in program characteristics and in the ineffectiveness of much federal oversight of state administration.

Probably no more striking proof of the persistence of states' individuality exists than the SSI program, in which they are free to supplement the federal minimum payment. Congress on 1973 required supplementation to the extent necessary to hold current recipients harmless against the changes associated with federalization, and some states have also provided optional supplements.   Only seven states do not supplement at all, according to a study done in 1984.[18] As of January 1985, the minimum federal payment for an aged individual living alone and having no countable income was $325, but differences in state supplements meant that the actual legal minimum ranged from $325 to a high of $586 in Alaska.   Because many recipients have countable income, monthly payments are on average less than these minimums; in August 1985 they ranged from $90.95 per aged recipient in Maine to $252.83 in Alaska.[19]

The persistence of federalism is perhaps even more vividly demonstrated, though, by the administrative features of SSI. Twenty-seven states administer their own supplements. No federal regulations apply to supplements in these states, which remain free to supplement whomever they please in whatever amounts they please. As one would expect, practices vary widely. At an extreme, Illinois continues to calculate an individual budget amount for each of its nearly 30,000 recipients of state supplements.

Nor is the situation vastly different in those 16 states (plus the District of Columbia) that have accepted Congress's offer to have the Social Security Administration administer supplements for them. Eager to get the program under way with the states' cooperation, SSA at the outset agreed to administer a number of variations in supplementation. Variations are permitted among benefit categories, three geographic divisions within a state, and five different living arrangements. One analyst has calculated that there are about 300 different SSI benefits nationally; he counted 158 state-administered variations and 130 federally-administered variations.[20] Perversely, the result of the "national" takeover has been to burden a national administrative agency, the SSA, with many of the accommodations to local circumstances that ordinarily take place through the medium of state administration. The SSA has found this to be a very large burden indeed, as a history of administrative troubles in SSI shows.

In Aid to Families with Dependent Children, which is still basically a state-run program despite prolonged attempts under both Nixon and Carter to achieve a "welfare reform" that would federalize it, interstate payment differences likewise persist, of course. In the second quarter of 1984, the average monthly payment per recipient ranged from $31 in Mississippi to $217 in Alaska. Twenty-three states were providing AFDC-UP—that is, were using welfare to compensate for parental unemployment as well as the absence of an employed adult from the home—but the rest were not.[21] Encouraged by Congress after 1981 to set up work programs for welfare recipients, the states adopted "a flurry of initiatives," according to a report in *The National Journal*. In most states, however, work and training programs were limited to a few counties and to small subgroups of those eligible because of financial, administrative, or geographical constraints.[22] In short, after a decade or more of the most intense effort in Washington to supplant AFDC, the program survived, interstate and even intrastate variations in it remained the norm, and states were quite conspicuously functioning as "laboratories of experiment."

These laboratories were only lightly supervised by federal administrators. Close, detailed supervision of state administration of welfare, which had been attempted by the Bureau of Public Assistance in the years following passage of the Social Security Act, had collapsed by the end of the 1960s, to some extent destroyed by the growth of caseloads, to some extent deliberately abandoned by leaders of the Department of Health, Education and Welfare who believed that the BPA's administrative style had produced too much red tape while failing to contain the caseloads. In the late 1960s, the very detailed guidance developed by the BPA over decades was cancelled in favor of much more general and permissive regulations.[23]

However, in the face of caseloads which continued to mount along with pressures to contain federal spending, the new permissiveness and simplicity did not last long. HEW in the early 1970s initiated an effort to control error rates in AFDC by designing sample studies, setting performance objectives, and manipulating incentives—rewards *and* penalties—in the fashion of new-style management experts and policy analysts rather than old-style social workers, who had had a more patronizing and less scientific approach to dealing with the states. The idea, incorporated in HEW regulations promulgated at the end of 1972, was that the states would be penalized with the loss of federal funds if they had excessive error rates. But thereafter various secretaries of HEW kept postponing sanctions while various subordinates negotiated with one another and with the states over what would be practicable and acceptable. Eventually, 13 states won a judgment from the U.S. District Court in the District of Columbia that the tolerance levels for error set by HEW were arbitrary and capricious. Negotiations resumed, and weak quality control regulations, with which most states would find it easy to comply, were promulgated in 1979.[24] In the Tax Equity and Fiscal Responsibility Act of 1982, Congress set 4 percent as an allowable error rate in AFDC payments for 1983 and 3 percent thereafter, with the proviso that the secretary of health and human services should make no reimbursements for erroneous payments in excess of that rate. However, the Secretary might waive all or part of the reduction in grants if "a State is unable to reach the allowable error rate . . . despite a good faith effort. . . ."[25]

Bargaining and negotiation, not command and obedience, appear to characterize the practice of intergovernmental programs now as in the past, even if the past was far more mindful of a tradition called states' rights. To these negotiations, states bring some newly-acquired strengths that partially offset Congress's diminished sensitivity to their interests, and federal administrative agencies bring some weaknesses of long standing.

State Strengths and Federal Weaknesses

One of the states' strengths consists of organization. Both state and local governments have banded together in various organizations which perform service and lobbying functions on their behalf. When HEW officials were seeking to develop their AFDC quality control program in the 1970s, they negotiated with a group composed of representatives of the National Association of Counties, the National Conference of State Legislatures, National League of Cities/U.S. Conference of Mayors, the National Governors Conference, and the American Public Welfare Association, in which the NGC took the lead. The rise of the "intergovernmental lobby" is well documented, and at least one influential article attributed to the passage of general revenue-sharing largely to its existence.[26] A second new-found strength of the states—one not unique to them but widely shared in our society—is their capacity to bring suit. Individually, in *ad hoc* groups or through their formal lobbying organizations, they resort to the courts when they feel that Congress or the executive agencies have transgressed constitutional or statutory bounds.

In general, their constitutionally-based challenges have not succeeded. Courts have found nothing constitutionally impermissible in partial preemptions or the newer grant-in-aid techniques. They typically hold that if a valid national purpose is being served (and under the commerce clause or the power to tax and spend for the general welfare, one always is), and if the states are not being coerced (and under grant-in-aid programs and partial preemptions, the states technically do retain the option of not participating), then the law is valid.

Statutory challenges are another matter, however, as the example of HEW's failed attempt to promulgate strict AFDC quality control regulations shows. Throughout their negotiations with the states, HEW officials in that case were hampered both by intradepartmental differences of view and by a well-founded apprehension over what the courts would permit. Courts are not loathe to find that federal executive agencies have exceeded their statutory authority in promulgating regulations for intergovernmental programs.

Probably the most telling and significant use of the courts' powers of statutory review came in the late 1970s in a set of cases that arose out of the Environmental Protection Agency's promulgation of standards for transportation control plans. Under threat of various civil sanctions, including injunctions, the imposition of receiverships on certain state functions, and fines and contempt citations for state officials, EPA would have required the states to adopt and enforce such measures as parking bans and surcharges, bus lanes, and computerized carpool matching. Three out of four appellate courts which reviewed these regulations found that they had exceeded Congress's intent and strongly hinted that they violated the Constitution as well. The states could be offered the choice of whether to participate in pollution control and could be fully preempted if they chose not to participate, but they could not be ordered to carry out federal regulations.[27]

If negotiation works well for the states, though, it is not just because they are well organized and sometimes victorious in the courts. It is because federal agencies bring serious weaknesses to the bargaining table. Neither of their principal weapons—to withhold funds in grant-in-aid programs, to take charge of enforcement in regulatory programs—is readily usable.

Withholding funds is self-defeating and risks congressional intervention and reprimand. (The HEW officials who struggled with AFDC quality control issues in the 1970s felt under pressure from Congress to do something yet doubted that Congress would come to their defense if they did anything drastic.) Withholding, though occasionally threatened, is rarely used. When issues arise, the contestants negotiate.[28]

The threat to take charge of administration likewise lacks credibility except in isolated cases because federal agencies generally lack the capacity to supersede the states, and everyone knows it. Congress is unwilling to spend the funds or otherwise to bear the onus of creating a large federal bureaucracy; that is why it chooses to rely so heavily on intergovernmental techniques.

Where partial preemption has been employed, giving states the option of assuming responsibility for enforcement and federal agencies' responsibility for approving state plans and supervising their execution, states in general have opted to participate, and federal agencies have in general made the necessary delegations. Among the new regulatory regimes, only that for occupational health and safety remains overwhelmingly a federal responsibility, and that is only because the AFL-CIO successfully challenged the Department of Labor's criteria for delegation in court during the Ford administration, raising a set of issues that have since remained unresolved. In practice, about half of the states run their own occupational safety and health programs even if the federal government remains nominally in charge almost everywhere.[29]

When state defiance or default requires federal agencies to assume enforcement responsibilities in regulatory programs based on partial preemption, the results are not invariable felicitous. One consequence of the use of partial preemption has been to demonstrate, through various "natural experiments," that federal administration is not necessarily superior to state administration.

In 1981 the Idaho legislature, irritated by the U.S. Environmental Protection Agency (EPA), voted not to fund the state's air quality program, forcing EPA to administer it. Both state and federal officials concluded after a year that the federal takeover caused more problems than it solved. EPA reportedly spent almost five times as much to maintain the Idaho program that year as the state would have spent to do the same job. In another case, Iowa's environmental budget was cut 15 percent in 1982, causing a loss of federal matching funds. The state then returned responsibility for its municipal water-monitoring program to EPA, which managed to conduct only about 15 percent of the inspections formerly performed by the state.[30]

The Office of Surface Mining in 1984 found it necessary to reclaim responsibility from Tennessee and

Oklahoma, but nothing in the administrative performance of the federal agency gives grounds for confidence that it can do much better.[31]

A study by the Congressional Research Service in 1983 sought systematically to compare occupational injury rates in states with federally-run programs with those where state agencies remained in charge, in a tentative test of the effectiveness of programs in the two sets. The study concluded that states with state-run programs had a somewhat better performance record.[32] Organized labor has complained that inspections are fewer in states where the Occupational Safety and Health Administration (OSHA) remains responsible for enforcement, although this has not caused it to reexamine its abiding preference for a federal regime. Current failures of federal performance can be blamed on the Republican administration.[33]

The new regulatory regimes are still new enough that one cannot be sure that they have stabilized. The arrival of the Reagan administration, committed to a sharp reduction in federal spending and a revival of states' rights—or states' responsibilities, as Reagan officials sometimes insist—accelerated delegations to state governments and correspondingly contracted the size and hence administrative capacities of the federal regulatory agencies. Yet it is doubtful that a future change in the election returns would work more than marginal changes in the administrative arrangements that have emerged. Apparently, these arrangements leave much for the states to do and much room for them to negotiate with their federal-agency supervisors over how and how fast to do it.

The Role of the Courts

Insofar as centralization has occurred in the past decade or two, the courts have been at least as influential as Congress, arguably much more so. This is not so much because courts have preferred the national side in overt contests between the national government and the states as because federal courts have aggressively pursued the extension of individual rights with little regard for the effect on the states' prerogatives as governments in their own right.[34]

By steadily enlarging the application of the due process and equal protection clauses of the Fourteenth Amendment, the Supreme Court carried into the late 1960s and early 1970s the vigorous extension of the constitutional rights of individuals begun in the 1950s with *Brown vs. Board of Education* (or, if one prefers, in 1925 with *Gitlow vs. New York* , in which the Court first read the Bill of Rights into the Fourteenth Amendment). Such celebrated cases as *Roe vs. Wade* (1973), which struck down state laws prohibiting abortion; *Goldberg vs. Kelly* (1970), which required that a welfare recipient be afforded an evidentiary hearing *before* the termination of benefits; and *Shapiro vs. Thompson* (1969), which invalidated state residency requirements for welfare applicants, boldly asserted national power at the states' expense.[35]

In the area of voting rights, statutory construction as well as constitutional interpretation has been the Court's route to a radically altered federalism. Since its decision in 1969 in *Allen vs. State Board of Elections*, the Department of Justice has had power to review municipal annexations, the redrawing of district lines, and the choice of at-large versus district elections in jurisdictions covered by the Voting Rights Act—power that it has used to increase the probability that minority candidates will win office. Such methods of protecting the franchise of blacks and other minorities to whom the law's protection has been extended are far more problematic and intrusive than those contemplated when it was passed in 1965.[36]

Rather less publicized than Supreme Court decisions, yet arguably at least as intrusive, have been the numerous decisions of lower federal courts in the so-called institution cases, in which state governments were ordered to increase their expenditures on facilities for the mentally ill or retarded, criminals, and juvenile detainees. The decrees in these cases have mandated massive and often detailed changes in the operation of institutions and their programs—changes involving the physical condition of the facility, staffing, and quality of services.[37]

In some especially intrusive grant-in-aid programs, notably the Education for All Handicapped Children Act of 1975, Congress has been emboldened by courts. That act requires, as a condition of grants-in-aid, that states have in effect a policy assuring all handicapped children between the ages of 3 and 21 the right to a free appropriate public education and that local educational agencies maintain and annually review an individualized program for each handicapped child. This law built upon federal district court decisions of 1971 in Pennsylvania and 1972 in the District of Columbia.[38]

Where newly-sweeping grant-in-aid conditions have been particularly effective, it has ordinarily been because courts have reinforced and elaborated them, in effect working in tandem with the administrative agency. *Together*, the courts and the Office of Education (and then the Office of Civil Rights, after it was separately constituted) brought about the extraordinary desegregation of Southern schools in the late 1960s. Title VI of the Civil Rights Act of 1964, with a "cross-cutting requirement" which prohibited racial discrimination in the use of federal grants-in-aid, when combined with the grants to elementary and secondary schools that were freshly enacted in 1965, complemented *Brown vs. Board* and the successor decisions. Also, it was crucially complemented by them. As Gary Orfield notes in his definitive study of the application of TItle VI to Southern schools, the decisive federal response came in 1968 in a case involving the schools of New Kent County, Virginia. "Once again the work of black attorneys and the response of the judiciary [created] a shield behind which the administrative techniques of HEW could be effectively employed."[39]

The influence of the courts is shown not just in what they have done, but, less directly, in what they have declined to prevent Congress from doing. For a fleeting moment, in *National League of Cities vs. Usery* (1976), the Supreme Court seemed willing to revive *and apply* the precept that states' sovereignty imposes some limit on Congress's exercise of the commerce clause. In that decision it held that Congress could not use the Fair labor Standards Act to regulate the states' determination of their employees' wages and hours.[40] Successor decisions, however, rather than building on *National League of Cities*, led to the repudiation of it in *Garcia vs. San Antonio Metropolitan Transit Authority* in 1985.[41] While the Court has never said that states' sovereignty imposes *no* limit on Congress's commerce clause powers, it has backed away from trying to define one.

It is little wonder that the Reagan administration's attempt to construct protection for the states had by late

1985 come to focus on judicial appointments. In its own legislative and administrative choices, the Reagan administration has been far from consistent in its commitment to strengthening the states. When budget reduction and other objectives have conflicted with that aim, the administration's devolutionary objectives have often been compromised, as Timothy Conlan has shown in a careful analysis.[42] To that, Reagan officials might well reply that for the preservation of the states as a coordinate element of government, it is the federal bench that matters most.

Current Debates

As of the mid-1980s, the value of federalism was very much at issue within the Supreme Court and between the Court and the Reagan administration's second attorney general. Today's conservatives profess to value the federal principle highly, whereas liberals, in their preoccupation with perfecting individual rights, are either indifferent to questions of government structure or reflexively prefer national to state action.

The current debate, as yet imperfectly joined for lack of a full exposition on either side, appears to turn on essentially the issues which divided federalists and anti-federalists 200 years ago. Both sides profess to value liberty and democracy above all. They differ in their judgments of the distribution of governmental power that will best serve those ends.

"A substantive issue like abortion is a matter of public or civic morality," Attorney General Edwin Meese has argued, and "should be decided upon through a free and robust discussion at the level [of government] most appropriate to its determination." In his view, that is the level of state and local government, for "big government does not encourage a sense of belonging. . . . An essential sense of community is far more likely to develop at the local level." A proper understanding of federalism, in this view, would permit such matters as abortion, prayer in the schools, pornography, and aid to parochial schools to be deliberated on by state governments and resolved by the sense of the particular community, there to be incorporated in statutes, rather than being treated at the national level as subjects of constitutional doctrine.[43]

Much as Meese in these remarks argued the superior communal qualities of the states, Justice Lewis F. Powell in a dissent to *Garcia vs. SAMTA* argued the inferior quality of the federal government's policy processes. Federal laws are drafted by congressional committee staffs and federal regulations, often more important than the laws, by the staffs of agencies, he wrote. A realistic comparison of the operation of the different levels of government, in Powell's view, shows state and local governments to be more accessible and responsive, hence more democratic, than the government based in Washington. That government in the national capital would become remote and alienated from ordinary people was one of the fears of the anti-federalists. Their intellectual heirs on the Supreme Court say it has happened.

Perhaps the most important events in the federal system in the recent past are those which bear on the potential power of such arguments as Meese's and Powell's by affecting either the public's receptivity to them or their plausibility. Even as centralization proceeds—indeed, perhaps because it has proceeded as far—the federal government seems to have suffered a decline in popular esteem. Confidence in its performance dropped sharply in the 1970s, and by the mid-1980s it was doing poorly in pools asking the public to compare it to state and local governments.[44] By contrast, scholarly and journalistic accounts of the performance of state governments uniformly judge it much improved over two or three decades ago, enhanced by legislatures more active, more professional, and better-staffed than formerly—*and* more representative of their constituencies, with ironic thanks to the reapportionment decisions of the Supreme Court.[45]

Governmental competence and perceptions of it aside, all discussions of American federalism must henceforth be altered by what is arguably the most important new social and political datum of our times: the end of Southern exceptionalism. Until now, arguments favoring the states' side in any dispute over federalism suffered fatally from the burden of the South's deviant social system. Whether or not blacks have been successfully integrated into American society (a separate question), there can be little doubt that the South as a region has been integrated. That change, even if achieved very largely by the instrumentalities of the federal government, holds the possibility that the case for the states can at last begin to be discussed on its merits.

That case deserves a more careful contemporary exposition than it has yet received, with due regard for the purposes and expectations of the Founders. The Founders did not make a strong argument for the federal aspects of their "composition." *The Federalist* is "rather inexplicit and ambiguous in its treatment of federalism," for the reason that its authors were at heart nationalists.[46] Madison saw the size of the new republic, not its compound quality, as crucial to the achievement of liberty. His most eloquent and memorable statements were made in support of "extending the sphere."[47] He told the convention that "Were it practicable for the General Government to extend its care to every requisite object without the co-operation of the State Governments, the people would not be less free as members of one great Republic, than as members of thirteen small ones."[48]

Yet Madison's willingness to preserve the states was more than a concession to the fact that their abolition, then as now, was politically unacceptable. Prudent and practical, he thought they would be useful, even if subordinately. He doubted that the national government would be suited to the entire task of governing "so great an extent of country, and over so great a variety of objects."[49]

In this, as in so much else, Madison was very wise. As the burdens of governing grow, the inability or unwillingness of the federal government to bear them alone is manifest.[50] The states therefore remain vigorous, although they are more nearly the subordinately useful governments that Madison anticipated in 1787 than the coordinate ones posited by Wheare's definition.

ENDNOTES

1.   Cited in Irving Brant, *The Fourth President: A Life of James Madison* (Indianapolis: The Bobbs-Merrill Company, 1970), p. 146.

2.   "[A] consolidation of the States is not less unattainable than it would be inexpedient," the nationalist Madison wrote, in the same letter to Randolph.

3.   The leading statement is No. 39. For an interpretation, see Martin Diamond, "What the Framers Meant by Federalism," in Robert A. Goldwin, ed., *A Nation of States: Essays on the American Federal System* (Chicago: Rand McNally & Co., 1963), pp. 24-41.

4.   *Federal Government* (New York: Oxford University Press, 1953), p. 2. Wheare defines the federal principle by reference to the particular features of the United States government, for "The modern idea of what federal government is has been determined by the United States of America," p. 1.

5.   *Journal of the Federal Convention Kept by James Madison* (Chicago: Albert, Scott & Co., 1893), p. 74.

6.   *Ibid.*, p. 120.

7.   *Ibid.*, p. 280.

8.   *The Letters and Other Writings of James Madison* (Congress edition: R. Worthington, 1884), vol. III, p. 625.

9.   Cf. Edward S. Corwin, "The Passing of Dual Federalism," *Virginia Law Review*, vol. 36 (1950).

10.   The Advisory Commission on Intergovernmental Relations (ACIR), in studies of the intergovernmental grant system done in the late 1970s, also counted as

block grants those authorized by the Partnership for Health Act of 1966, which had consolidated seven categorical grants, and the Omnibus Crime Control and Safe Streets Act of 1968. See Advisory Commission on Intergovernmental Relations, *Block Grants: A Comparative Analysis* (Washington: ACIR, 1977).

11. Advisory Commission on Intergovernmental Relations, *Regulatory Federalism: Policy, Process, Impact and Reform* (Washington: ACIR, 1984), pp. 8, 71-78.

12. In truth, the technique was not altogether new but had antecedents as old as the Hatch Act, which was amended in 1940 to prohibit partisan political activity by any "officer or employee of any State or local agency whose principal employment is in connection with any activity which is financed in whole or in part by loans or grants made by the United States. . . ." Failure to comply was punishable by the withholding of funds. *54 Stat. 767* (1940). Cross-cutting requirements did not become common until the 1960s, however.

13. *Ibid.*, pp. 9, 78-82.

14. *Ibid.*, pp. 9, 82-88. I am much indebted to David R. Beam for enlightenment on the newer techniques of federal influence vis-a-vis the states, derived both from personal conversations and from his work at the ACIR as one of the authors of *Regulatory Federalism*.

15. *84 Stat.* 1676 (1970). The law says that "Each State . . . shall . . . adopt . . . a plan. . . ."

16. *91 Stat.* 445 (1977).

17. *84 Stat.* 1590 (1970).

18. Renato A. DiPentima, "The Supplemental Security Income Program: A Study of Implementation," Ph.D. dissertation (University of Maryland, 1984), p. 80.

19. *Social Security Bulletin*, vol. 48 (October 1985), p. 19, and (November 1985), p. 42. These data published by the federal government cover only those states—slightly

more than half of the total—in which the Social Security Administration has responsibility for administering supplemental payments. The SSA lacks comparable data from states that have chosen to administer themselves whatever program of supplementation exists. See the text, *infra*, for further explanation of federal versus state administration of supplements.

20. DiPentima, *op. cit.*, p. 85.

21. U.S. Department of Health and Human Services, *Quarterly Public Assistance Statistics* (April-June 1984), Tables 7 and 15.

22. Julie Kosterlitz, "Liberals and Conservatives Share Goals, Differ on Details of Work for Welfare," *National Journal* (October 26, 1985), pp. 2418-22.

23. Martha Derthick, *The Influence of Federal Grants: Public Assistance in Massachusetts* (Cambridge: Harvard University Press, 1970), pp. 225-29, and *Uncontrollable Spending for Social Services Grants* (Washington: The Brookings Institution, 1975), pp. 15-24.

24. "Controlling AFDC Error Rates," Kennedy School of Government Case C 14-80-302 (copyright by President and Fellows of Harvard College, 1980).

25. H. Rept. 97-760, p. 79.

26. Donald H. Haider, *When Governments Come to Washington: Governors, Mayors, and Intergovernmental Lobbying* (New York: Free Press, 1974); Samuel H. Beer, "The Adoption of General Revenue Sharing: A Case Study in Public Sector Politics," *Public Policy*, vol. 24 (Spring 1976). The impending demise of general revenue-sharing calls into question the hypothesis that the intergovernmental lobby was responsible for its passage, for there is no reason to suppose that the lobby is less well-organized today than it was in the early 1970s.

27. *Brown vs. Environmental Protection Agency*, 521 F. 2nd
827 (9th Cir., 1975); *Maryland vs. Environmental
Protection Agency*, 530 F. 2nd 215 (4th Cir., 1975);
District of Columbia vs. Train, 521 F. 2nd 971 (D.C.
Cir., 1975); *Pennsylvania Vs. Environmental Protection
Agency*, 500 F. 2nd 246 (3rd Cir., 1974).

28. Cf. Derthick, *The Influence of Federal Grants*, chap. 8.
However, the willingness of courts since 1970 to
discover private rights of action in federal statutes has
to some extent offset the weakness of federal agencies
in regard to the use of withholding. As R. Shep
Melnick has written, "The private right of action has
special significance in joint federal-state spending
programs. If an alleged beneficiary could only bring
suit against a federal administrator for failing to
enforce federal standards, the only relief the court
could offer successful plaintiffs would be an injunction
cutting off federal funds to the state. . . . But when
potential recipients can bring suit against the state for
failure to comply with federal requirements, the court
can compel the state to pay the plaintiff the money
owed. The private right of action, thus, significantly
alters the balance of power between the federal
government and the states." "The Politics of
Partnership," *Public Administration Review*, vol. 45
(November 1985), pp. 656-57.

29. On intergovernmental relations in occupational safety
and health, see the oversight hearings held annually by
the Subcommittee on Health and Safety of the Committee on Education and Labor, U.S. House of
Representatives. The most important titles are: *OSHA
Oversight—State of the Agency Report by Assistant
Secretary of Labor for OSHA*, 97 Cong. 2 sess. (1983),
pp. 212-36; *OSHA Oversight—Staffing Levels for OSHA
Approved State Plans*, 98 Cong. 1 sess. (1983); and
Oversight on OSHA: State of the Agency, 99 Cong. 1
sess. (1985), serial no. 99-12.

30. *State of the Environment: An Assessment at Mid-
Decade* (Washington: The Conservation Foundation,
1984), p. 458.

31. Rochelle L. Stanfield, "Mine Disaster," *National Journal* (October 12, 1985), p. 2342.

32. U.S. House of Representatives, Committee on Education and Labor, *OSHA Oversight—Staffing Levels for OSHA Approved State Plans*, Hearings before the Subcommittee on Health and Safety, 98 Cong., 1 sess. (1983), pp. 295-327. See also the work of Frank J. Thompson and Michael J. Scicchitano: "State Implementation Effort and Federal Regulatory Policy: The Case of Occupational Safety and Health," *Journal of Politics*, vol. 47 (1985), pp. 686-703, and "State Enforcement of Federal Regulatory Policy: The Lessons of OSHA," *Policy Studies Journal*, vol. 13 (March 1985), pp. 591-598.

33. Michael Wines, "Auchter's Record at OSHA Leaves Labor Outraged, Business Satisfied," *National Journal* (October 1, 1983), pp. 2008-13.

34. For a critique, see Robert F. Nagel, "Federalism as a Fundamental Value: National League of Cities in Perspective," *Supreme Court Review* (1981), pp. 81-109.

35. For a good summary of the Court's use of the Fourteenth Amendment to extend civil liberties, see David Fellman, "The Nationalization of American Civil Liberties," in M. Judd Harmon, ed., *Essays on the Constitution of the United States* (Port Washington, NY: Kennikat Press, 1978), pp. 49-60.

36. Abigail M. Thernstrom, "The Odd Evolution of the Voting Rights Act," *Public Interest* (Spring 1979), pp. 49-76.

37. Gerald E. Frug, "The Judicial Power of the Purse," *University of Pennsylvania Law Review*, vol. 126 (April 1978), pp. 715-794.

38. Erwin L. Levine and Elizabeth M. Wexler, *PL 94-142: An Act of Congress* (New York: Macmillan, 1981), pp. 38-41. In the field of voting rights, statutory amendments and court decisions have interacted to produce the surprisingly far reach of federal action

described above. These events are analyzed in detail in a forthcoming book by Abigail M. Thernstrom.

39. Gary Orfield, *The Reconstruction of Southern Education: The Schools and the 1964 Civil Rights Act* (New York: John Wiley and Sons, 1969), p. 262. See also Jeremy Rabkin, "Office for Civil Rights," in James Q. Wilson, ed., *The Politics of Regulation* (New York: Basic Books, 1980), chap. 9.

40. 426 U.S. 833.

41. Slip opinion No. 82-1913, decided February 19, 1985.

42. Timothy J. Conlan, "Federalism and Competing Values in the Reagan Administration," in Laurence J. O'Toole, Jr., ed., *American Intergovernmental Relations* (Washington: CQ Press, 1985), pp. 265-80.

43. Address before the American Enterprise Institute, Sept. 6, 1985.

44. Seymour Martin Lipset and William Schneider, *The Confidence Gap: Business, Labor and Government in the Public Mind* (New York: Free Press, 1968), and Advisory Commission on Intergovernmental Relations, *Changing Public Attitudes on Governments and Taxes: 1984* (Washington: ACIR, 1984).

45. Alan Rosenthal, *Legislative Life: People, Process, and Performance in the States* (New York: Harper & Row, 1981), and William K. Muir, Jr., *Legislature: California's School for Politics* (Chicago: University of Chicago Press, 1982).

46. Martin Diamond, "The Federalist's View of Federalism," in *Essays in Federalism* (Claremont, CA: Institute for Studies in Federalism, 1961), pp. 21-62. The quotation appears at p. 24. It was left to the anti-federalists to make the case for the states at the time of the founding. See Herbert J. Storing, *What the Anti-Federalists Were For* (Chicago: University of Chicago Press, 1981), chap. 3.

47. The classic statement is contained in *Federalist* No. 10.

48. *Journal*, p. 212.

49. *Ibid.* Later, as the author of the Virginia resolution of 1798 protesting the Alien and Sedition Acts, Madison would find the states to be useful more fundamentally, as a medium for resisting unconstitutional acts of the general government. According to his biographer, Irving Brant, this was an instance of putting "political objectives ahead of abstract thought. . . . He had no desire to exalt state sovereignty, but used it as a weapon. . . ."

50. Cf. Martha Derthick, "Preserving Federalism: Congress, the States, and the Supreme Court," *The Brookings Review*, vol. 4 (Winter/Spring 1986), pp. 32-37.

CHAPTER EIGHT

Public Administrators and the Judiciary: The "New Partnership"

DAVID H. ROSENBLOOM*

The bicentennial of the framing of the Constitution witnesses the emergence of a new relationship between public administrators and the judiciary. This relationship grows out of the convergence of two of the great historical developments of the past half century—developments which are so central as to define much of the character of the United States polity today. One is the establishment of a full-fledged administrative state during the period since the inception of the New Deal in 1933. The importance of the modern administrative state is attested to not only by the number of personnel it employs and the amount of resources it uses, but also by the extent to which it has become a critical element in the operation of government and

---

* **David H. Rosenbloom** is Professor of Public Administration, The Maxwell School, Syracuse University. He specializes in the politics, personnel, and law of public bureaucracy. Among his books are *Federal Service and the Constitution* (Cornell, 1971), *Federal Equal Employment Opportunity* (Praeger, 1977), *Public Administration and Law* (Marcel Dekker, 1983), and *Public Administration* (Random House, 1986). He is coauthor with David Nachmias of *Bureaucratic Government, USA* (St. Martin's, 1980), and with Samuel Krislov of *Representative Bureaucracy and the American Political System* (Praeger, 1981). He is currently Coeditor-in-Chief of *Policy Studies Journal*.

politics.[1]   In fact, it is now a commonplace that other political institutions, including Congress and the presidency, have been reorganized and otherwise adjusted in efforts to deal more effectively with public bureaucracies. The second development has been the expansion of individual civil rights and liberties under the Constitution.   Although sometimes attributed to the "Warren Court" (1953-1969), which contributed a great deal to it, this trend has continued and appears to be deeply embedded in constitutional law.[2]

Neither of these contemporary developments is without important historical antecedents.   Both public administration and individual liberty were of great concern to the Framers. Alexander Hamilton wrote in *Federalist No. 68* that " . . . the true test of a good government is its aptitude and tendency to produce a good administration," while in *Federalist No. 10*, James Madison called liberty "essential to political life" and declared that the protection of individuals' "faculties" is "the first object of government."[3]   Hamilton apparently saw little conflict between good public administration and individual liberty.   In *Federalist No. 1*, he argued that ". . . the vigor of government is essential to the security of liberty. . . ."[4]   But since the emergence of an administrative state and a more expansive interpretation of individual constitutional rights, far greater attention has been devoted to the complex problem of protecting individual liberty against encroachments by public administrators.   It is precisely this concern that has prompted the judiciary to intervene more directly and extensively in public administration.

The judiciary has always exercised a varying degree of review of public administration, but today it is more apt to assert the constitutional rights of individuals who are subject to administrative action and to become directly involved in the management of public facilities.   The new relationship between public administration and the judiciary differs qualitatively from the old.   As Judge David Bazelon described it, today public administrators ". . . find themselves locked into involuntary partnerships with the courts."[5]   What are the dimensions of this "new partnership"?   What challenges does it pose to public administration?   Does it encourage the development of a new foundation for public administration?

The Dimensions of the New Partnership

The extent of judicial involvement in public administration has been summarized succinctly by James D. Carroll,
who noted that:

> . . . in the last decade [1970s] several thousand
> damage suits have been filed by Americans against
> hundreds of state and local governments and
> thousands of state and local government officials.
> The face amount of the damages claimed adds up
> to billions of dollars. In over half of the states,
> one or more institutions—prisons, mental insti-
> tutions, institutions for the retarded, juvenile
> homes—have been declared unconstitutional, as
> structured and administered. Many state and
> local government officials have found themselves
> subject to demands that they be held personally
> liable in money damages to individuals and
> organizations claiming they have been harmed by
> the actions of these officials.[6]

Sometimes judicial intervention in a single jurisdiction can
have very pronounced effects. For instance, in 1981, 48
percent of Boston's budgetary appropriations were "presided
over" by federal and state judges.[7] Among the functions
affected were public education, public personnel selection,
jails, public housing, and care for the mentally retarded.
Remarkably, such an extensive judicial "partnership" with
public administrators has been established very largely by
the courts themselves, rather than through legislation or
constitutional amendment.

The new partnership is probably best viewed as a
response by the judiciary to the development of the
administrative state.[8] Since the 1950s, several Supreme
Court justices and federal judges have noted the challenges
that large-scale and ubiquitous public administration poses
to the constitutional and political order. For instance, in
various dissenting opinions Justice William Douglas wrote
that "the bureaucracy of modern government is not only
slow, lumbering, and oppressive; it is omnipresent," "today's
mounting bureaucracy, both at the state and federal levels,
promises to be suffocating and repressive unless it is put
into the harness of procedural due process," and "the

sovereign of this Nation is the people, not the bureaucracy."[9]   In *Branti vs. Finkel* (1980), Justice Lewis Powell
was joined by Justice William Rehnquist in a dissent that
chided the Court's majority for neglecting that "the growth
of the civil service system already has limited the ability of
elected politicians to effect political change."[10]   In another
case, Justice Byron White noted that "there is no doubt that
the development of the administrative agency in response to
modern legislative and administrative need has placed severe
strain on the separation-of-powers in its pristine
formulation."[11]

Such expressions of judicial concern with individual
liberty, popular sovereignty, and the separation of powers in
the administrative state indicate that the growth of public
bureaucratic power has been salient to the courts.   The
judiciary's overall reaction has been to develop a legal
framework within which it can compel public administrators
to be more responsive to judges' views pertaining to
individuals' constitutional rights.   This framework makes the
judiciary the *senior* partner in its relationships with public
administrators: the courts determine what the Constitution
requires or permits public administrators to do, they control
a forum in which individuals may contest administrative
action, and they define the liabilities that public
administrators may face for violating individuals' constitutional rights.   The framework for the new partnership is
coherent enough to make it an equivalent to the major
institutional reforms adopted by the presidency and Congress
in their efforts to constrain and control the exercise of
administrative power.   Although at present the judiciary may
have completed its own definition of the formal terms of its
new partnership with public administrators,[12] in the future
it may exercise its prerogatives with greater or lesser vigor
as the occasion seems to demand.

Conditions of the New Partnership

Contemporary judicial involvement in public
administration rests primarily upon three broad legal changes
developed incrementally by the courts themselves.   These
changes place the relationship between the judiciary and
public administration on a basis that extends far beyond the

traditional concerns of American administrative law with officials' discretion and the scope of judicial review.[13]

The first change has been the declaration of new constitutional rights for individuals as they come into contact with public administration. Since the 1960s, clients of administrative agencies, such as welfare recipients, have been afforded far greater substantive, equal protection, and procedural due process constitutional rights.[14] Government benefits that were once defined as a privilege to which one had no constitutional right, were redefined as a "new property" in which one does have a constitutionally cognizable interest.[15] The constitutional rights of public employees to freedom of speech and association, procedural due process, and equal protection have also been vastly expanded.[16] Individuals involuntarily confined in public mental health facilities have been granted a constitutional right to treatment or training, and some of their ordinary constitutional rights as members of the political community have been granted greater protection.[17] The Eighth Amendment and equal protection rights of prisoners have also been dramatically strengthened through radical departure from earlier legal doctrines.[18] Additionally, some constitutional protections have been developed for individuals engaged in "street-level" encounters with police or other public administrators.[19] Taken together, these constitutional developments are a kind of "bill of rights" for the individual in the administrative state that places new constraints on public administrative activity in many areas of public policy.

The second legal change has been the development of the "public law litigation" suite, which is a vehicle for efforts to use adjudication to obtain broad reforms of public institutions such as schools, mental health facilities, and prisons. It has also been common in cases involving the selection, promotion, or retention of public employees. As Abram Chayes explains, public law litigation has several features that developed gradually over the past century, but did not crystallize into a systematically new form of suit until the 1970s.[20] It differs from the traditional lawsuit in very significant ways.

First, the public law litigation suit is not bipolar but rather may involve whole communities and administrative operations. Consequently, it is not controlled by the parties initiating it, that is, the original plaintiff may no longer be a party to the suit when a court hands down its decision or while a remedy requiring continuing reform is being implemented. Public law litigation is prospective as opposed to retrospective. When the plaintiffs are successful, the court's decree " . . . seeks to adjust future behavior, not to compensate for past wrong. It is deliberately fashioned rather than logically deduced from the nature of the legal harm suffered. It provides for a complex, on-going regime of performance rather than a simple, one-shot, one-way transfer. . . . [I]t prolongs and deepens, rather than terminates, the court's involvement with the dispute.[21] The judge may be active in " . . . organizing and shaping the litigation to ensure a just and viable outcome."[22] Accordingly, public law litigation suits often result in consent decrees rather than judicial decisions issued after full-fledged trials. Such decrees are formulated through negotiations between the legal representatives of the parties—negotiations in which the judge may play a key role. Where extensive reforms in administrative institutions or operations are required, a judge may appoint a special master or create a committee of some kind to oversee their implementation.

The public law litigation suit was developed by the judiciary itself. It has the potential to involve judges very directly and deeply in a variety of public administrative operations. Decrees may be highly detailed in their requirements. Judges have mandated certain air and water temperature ranges and ratios for staffing, patients per sanitary facility, and square footage per patient in public mental health institutions.[23] Public schools have been closed and attendance zones have been created by judicial decree.[24] Judges have determined where prison guards will be stationed.[25] But the essence of such decrees is conceptual. The decision in *Wyatt vs. Stickney* (1971) guaranteed involuntarily confined patients in Alabama's mental health system ". . . the right to confinement in 'the least restrictive conditions necessary to achieve the purposes of commitment,' freedom 'from unnecessary or excessive medication,' 'prompt and adequate medical treatment for any physical ailments,' 'an adequate allowance of clothing,' 'regular physical exercise,' and 'an individualized treatment plan.'"[26]

The third legal change comprising the framework of the new partnership between the judiciary and public administrators has been a broad switch from a presumption that public administrators have an *absolute* immunity from civil suits seeking damages for tortuous behavior within the scope of their official duties to a presumption of only *qualified* immunity.[27] This doctrinal change has dramatically increased the personal liability of public administrators for violating individuals' constitutional and federally protected statutory rights. In a series of cases reaching back through the 1970s and continuing to the present time, the Supreme Court resurrected what had been regarded as a moribund provision of the Civil Rights Act of 1871 by making it the basis for holding that public administrators who violate individuals' constitutional rights, of which they are cognizant or should reasonably be aware, may be held personally liable for compensatory and possibly punitive money damages. Moreover, the Court held that even though the 1871 act applies specifically to persons acting under state or local governmental authority, federal officials may face similar liabilities directly under the Constitution.[28] Municipalities are treated as persons for the purposes of liability, and therefore cities can be held liable for the acts of their officials, including breaches of individuals' constitutional rights.[29]

The new liabilities faced by public administrators serve as a capstone to the judiciary's "bill of rights" for individuals in the administrative state and its development of the public law litigation suit. Liability is an enforcement mechanism. In *Carlson vs. Green* (1980), the Supreme Court emphasized that administrators' new liability ". . . in addition to compensating victims, serves a deterrent purpose."[30] In *Owen vs. City of Independence* (1980), the Court reasoned that "the knowledge that a municipality will be liable for all of its injurious conduct, whether committed in good faith or not, should create an incentive for officials who may harbor doubts about the lawfulness of their intended actions to err on the side of protecting citizens' constitutional rights."[31] The broader implication of such liability is that it virtually requires public administrators to consider knowledge of constitutional rights, principles, and values as a central aspect of professional competence.

The Traditional Public Administrative Culture

Judge Bazelon called for efforts ". . . to forge a better relationship between the partners,"[32] judicial and administrative, in contemporary public administration. He posed a serious challenge. A broad divergence often separates public administrative and judicial values, cognitive styles and methods, and approaches to the evaluation of public policy.

Perhaps the core of the tension between public administrators and judges can be explained best in historical terms. During the period from 1877 to 1920, a persistent and comprehensive "administrative culture" developed in the United States through the confluence of the civil service reform, Progressive, and Scientific Management movements.[33] This culture continues to inform much of the operation of and discourse concerning public bureaucracy, but ironically its formation *predated* the emergence of the full-fledged administrative state, especially in its social welfare aspects. Accordingly, the prevailing administrative culture may be imperfectly suited to present-day public administration. Moreover, as the scope of constitutional rights expanded generally, this administrative culture seemed increasingly at odds with the principles and requirements of constitutional law.

Why a new and more suitable administrative culture has not developed remains something of a mystery. Certainly, the intellectual adequacy of the orthodoxy that espoused it was severely challenged by Herbert Simon, Robert Dahl, Dwight Waldo, and Paul Appleby in the late 1940s.[34] But Harold Seidman is equally correct in observing that if 1937 marked the "high noon" of the orthodoxy, then "someone apparently stopped the clock."[35] Perhaps Waldo described the persistence of the orthodox approach best: ". . . a social theory widely held by the actors has a self-confirming tendency and the classical theory is now deeply ingrained in our culture."[36] Hence, neither the new public administration movement[37] nor vast changes in administrative activities and technologies have dislodged it. However, the judiciary's recent imposition of itself as a partner in public administration does carry with it considerable potential for promoting the development of a new administrative culture because it challenges public administration's dominant values, cognitive approaches, and political authority.

The present administrative culture was forged through a protracted struggle for political and organizational change, but in retrospect its development can be explained in straightforward terms. The civil service reform movement (1870s-1890s) sought to destroy the earlier patronage-based administrative culture as a means of promoting fundamental political change.[38] For the reformers, the merit system and political neutralization of the public service were means of depriving political machines and professional politicians of electoral and financial support. Administrative reform was valued for the efficiency and public morality it would promote, but it was most centrally a vehicle for political reform. The Progressives, on the other hand, sought political reform directly while recognizing that it would also lead to administrative improvement. In public administration's intellectual tradition, it was Frank Goodnow's classic book, *Politics and Administration* (1900),[39] that provided the bridge between nineteenth century reform and twentieth century Progressivism. Goodnow argued that civil service reform could promote the kind of anti-machine politics favored by the Progressives and that Progressive political reforms, by weakening the grip of political parties on government, could enhance the prospects for the emergence of a public-interest oriented, technically competent civil service that would be respected by the public for its efficient and effective execution of the people's will. It is interesting to note that Goodnow, who subsequently published another classic, *Principles of the Administrative Law of the United States* (1950),[40] anticipated that the judiciary would share with public administrators responsibility for execution of the will of the state.

Frederick Taylor's Scientific Management added a key ingredient to the mix of civil service reform and Progressivism.[41] Taylor was widely believed to be developing management as a distinct function and making it an applied science. Scientific Management would promote efficiency, which was not only desirable materially, but also morally as it would reduce waste. The implications of Scientific Management for the public sector were not lost on the Progressives. Public management could also be scientifically based, thereby further reducing the appropriateness of partisan intrusion on public administration. The second edition of the "Model City Charter" produced by the National Municipal League in 1916 serves as a monument to the connection between Progressivism and Taylorism:

> The city manager shall be the chief executive officer of the city. He shall be chosen by the council solely on the basis of his executive and administrative qualifications. The choice shall not be limited to inhabitants of the city or state. . . .
>
> Neither the council nor any of its committees or members shall dictate the appointment of any person to office or employment by the city manager, or in any manner interfere with the city manager or prevent him from exercising his own judgment in the appointment of officers and employees in the administrative service.[42]

The administrative culture that developed through the confluence of these movements is familiar. Nevertheless, a brief review of its main values and orientations serves to highlight its tension with contemporary judicial perspectives. First, as Woodrow Wilson insisted, the administrative culture maintains that ". . . administration lies outside the proper sphere of *politics*. Administrative questions are not political questions."[43] Administration is best seen as "a field of business" that "at most points stands apart even from the debatable ground of constitutional study."[44] Leonard White's *Introduction to the Study of Public Administration* (1926), the first major American textbook on the subject, reiterated that ". . . the study of administration should start from the base of management rather than the foundation of law, and is therefore more absorbed in the affairs of the American Management Association than in the decisions of the courts."[45] Little notice was taken that unlike public management, with the exception of the Thirteenth Amendment, private management is not directly constrained by the Constitution.

The values of management were efficiency and economy, as articulated by Wilson, Taylor, and others. The method for achieving them was science. Frederick Mosher notes that the following objectives of the New York Bureau of Municipal Research in 1915 serve as "a good summation of the nature of the management movement as a whole": "To promote efficient and economical municipal government; to promote adoption of scientific methods of accounting and of reporting the details of municipal business. . . .; to collect, to classify, to analyze, to correlate, to interpret and to publish facts as to the administration of municipal government."[46] The emphasis on science was fully evident at the "high noon" of the orthodoxy, which was marked by the publication of the very influential volume, *Papers on Science of Administration* (1937).[47]

The New Partnership's Challenge to the Administrative Culture

As partner in public administration, the judiciary has frequently found this administrative culture unsuitable, especially in the realm of values.   Luther Gulick was precisely in the mainstream of the administrative culture when he asserted in 1937 that "Efficiency is . . . axiom number one in the value scale of administration."[48] However, Chief Justice Warren Burger, writing for the Supreme Court in *Immigration and Naturalization Service vs. Chadha* (1983), was just as assuredly in the mainstream of constitutional interpretation when he noted that ". . . it is crystal clear from the records of the [Constitutional] Convention, contemporaneous writings and debates, that the Framers ranked other values higher than efficiency."[49] Whereas Woodrow Wilson could call for a public administration that would accomplish its tasks "at the least possible cost either of money or of energy,"[50] several judicial opinions have rejected economy as a basis for encroaching upon constitutional rights.   As one federal court put it, "inadequate resources can never be an adequate justification for the state's depriving any person of his constitutional rights."[51]

These tensions over the relative importance of values have been central to recent judicial involvement in public administration. The growth, in absolute numbers, of public administrators, lawyers, and lawsuits involving public administration has afforded the courts ample opportunity to confront the traditional administrative culture. Administrative efforts to promote efficiency and/or economy are often complicated and frustrated by very inadequate funding. However, administrative doctrines and practices have also contributed independently to unconstitutional conditions in many prisons and public mental health facilities. Administrative values have likewise fostered unconstitutional abridgements of the rights of public employees, those of recipients of social welfare and other governmental benefits, and the rights of applicants for such benefits. In many of the cases in which their actions were declared unconstitutional by the courts, public administrators were acting well within the bounds of the administrative culture.[52] For instance, it may be more efficient or economical to deprive an individual of welfare benefits without affording him/her a hearing, to erect strict residency requirements for eligibility for such benefits, or to prohibit public employees from joining labor unions, but it is also unconstitutional to do so.

The judiciary has also challenged the administrative culture's insistence on an apolitical public service. The Supreme Court has clearly accepted the value of *non-partisanship* in the public service by upholding prohibitions on the partisan activity of public employees.[53] It has even held that patronage dismissals from rank-and-file public sector jobs are unconstitutional.[54] However, the Court has also unequivocally held that the Constitution protects the right of public employees to express their views publicly or to their supervisors on matters of public policy or public concern.[55]

In drawing what amounts to a distinction between partisan activity and politics involving public policy, the judiciary poses a challenge to the legitimization of the selection and the authority of public administrators on the grounds that they are politically neutral and technically expert. Once public administrators speak out publicly on matters of public policy, their neutrality is compromised. Should they disagree with one another, their technical expertise will appear an insufficient basis for delegating authority to them or permitting them to exercise broad discretion in the implementation of public policies. Consequently, public administrators' legitimacy according to the administrative culture may be impugned and another basis for it—such as representation—may be developed. In either event, the existing administrative culture may face a very serious test.

The judiciary's dominant cognitive approach also tends to be in tension with the scientific method favored by the administrative culture. Judicial reasoning rests heavily upon the application of legal principles to individual cases, whose particularistic fact-patterns are developed in accordance with elaborate rules of evidence and adversary procedure. Judicial reasoning is often explicitly normative and engaged in the ranking or balancing of competing values. Each case is treated more or less on its own merits. Violations of legal right must be remedied. Consequently, judges define the problem of establishing priorities among claimants for scarce public resources and statuses differently than do legislatures or public administrators engaged in budget making.[56] There is a reluctance to go much beyond the facts and available remedies for the case at hand or to construct social categories as a means of predicting or imputing individual behavior. Indeed, racial categories are considered constitutionally suspect, and the courts have "invalidated statutes employing gender as an inaccurate proxy for other, more germane bases of classification."[57] Donald Horowitz argues that traditional judicial reasoning rests on "legal facts" and that accordingly judges may face serious cognitive limitations when dealing with "social facts," or social scientific generalization, as they often must in public law litigation.[58] On the other hand, to the extent that contemporary public administration is scientific, it rests on categorization and application of statistical probability as a means of generalizing about social and economic phenomena.

Craig vs. Boren (1976) presented a clear judicial statement on the divergence between traditional legal reasoning and statistical generalization. The case concerned an Oklahoma regulation prohibiting males under the age of 21, and females under 18, from purchasing "3.2 percent" beer. The plaintiffs claimed that it deprived males in the 18-20 year old category of equal protection of the law. The Supreme Court reasoned:

> . . . the only survey that explicitly centered its attention upon drivers and their use of beer— albeit apparently not of the diluted 3.2% variety— reached results that hardly can be viewed as impressive in *justifying* either a gender or age classification.

There is no reason to belabor this line of [statistical] analysis. It is unrealistic to expect either members of the judiciary or state officials to be well versed in the rigors of experimental statistical technique. But this merely illustrates that proving broad sociological propositions by statistics is a dubious business, and one that *inevitably is in tension with the normative philosophy that underlies the Equal Protection Clause.*[59]

The divergence between traditional legal reasoning and reliance on social scientific generalization has important implications for the public administrative culture. The courts have been skeptical of generalizations that *constrain* the constitutional rights of specific individuals. Public sector affirmative action, mandatory maternity leaves, and some policies using residency as a proxy for attitudinal or other individual attributes have been outstanding examples.[60] Judicial decisions in these areas express a preference for an individualized determination of a person's status when he/she may be particularly injured by administrative action. Such determinations may involve investigations, extensive documentation, assessment of an individual's intent or physical or emotional condition, and administrative hearings. They promote the use of adjudication as an administrative process. This "judicialization" of public administration challenges the administrative culture not only due to its resistance to a scientific approach, but also because the necessary independence of administrative hearing examiners stands in opposition to the culture's concepts of management and managerial authority.[61] Adjudication can also be time consuming and expensive.

Finally, the administrative culture dating from the 1877-1920 period evaluates the effectiveness of government operations in terms of a combination of costs and results. It recognizes that although universal compliance with a policy may be desirable in the abstract, at some point the marginal cost of achieving additional compliance may rise too sharply to be economical or practicable. The judiciary's approach to the evaluation of public policy may also embrace considerations of cost-effectiveness or costs and benefits.[62] However, the courts are the preeminent governmental forum in which individuals whose treatment is at variance with the norm may seek redress for particularistic violations of their rights. Moreover, when fundamental rights are at stake, the courts are apt to apply a stringent requirement that the government show a "compelling interest" for abridging them, whereas administrators are likely to employ a more pragmatic or utilitarian "reasonableness" test. Overall, the judiciary may also be more concerned than public administrators with "outlying" cases. *Connecticut vs. Teal* (1982) presents a recent example.[63] Albeit somewhat reluctantly, the Equal Employment Opportunity Commission (EEOC) propounded a "bottom line" approach to the enforcement of equal opportunity law. The EEOC's rule assumed that an employer would be in full compliance with the law if its selection rate of minorities was equal to at least 80 percent of its selection rate among nonminority applicants. However, by a five-to-four majority, the Supreme Court rejected the contention that meeting such a bottom line could "immunize an employer from liability for *specific* acts of discrimination."[64] Firmly within the American tradition of viewing government as instituted to secure individual rights, the majority reasoned that the law "guarantees . . . individual respondents the opportunity to compete equally with white workers on the basis of job-related criteria."[65] Consequently, individual minority group members retain a right to challenge specific acts of discrimination against them even though from an administrative perspective the employer's overall compliance with the law is deemed fully adequate.

The New Partnership and the Future

The judicial response to the rise of the contemporary administrative state and the disparity between the judiciary's orientations and those of the still prevailing administrative culture make for an uneasy partnership between judges and public administrators. Deep tensions exist between the judiciary and public administrators concerning individual rights and the values and cognitive and evaluative approaches that ought to inform public administration. What might the future bring? A few models can be gleaned from recent discourse.

One model is based on coping.[66] The tensions between the partners may be irresolvable and last indefinitely. The courts and public agencies will have to learn to cope with one another. The judiciary will recognize the limits of its ability to control public administrative behavior. There has now been enough experience with and analysis of the implementation of public law litigation decrees to suggest that judges cannot expect their involvement in the reform of public institutions to go smoothly or to be fully successful. Judges, like chief executives and legislators, may have to adjust their demands and expectations of public administrators. For the judiciary, coping may mean reluctance to expand or deepen intervention in public administration in the future.

On the administrative side, the coping model suggests finding ways of reducing the intrusiveness of the new judicial partners. For instance, if personal liability is increased due to judicial decisions, insurance or governmental indemnification can be sought. If due process is required prior to terminating individuals' welfare benefits, eligibility can be certified for relatively short periods of time and made self-terminating. Denial of recertification may require a hearing at some point, if the individual reapplies and persists; but in the meantime the benefits are unavailable to him/her and public funds are preserved. Court mandated staffing ratios in public mental health facilities can be made by "dumping" patients in the surrounding counties.[67]

The coping model may not have much to recommend it—except experience. It is essentially a form of "muddling through"[68] that is characteristic of public administration in the United States. Experience with presidential and congressional direction of federal administration suggests that coping is a pervasive tendency. Coping is a way of dealing with problems that cannot be solved, and it is not clear that the tensions between public administration and democratic constitutionalism can be resolved in any permanent sense.[69]

A second model is one of convergence. It assumes that the interaction of judges and public administrators will produce greater harmony between the new partners. Rather than each partner simply adjusting to the demands of the other, the partnership may produce greater consensus on administrative matters. For instance, the judiciary may become more facile with cost-effective and cost-benefit analysis and more favorably inclined toward statistical generalization if it gains more experience with public law litigation. Public administrators may also gain greater appreciation of the desirability of developing programs with regard to individual constitutional rights as well as traditional administrative values.[70] Judicialization of public administration and the bureaucratization of the courts, primarily in response to heavy caseloads, may eventually make the concerns of public administrators and judges converge.[71]

A third model is one of judicial withdrawal from the new partnership. The courts have been strongly criticized by scholars, practitioners, and segments of the public for their involvement ("interference") in public administration.[72] Judicial opposition to the growth of public administrative power during the New Deal was costly to the courts. It was followed by a period of judicial deference and acquiescence toward public administration.[73] Although the issues have changed, a similar institutional response is possible in the future. For instance, the judiciary could more or less refuse to entertain public law litigation suits and reduce the scope of its involvement in the reform of public administrative institutions.[74]

A fourth model assumes that the long-standing judicial trend of strengthening and expanding individual constitutional rights will continue. The expanding rights model raises the possibility that in the future constitutional law will broaden its concept of liberty to include "positive liberty," or the freedom to enjoy living conditions that enable the individual to be his/her "own master."[75] Among such conditions, for example, might be adequate housing and nutrition, some level of education, and, insofar as practicable, good mental and physical health. An expansion of rights along these lines would not be antithetical to public administration, which is often concerned with sociotherapy and the maintenance of individuals' health. However, a constitutional emphasis on positive liberty would prompt substantial change in public administrative structures, processes, and value choices.

Thus, the development of a new administrative culture is another possible future. The values of the "new public administration" movement are still relevant in this regard and offer considerable potential for combination with those underlying the judicial response to the administrative state. A new administrative culture might base legitimacy on public representation and participation in public administration. It might favor due process and equity over efficiency and economy. Hierarchical authority could be reduced through several developments: judicialization of public administration, greater constitutional and legal rights for public employees, and the requirement that individual public administrators be held personally responsible for their official actions. Important changes along these lines have already occurred. For instance, "whistleblowing," which was once considered "insubordination," is currently viewed as a civic virtue and almost legally obligatory.[76] The Civil Service Reform Act of 1978 calls for a socially representative work force and requires efforts to eliminate the "underrepresentation" of social groups. In the wake of the new partnership, the new public administration, various administrative reforms, and the development of the "right to treatment" (which is suggestive of positive liberty), terms such as "representative bureaucracy," "participatory bureaucracy," and "humane bureaucracy" may no longer appear as oxymora.

Any of these futures seems possible. But much depends on the future that the public administrative community itself seeks. In 1787, the Framers of the Constitution had great prescience in matters of government generally without exposure to more than the rudimentary antecedents of the contemporary administrative state. We have the benefit of hindsight. Can we attempt to match their prescience?

ENDNOTES

1. See Dwight Waldo, *The Administrative State*, 2nd ed. (New York: Holmes and Meier, 1984); James Q. Wilson, "The Rise of the Bureaucratic State," *Public Interest*, vol. 41 (Fall 1975), pp. 77-103.

2. Malcom Feeley and Samuel Krislov, *Constitutional Law* (Boston: Little, Brown, 1975), p. vii, write: "Beginning in the 1950s under Chief Justice Earl Warren, the Supreme Court set in motion an agenda for social reform. The process continues today. . . . [T]he Burger Court has been swept along by the tide of social change; at times it has been even more creative and activist than its predecessor."

3. *The Federalist Papers*, edited by Clinton Rossiter (New York: New American Library, 1961), pp. 414,78.

4. *Ibid.*, p. 35.

5. David Bazelon, "The Impact of the Courts on Public Administration," *Indiana Law Journal*, vol. 52 (1976), p. 105.

6. James D. Carroll, "The New Juridical Federalism and the Alienation of Public Policy and Administration," *American Review of Public Administration*, vol. 16 (Spring 1982), p. 90.

7. Robert Turner, "Governing from the Bench," The *Boston Globe Magazine* (November 8, 1981), pp. 12ff.

8. David H. Rosenbloom, *Public Administration and Law* (New York: Marcel Dekker, 1983); Richard Neely, *How Courts Govern America* (New Haven: Yale University Press, 1981).

9. *Wyman vs. James*, 400 U.S. 309, 335 (1971); *Spady vs. Mount Vernon*, 419 U.S. 983, 985 (1974); *U.S. vs. Richardson*, 418 U.S. 166, 201 (1974).

10. *Branti vs. Finkel*, 445 U.S. 507, 530 (1980).

11. *Buckley vs. Valeo*, 424 U.S. 1, 280-281 (1976).

12. Philip Cooper, "Conflict or Constructive Tension: The Changing Relationship of Judges and Administrators," *Public Administration Review*, vol. 45 (November 1985), pp. 643-652.

13. For problems of the traditional model, see Richard Stewart, "The Reformation of American Administrative Law," *Harvard Law Review*, vol. 88 (1975), pp. 1667-1813.

14. See generally, Rosenbloom, *Public Administration and Law*, chap. 3, and the cases cited therein.

15. See Charles Reich, "The New Property," *Yale Law Journal*, vol. 73 (1964), pp. 733-787; William Van Alstyne, "The Demise of the Right-Privilege Distinction in Constitutional Law," *Harvard Law Review*, vol. 81 (1968), pp. 1439-1464.

16. For a recent review, see "Developments in the Law—Public Employment," *Harvard Law Review*, vol. 97 (1984), pp. 1611-1800. For the development of the changing approach, see David H. Rosenbloom, *Federal Service and the Constitution* (Ithaca: Cornell University Press, 1971).

17. *Wyatt vs. Stickney*, 325 F. Supp. 781 (1971); *Youngberg vs. Romeo*, 457 U.S. 307 (1982). Bruce Ennis and Richard Emery, *The Rights of Mental Patients* (New York: Avon, 1978).

18. "Confronting the Conditions of Confinement: An Expanded Role for the Courts in Prison Reform," *Harvard Civil Rights-Civil Liberties Law Review*, vol. 12 (1977), pp. 367-404.

19. *U.S. vs. Brignoni-Ponce*, 422 U.S. 873 (1975); *Delaware vs. Prouse*, 440 U.S. 648 (1979); *Kolender vs. Lawson*, 461 U.S. 352 (1983). See also Michael Lipsky, *Street-Level Bureaucracy* (New York: Russell Sage Foundation,

1980).

20. Abram Chayes, "The Role of the Judge in Public Law Litigation," *Harvard Law Review*, vol. 89 (1976), pp. 1281-1316.

21. *Ibid.*, p. 1298.

22. *Ibid.*, p. 1302.

23. *Wyatt vs. Stickney*, 325 F. Supp. 781 (1971); 344 F. Supp. 1341 (1982).

24. *Morgan vs. Kerrigan*, 401 F. Supp. 216 1975).

25. *Hamilton vs. Landrieu*, 351 F. Supp. 549 (1972).

26. Tinsley E. Yarbrough, "The Political World of Judges as Managers," *Public Administration Review*, vol. 45 (November 1985), p. 665.

27. The classic discussion is "Developments in the Law—Section 1983 and Federalism," *Harvard Law Review*, vol. 90 (1977), pp. 1133-1361. Recent cases include *Smith vs. Wade*, 461 U.S. 30 (1983) (punitive damages); and *Cleavinger vs. Saxner.* See *Law Week*, vol. 54 (No. 84-732, December 10, 1985), pp. 4048.

28. *Butz vs. Economou*, 438 U.S. 478 (1978), discusses this point directly while holding that federal public administrators with adjudicatory functions retain absolute immunity. See also *Harlow vs. Fitzgerald*, 457 U.S. 800 (1982); *Carlson vs. Green*, 446 U.S. 14 (1980); *Davis vs. Passman*, 442 U.S. 228 (1979); and *Bivens vs. Six Unknown Named Federal Narcotics Agents*, 403 U.S. 388 (1971).

29. *Monell vs. Department of Social Services*, 436 U.S. 658 (1978); *Owen vs. City of Independence*, 445 U.S. 622 (1980). See also *Pembaur vs. City of Cincinnati*, 89 L. Ed. 2nd 452 (1986).

30. *Carlson vs. Green*, 446 U.S. 14, 21 (1980).

31. *Owen vs. City of Independence*, 445 U.S. 622, 651-652 (1980). See also *Malley vs. Briggs*, 89 L. Ed. 2nd 271 (1986).

32. Bazelon, *Indiana Law Journal, supra*, p. 105.

33. "Administrative culture" refers to the values, cognitive approaches and methods of developing knowledge, and evaluative perspectives that dominate public administration's theoretical and practical orientation in a given political system. See David Nachmias and David H. Rosenbloom, *Bureaucratic Culture* (New York: St. Martin's Press, 1978); Gerald Caiden, *Israel's Administrative Culture* (Berkeley: Institute of Government Studies, University of California, 1970). Stephen Skowronek, *Building a New American State: The Expansion of National Administrative Capacities, 1877-1920* (New York: Cambridge University Press, 1982), presents an excellent discussion of public administration during the period in which the American administrative culture was formed. This culture was solidified during the 1920s by the federal Budget and Accounting Act of 1921, the Classification Act of 1923, and the publication of the first major American textbook on public administration, Leonard White's *Introduction to the Study of Public Administration* (New York: Macmillan, 1926).

34. Herbert Simon, *Administrative Behavior* (New York: Free Press, 1947); Robert A. Dahl, "The Science of Public Administration: Three Problems," *Public Administration Review*, vol. 7 (Winter 1947), pp. 1-11; Dwight Waldo, *The Administrative State* (New York: Ronald Press, 1948); Paul Appleby, *Policy and Administration* (University, AL: University of Alabama Press, 1949).

35. Harold Seidman, *Politics, Position, and Power*, 2nd ed. (New York: Oxford University Press, 1975), p. 9.

36. Dwight Waldo, "Organization Theory: An Elephantine Problem," *Public Administration Review*, vol. 21 (Autumn 1961), p. 220. See also David R. Beam, "Public Administration is Alive and Well and Living in

the White House," *Public Administration Review*, vol. 38 (January/February 1978), pp. 72-77.

37. Frank Marini, ed., *Toward a New Public Administration* (Scranton, PA: Chandler, 1971).

38. Rosenbloom, *Federal Service*, chap. 3; Skowronek, *Building a New American State*, chap. 3.

39. New York: Macmillan, 1900.

40. New York: G. P. Putnam's Sons, 1905.

41. Frederick Taylor, *The Principles of Scientific Management* (New York: Norton, 1967); originally published in 1911.

42. Frederick Mosher, ed., *Basic Documents of American Public Administration, 1776-1950* (New York: Holmes and Meier, 1976), pp. 82-83. The first Model City Charter was issued in 1900 and advocated a "strong" mayor form of government. The Charter, now undergoing its seventh revision, has remained much the same.

43. Woodrow Wilson, "The Study of Administration," *Political Science Quarterly*, vol. 56 (December 1941), p. 494; originally published in 1887.

44. *Ibid.*, pp. 493-494.

45. White, *Study of Public Administration*, pp. vii-viii.

46. Mosher, *Basic Documents*, p. 45.

47. Luther Gulick and L. Urwick, eds., *Papers on the Science of Administration* (New York: Institute of Public Administration, Columbia University, 1937).

48. Luther Gulick, "Science, Values and Public Administration," *ibid.*, p. 192.

49. 462 U.S. 919, 958-959 (1983). See Louis Fisher, "The Efficiency Side of Separated Powers," *Journal of American Studies* [U.K.], vol. 5 (August 1971), pp. 113-131 for an opposing view of the Framers' intent.

50. Wilson, *Political Science Quarterly*, vol. 56, p. 481.

51. *Hamilton vs. Love*, 328 F. Supp. 1182, 1194 (1971).

52. See Rosenbloom, *Public Administration and Law*, chaps. 3-5.

53. *United Public Workers vs. Mitchell*, 330 U.S. 75 (1947); *Civil Service Commission vs. National Association of Letter Carriers*, 413 U.S. 548 (1973); *Broadrick vs. Oklahoma*, 413 U.S. 601 (1973).

54. *Elrod vs. Burns*, 427 U.S. 347 (1976); *Branti vs. Finkel*, 445 U.S. 507 (1980).

55. See *Pickering vs. Board of Education*, 391 U.S. 563 (1968); *Givhan vs. Western Line Consolidated School District*, 439 U.S. 410 (1979); *Bush vs. Lucas*, 462 U.S. 367 (1983); *Leonard vs. City of Columbus*, 705 F. 2nd 1299 (1983); *Connick vs. Myers*, 461 U.S. 138 (1983), discusses some limits.

56. Donald Horowitz, "Decreeing Organizational Change: Judicial Supervision of Public Institutions," *Duke Law Journal*, vol. 1983 (1983), pp. 1265-1307; especially pp. 1303-1306.

57. *Craig vs. Boren*, 429 U.S. 190, 198 (1976).

58. Donald Horowitz, *The Courts and Social Policy* (Washington: Brookings Institution, 1977), especially pp. 31-32.

59. 429 U.S. 190, 203-204; emphasis added.

60. *Regents vs. Bakke*, 438 U.S. 265 (1978); *Cleveland Board of Education vs. LaFleur*, 414 U.S. 632 (1974); *Zobel vs. Williams*, 457 U.S. 55 (1982); *Shapiro vs. Thompson*, 394 U.S. 618 (1969); *Memphis vs. Stotts*, 104

S.Ct. 2576 (1984). See also Robert Roberts, "The Public Law Litigation Model and *Memphis vs. Stotts,*" *Public Administration Review,* vol. 45 (July/August 1985), pp. 527-532; and *Wygant vs. Jackson Board of Education,* 90 L. Ed. 2nd 260 (1986).

61. Marshall Dimock, *Law and Dynamic Administration* (New York: Praeger, 1980), chap. 10.

62. *Mathews vs. Eldridge,* 424 U.S. 319 (1976). See also Stuart Taylor, "When is Justice a Bargain and When Isn't It?" *New York Times* (March 21, 1986), p. B4.

63. *Connecticut vs. Teal,* 457 U.S. 440 (1982). See also Donald Crowley, "Selection Tests and Equal Opportunity: The Court and the EEOC," *Administration and Society,* vol. 17 (November 1985), pp. 361-384.

64. *Connecticut vs. Teal,* 457 U.S. 440, 454 (1982), emphasis added.

65. *Ibid.,* p. 451.

66. Theodore J. Lowi, *The Personal President* (Ithaca: Cornell University Press, 1985), pp. 210-211.

67. "The *Wyatt* Case: Implementation of a Judicial Decree Ordering Institutional Change," *Yale Law Journal,* vol. 84 (1975), pp. 1338-1379.

68. Charles Lindblom, "The Science of 'Muddling Through,'" *Public Administration Review,* vol. 19 (Spring 1959), pp. 79-88.

69. Dwight Waldo, *The Enterprise of Public Administration* (Novato, CA: Chandler and Sharp, 1980), chap. 6.

70. *Parrish vs. Civil Service Commission,* 425 P.2nd 233 (1967); see also "School Case Backs an Ancient Ritual," *New York Times* (December 9, 1984), p. 84.

71. Donald Horowitz, *The Jurocracy* (Lexington, MA: Lexington Books, 1978); David Nachmias and David H. Rosenbloom, *Bureaucratic Government, USA* (New York:

St. Martin's Press, 1980), chapter 6; Dimock, *Law and Dynamic Administration.*

72. Horowitz, *Courts and Social Policy*; Edwin Meese III, "The Attorney General's View of the Supreme Court," *Public Administration Review*, vol. 45 (November 1985), pp. 701-704.

73. Martin Shapiro, *The Supreme Court and Administrative Agencies* (New York: Free Press, 1968), pp. 264-275.

74. See Fred Strasser, "U.S. Limits Decrees, Masters," *National Law Journal* (April 7, 1986), p. 29 for an example of current efforts to reduce judicial activity in public administration.

75. Isaiah Berlin, *Four Essays in Liberty* (London: Oxford University Press, 1969), chap. 3.

76. Robert Vaughn, "Statutory Protection of Whistleblowers in the Federal Executive Branch," *University of Illinois Law Review*, vol. 1982 (1982), pp. 615-667.

CHAPTER NINE

Paradox, Ambiguity, and Enigma:
The Strange Case of the Executive Budget
and the United States Constitution

NAOMI CAIDEN[*]

What has become of the executive budget? Drawn from European experience, it was a popular proposal at all levels of government in the United States at the beginning of the century, a keystone in a Progressive agenda of reform. Adopted at the federal level in 1921, it stood for 50 years or more as a dominant institution in national economic and fiscal policy-making. But in the mid-1980s, the federal budget process is widely perceived as in a state of crisis, and the meaning and significance of the executive budget are open to question.

Current confusions may often be traced to past misunderstandings and unfounded expectations. The place of the executive budget in the United States constitutional context has never really been clear, and the institution as adopted and developed differed from the initial proposal. The original concept espoused by budget reformers implied an executive budget monopoly, justified by a doctrine of

---

[*] **Naomi Caiden** is Chair of the Department of Public Administration at California State University, San Bernardino. She is the author of numerous articles on comparative public budgeting and the coauthor (with Aaron Wildavsky) of *Planning and Budgeting in Poor Countries* (Transaction, 1980).

administrative neutrality, at odds both with contemporary practice and the separation of powers. In this sense the executive budget was a paradox. The Budget and Accounting Act of 1921 modified this concept by retaining legislative initiative in appropriations and stressing the executive budget as a means of gaining executive responsibility and strengthening legislative budgetary control. Later the justification of policy-making capacity was added to that of administrative efficiency. In this sense, the executive budget was an integral part of the separation of powers, reflecting constitutional ambiguities regarding the place and limits of executive power, though these were overshadowed by acceptance of executive leadership.

Presently, neither original nor later meaning appears accurate. Assertions of executive budget monopoly on grounds of administrative neutrality seem inapposite, but expectations of executive prerogative from the original concept linger. Responsibility, the foundation of the modified executive budget, also seems to have evaporated: the executive budget is now simply a bargaining counter in a complex game in which the legislature often takes the initiative and the executive adopts a reactive stance. The result is the opposite of intention. Orderly processes break down or are bypassed; budget figures are open to a variety of interpretations; and budget outcomes appear to be beyond control of either branch of government. The executive budget still exists in form, but its significance as an institution has become an enigma.

The Executive Budget As Paradox

Nothing is said about the executive budget in the Constitution. In an understandable reaction to colonial experience, Congress was given the power to raise revenue and enact appropriations [Article I, Section 7 (1); Section 8 (1); Section 9 (7)]. But constitutional vagueness on the meaning of executive power [Article I, Section 1 (1)] extended to the question of financial management. The Constitution required that "a regular Statement and Account of the Receipts and Expenditures of all public Money shall be published from time to time" [Article I Section 9 (7)], but as Frederick Mosher has pointed out, "the Constitution was silent on who should initiate financial plans and proposals, who should manage the finances, who should keep the accounts, and who should audit transactions."[1]

The vagueness is not really surprising, since at the time public budgets in the sense we know them today did not exist, and a model of responsible constitutional government had not yet emerged. *The Federalist Papers* shed little light on the issue. Madison's distaste for factions extended to any faction in control of a legislative majority and ruled out an executive dependent on the legislature.[2] His advocacy of shared and overlapping powers made no mention of budgetary control. In contrast, Hamilton believed that most government was limited to executive details "and falls peculiarly within the province of the executive department," including "the preparatory plans of finance, the application and disbursement of the public moneys in conformity to the general appropriations of the legislature."[3]

The initial legislation establishing the Treasury, however, made no mention of the president, required Senate confirmation for the appointment of the secretary to the treasury, and gave the secretary the responsibility of submitting estimates directly to Congress. In Mosher's words, "Insofar as there was a budget at all, it was a congressional budget."[4]

One hundred years later, Woodrow Wilson criticized financial administration, contending that it had developed without real acknowledgement from one of balanced powers to congressional supremacy, resulting in a divorce between the formal and the living constitutions. Congress had entered more and more into the details of administration until the secretaries of departments were the real executives responsible only to the powerful committees of Congress to the point where "the Committees are the ministers and the titular ministers only confidential clerks."[5] The charges against Congress were many. It had no direct contact with finances and no grasp of details; each committee went its own way; financial policy was unstable and strayed from the paths of wisdom and providence; the major concern was commercial policy protecting manufacturing interests, not regular financial administration. The president was head of the administration but did not have control.

The "vast alteration in the conditions of government" and constraints in revenue necessitated, in Wilson's view, quite a different kind of financial administration, centered "in the hands of a few highly-trained and skillful men acting subject to a very strict responsibility."[6]   Congress needed to have "the estimates translated and expanded in condensed statements by skilled officials who have made it their business . . . to know thoroughly what they are talking about."[7]   Revenues and expenditures should be treated as "initially adjustable parts of a single, uniform, self-consistent system.   They can be so treated only when they are under the management of a single body; only when all financial arrangements are based upon schemes prepared by a few men of trained minds and accordant principles, who can act with easy agreement and with perfect confidence in each other."[8]

How much of all this rhetoric was an accurate portrayal or a caricature either in Wilson's time or subsequently is unclear.   Aaron Wildavsky has pointed out that as far as can be ascertained, nineteenth century appropriations appeared to be more or less stable, and despite lack of a central budget there was a powerful though informal ability to coordinate expenditure and revenue.[9]   Through its committees Congress did control the budget and consistently pressed for economy.[10]   Its appropriations decisions were guided by the Book of Estimates (the combined estimates of departments) and other executive proposals.[11]

But by the beginning of the twentieth century arguments for an executive budget were gaining force as part of a Progressive agenda of governmental reform. Issues of conservation of natural resources, railroad regulation, revision of banking and currency laws, and tariff reform appeared to demand national solutions for which, it was believed, the federal government as currently organized was ill-prepared.[12]   In the reformers' diffuse program for change, the exercise of governmental power was a key element.[13]   It followed that government had to be made efficient, in the sense of optimal use of resources to achieve social good.[14]   Administration should be expert, scientific, and neutral, the domain of trained professionals. It was a separate function, quite distinct from politics.

The reformers drew on their successful reforms in municipal government where the executive assumed primary responsibility for city business. They were also influenced by the example of rising business firms whose increased scale and complexity had brought about a managerial revolution. Administrative modernization required executive management, so that lines of authority flowed smoothly from central authority according to a hierarchical model of bureaucracy.

Finally, the reformers looked to the practices of foreign governments where centralized budgets had become ubiquitous. Rene Stourm's authoritative text, *The Budget*, extolled executive monopoly over the budget function.[15] Admiringly United States reformers compared the British Cabinet system in which a unified executive dominated Parliament and commanded administration, including the budget, with the dispersal of power in their own government where lines of communication ran from departments directly to the powerful committees of Congress. In the view of a leading reformer, Frederick Cleveland, modern society required executive government, which in the United States meant that administration should be headed by a popularly-elected, effective president.[16]

The executive budget idea was most clearly spelled out by William Willoughby in *The Problem of a National Budget*. Willoughby saw the budget as essential for efficient and economical administration of public affairs, and he saw the President as responsible for government. The budget should be formulated by the executive alone, and only the executive should propose expenditures because "account-ability can be enforced and efficiency secured only when responsibility is definitely located in a single authority."[17] The executive was superior to the legislature in budgetary matters because "The executive alone is in a position to determine in detail the administrative needs of the governed and intelligently to formulate an annual work program."[18]

It followed that the chief executive must be recognized as the head of the administration, which should be organized as an integrated hierarchy. Heads of departments should not be allowed to bring financial proposals before the legislature. Whereas contemporary theory cast the chief executive in the negative role of reviewing and reducing estimates as submitted by the spending departments, his role should now be affirmative: "a positive, constructive work program emanating from a responsible administrator in chief."[19]

Willoughby believed that "the legislature should be largely if not wholly excluded from the direct determination of the appropriation of funds."[20] Ideally the legislature's role should be only to discuss and criticize the budget, acting as a strong moral check on the executive. But realizing that total legislative exclusion was impractical, Willoughby wished to restrict legislative determination to "such large questions of appropriation only as can in any sense be regarded as legislative" allowing considerable administrative discretion through lump sum appropriations and transfers.[21]

How did all this relate to the Constitution and, in particular, the separation of powers? The problem of constitutional allocation of responsibility for administration, and whether the president should be regarded as chief administrator, has been much debated between those who see executive power as a highly limited grant from Congress, and those who believe the Founders sought an effective administration. In general the reformers were hostile to the separation of powers.[22] Cleveland went so far as to assert that the Constitution erred and that it must give way to modern exigencies.[23] Willoughby, less extreme, thought that power over administration was clearly allocated to Congress, but modern administration required that it be delegated to the president. But there was no need to reform the Constitution, as the reformers proposed "mere administrative changes, rationalized by principles of efficiency and the value of good order."[24] The constitutional question was effectively bypassed through "a narrow and apolitical administrative solution."[25]

From a constitutional perspective, the paradox of the executive budget lay in the juxtaposition of a virtual executive monopoly of power over the budget with the separation of powers. In the British system, executive command over policy and administration was justified by Cabinet collective responsibility to the House of Commons: a government that failed to gain enough votes to pass its budget, an avowedly political program, might be forced to resign. In the United States, the separation of executive and legislature precluded such a check on the proposed wide powers of the executive: an executive could continue in office without the confidence of the legislature, even if it could not obtain passage of its budget. The proposal for an executive budget might thus be seen as a grab for power, concealed in the language of administrative neutrality. But this paradox was averted, though it remained a possibility, since the executive budget was not adopted in its pure form.

The Ambiguity of the Executive Budget

The eventual enactment of the executive budget by Congress in the 1921 Budget and Accounting Act represented a triumph of persuasion by the reformers. Their victory may be attributed to a general acceptance of the virtues of management related to perceived administrative and budgetary defects, of a plausible division of labor between president and Congress, and of the idea of responsibility. In addition, the form of the executive budget in the Act departed somewhat from the original model. As time passed, the executive budget came to fit in well with an expanded concept of presidential power, and its ambiguities were temporarily overshadowed.

The progenitor of the Budget Act was the 1912 Report of the President's Commission on Economy and Efficiency.[26] Although rejected by Congress at the time, it set out the premises and arguments for legislative action following World War I. The Report drew heavily on the efficiency movement with its emphasis on management and technical proficiency. Federal government operations had been the subject of concern since the 1880s, and persistent deficits in the early years of the twentieth century had focused attention on its financial management. The thrust of the Report was that managerial expertise and leadership would enhance congressional budgetary control. No other mechanism could produce efficient management which required government to choose priorities in the face of limited resources, to balance expenditures against revenues, and to coordinate estimates. The information provided to Congress fell well short of the constitutional requirement of "a regular statement and account of receipts and disbursements." Estimates of appropriations, receipts, and expenditures prepared and submitted by the secretary to the Treasury provided inadequate data for considering policy questions, used inconsistent classifications and lacked coordination.[27]

To reform the situation the Report envisaged a division of labor between Congress and the president in which the former retained ultimate power over appropriations and the president took on the role of general manager, proposing and implementing the decisions of Congress, in line with the classic policy-administration dichotomy. The key change would be in the nature of the budget. Up to this point, the Report explained, "the budget has been primarily an affair of the Congress rather than the President . . . the Book of Estimates, our nearest approach to a budget, is rather a more or less well-digested mass of information submitted by agents of the Legislature to the Legislature for the consideration of legislative committees to enable the Legislature both to originate and to determine the policy which is to be carried out by the Executive during the coming budgetary period." The Commission proposed a complete reversal of this procedure through the establishment of a budget: "a proposal to be prepared by the administration and submitted to the legislature." The executive branch would submit "a statement to the Legislature which would be its account of stewardship as well as its proposals for the future."[28] The budget would be "an instrument of *legislative control* over the administration." The act of appropriation would also enable the executive or its agents to exercise *administrative control* over the government's liabilities and expenditures.[29]

In short, the budget was to be an instrument for responsibility in government. The annual program would be prepared by the administration and submitted to the legislature. The administration would be responsible for proposals submitted, and Congress would be responsible for considering and acting on each proposal made.[30] To ensure efficiency and economy it was essential that executive responsibility be established for "the manner in which business is transacted in each of the departments and establishments."[31] Thus there should be central control over appointments, accounting, and reporting. Estimates of expenditure would be submitted to the president, who as head of the administration would present them as a definite administrative program.[32]

The Commission presented the executive budget not as a paradox in the separation of powers, but "an effective means whereby these constitutional principles may be maintained with integrity. . . ."[33] The legislature, whose role was consideration of questions of policy, would gain by receiving expert advice, enabling review of efficiency and economy based on facts, and by the assumption of responsibility by the executive for its proposals. The executive would gain through "his ability to bring together the facts and opinions necessary to the clear formulation of proposals for which he is willing actively to work as the responsible officer." The people would gain because "they are taken into the confidence of their official agents. . . . Therein" concluded the Commission, "lie the practical use and purpose of the mission, lie the practical use and purpose of the budget."[34]

All these arguments left plenty of room for ambiguity. For example, the Commission got into quite a tangle about whether the president had to spend money appropriated by Congress that had *not* been included in the executive budget, or whether appropriations were in fact mandatory or allowed him discretion to decide whether they should be spent. There was doubt about the position of the president as chief executive. At one point the Report referred to him as "part of the legislature" and later as prime minister, but more frequently he was regarded as "representative of the people at large,"[35] "the one officer of Government who represents the people as a whole,"[36] a concept far more than simply head of administration and one with possible plebiscitary overtones.

But such complexities aside, the Report, which also discussed comparative budget practices, was a remarkable document which paved the way for the modified executive budget adopted in 1921. At about the same time a single Appropriations Committee was established in both House and Senate. A Bureau of the Budget, under the control of the chief executive, was created to coordinate the estimates. Departments had to present estimates to Congress through the president's budget. A General Accounting Office was instituted to handle the audit function. But Congress retained the right to act as it wished on the president's budget, although the reformers would have preferred an end to its power to make spending proposals.[37]

The Budget and Accounting Act divided power between the president and Congress without deciding who should prevail. It also left open the question of presidential power over the executive branch. A "public administration" view, in Louis Fisher's words, saw the president as in complete charge of a hierarchy.[38] Congress, according to this model, could only consent and grant, while the executive had the function of planning expenditures. But it appears that the framers of the Act held an opposing view: Congress created the departments, and they were its agents. According to

Hugh Heclo, "Presidential capacities to coordinate the activities of the executive branch were created and countenanced because they met the needs of Congress, particularly the newly created appropriations process."[39] The Act recognized a relationship between finance and management and gave both executive and legislature some jurisdiction over each.

Despite the ambiguities of the Act, there was little problem in practice in the early years. The prevailing emphasis on economy in government meant an essentially negative role for the presidential budgetary function. The coordinative powers of the Bureau of the Budget (originally developed on the initiative of Congress) were directed to cutting back present outlays and avoiding new commitments.[40]   But the process was ill-adapted to substantive policy development,[41] and as the presidency moved to a positive role during the New Deal, moves were made to institutionalize and legitimize presidential power over the budget.

The Brownlow Committee, established during Franklin Roosevelt's second term in office, was the first of a number of official committees and commissions concerned with management of the executive budget. It saw the preparation and execution of the budget as essentially executive tasks, and the budget as a primary instrument for management in the executive branch. The purpose of a budget system was to provide in financial terms for planning, information, and control and to establish an integrated financial program in harmony with long-range and general economic policies. While the legislature should control general policy, the executive should be in charge of the details of administration. Executive control over the budget should be institutionalized in the Bureau of the Budget which would act as a general staff, the "right arm of the President for the central fiscal management of the vast administrative machine."[42]   This theme was echoed in the two Hoover Commissions, internal self-study reports of the Bureau of the Budget, two unpublished reports on government organization during the Johnson administration, and the Advisory Council on Executive Organization in 1969. The Bureau of the Budget gained important legislative and clearance functions. The logic of Keynesian control of the economy, the "permanent emergency" in foreign affairs and the role of the presidency in spearheading social programs, seemed to place the budget process as a major tool of executive policy-making.[43] The justification of policy-making capacity was thus added to that of administrative efficiency. The executive budget reflected an alliance between the values of neutral competence and executive leadership.[44]

The Enigma of the Executive Budget

The executive budget was accepted into the United States constitutional order during the first part of the twentieth century partly because it fitted well with an emphasis on presidential leadership and power and partly because of basic agreements between the executive and legislative branches that prevented raising the questions left unanswered by the 1921 Budget Act. But the presidency of Richard Nixon brought the issues of the president's relationship with the administration and with Congress to the forefront of public concern and sharply revealed the ambiguities of the executive budget.

Nixon, it seems, took the "public administration" view of the executive budget at face value. He sought to reorganize the executive branch as the domain of the managerial presidency.[45] He also sought to achieve his policy agenda through an administrative strategy. The budget became a crucial battleground between Congress and president and the understandings upon which the executive budget had been based broke down. Quite apart from his power to initiate a budget, the President did have extensive administrative powers over expenditures, including lump sum appropriations contingency funds, reprogramming, transfers between accounts, timing of obligations, and impoundments.[46] As long as these were used with restraint, with at least the tacit consent of Congress and not to implement independent policies, they were tolerated as necessary discretion on the part of the executive branch. But with the polarization of issues between a Republican President and a Democratic Congress, the politics of accommodation were disrupted. Both Congress and President grasped for spending control, Congress by requiring certain agencies to submit their requests directly to it at the same time as to the Office of Management and Budget,[47] Nixon through unacceptable policy impoundment of funds. The President's assertion of power, bypassing the normal budget process to achieve his objectives, underlined the fragility of the 1921 compromise. In Allen Schick's words, impoundment as unilateral action "offered no clear-cut procedure for resolving budgetary impasses between the two branches."[48] On the contrary, it "invited stalemate and protracted conflict," which were only resolved by the forced resignation of the President, regulation by Congress of future impoundments, and the establishment of a congressional budget process that provided Congress with institutional capacity that could potentially rival that of the presidency.[49]

There was no intrinsic reason why the strengthening of the congressional budget process should threaten the executive budget as set out in the 1921 Act. The 1974 Act provided Congress with the opportunity to vote upon significant budget totals—total budget authority, total outlays, surplus or deficit, and functional allocations—and to use these as a framework for the detailed appropriations decisions. Institutional reforms therefore established Budget Committees in each House and set up a timetable which "sandwiched" the budget process between first and second concurrent resolutions of Congress, the former proposing targets and the latter confirming ceilings. In order to bring appropriations totals in line with those of a preferred second resolution, a reconciliation process would enable Congress to instruct its authorizing and appropriations committees to meet stipulated expenditure goals. The Act established a Congressional Budget Office to provide analytical capacity, and to defeat the specific and contingent problems which had sparked reform, Congress took action to regulate impoundments.

The President's budget retained its function as a proposal upon which Congress would take action, and for the first six years there was little problem. Emphasis on both sides was primarily on economic stimulus and reduction of unemployment and later on expenditure restraint. Figures for budget authority and outlays in the first and second resolutions diverged from those of the President's budgets, but not in a consistent fashion, although Congress typically set defense targets lower and human resource targets higher.[50] Whereas congressional spending targets were set well above presidential requests under Ford, spending levels in the Carter administration and congressional budgets were almost indistinguishable.[51]

But there were already signs that the executive budget as a guiding and controlling force was no longer living up to expectations. Even in the 1960s, budget routines were acting as a constraint as order and regularity began to disappear from the political agenda and presidents "were forced to frequently adjust their spending and revenue targets in order to accommodate last-minute policy decisions and changing economic conditions." Both Kennedy and Johnson had developed their legislative programs independent of the budget process, and the legislative agenda and budget preparation had drifted apart. As presidents matured in office their interest in the budget tended to wane, and its routine turned into a grind, "a constraint on their ability to act and as an obstacle to achieving their objectives."[52]

By the late 1970s budgetary control, whether by executive or legislature, had become a serious problem. The dominance of indexed entitlements, debt interest and other multiyear commitments made federal expenditures rigid in nature and difficult to change in the short term. Because such a large part of expenditures was determined by the levels of key economic indicators—unemployment, inflation, economic growth, interest rates—budget outcomes were also hard to predict in conditions of economic volatility. As budget constraints had tightened, a growing area of "overspill" had emerged, hidden spending beyond the confines of the regular budget consisting of the spending of off-budget agencies, loans and loan guarantees, and a wide variety of tax expenditures or concessions. The budget seemed to be carried along by events more than it shaped them, when in 1980 a president was elected with a definite promise to change direction.

The so-called Reagan revolution might be regarded as a test case for the executive budget as the new President's agenda was to use the federal budget as a major tool for implementation of a program that included reductions in taxation, reversal of priorities between domestic and defense spending, and a general decrease in the level of federal spending. The success or failure of this revolution is still being debated, but the attempt once more brought to the fore the difficulties of the executive budget.[53]

It started out brightly enough along classical lines: a presidential program spelled out for deliberation in a detailed document. True, the budget represented a political program rather than the administrative justification of the original concept, but this use of the executive budget had long been legitimized. It was also possible to justify the use of an additional source of power, the integrating device of reconciliation as used with the congressional first budget resolution.[54] This *congressional* procedure (initially used under Carter) enabled the vexing questions of legislative entitlements to be dealt with within the budget framework and budget cuts to be presented and voted upon as a single package. It was used by the *Administration* to achieve unprecedented cuts in federal domestic expenditures, with of course the consent of Congress. But from this point, the executive budget began to unravel.

The first problem undoubtedly lay in the old question of separation of powers. Congress had to be reckoned with, and once again a Republican President faced a Democratic House of Representatives. While the administration was able to garner sufficient political support to gain passage of the reconciliation bill, the way the procedure was employed was seen by many as a manifestation of executive power overstepping the conventional boundaries of the executive role. Over one hundred pages of changes in authorizations and appropriations including legislative amendments were hurriedly pushed through Congress with virtually no debate on substance. Though reconciliation continued to be employed in subsequent years, it was no longer acceptable as a major device for shaping the budget.

The executive budget also lost credibility as a responsible document because of the quality of its figures. National budgets of the late twentieth century stand and fall on their assumptions and projections of how specific measures will affect revenues and outlays in the short and long term. Where these assumptions are wrong, as they undoubtedly were in 1981, or worse still, are cynically used for political purposes, as the director of the Office of Management and Budget (OMB) at the time has admitted, a budget will have a fictional quality, and those who took figures on trust once, will be unlikely to do so again.[55]

Once the damage was done, and a structural deficit beyond easy political repair had opened up, the ambiguities of the executive budget were fully revealed. The two potential dangers inherent in the concept—deadlock between the two branches and executive irresponsibility—began to characterize the budget process which became increasingly unpredictable from year to year as procedures broke down and trust eroded. It would be impossible to recount the complexities of the budget battle in these few pages, but it does appear that the executive budget no longer fulfills its expected role.

First, budgeting has become continuous, since it has become virtually impossible to resolve all the disputes in the course of a single budget cycle. Continuing resolutions have more often than not replaced appropriations. Budget initiatives take place throughout the year, and the regularity that used to characterize the cyclical budget process has been lost.

Secondly, while the budget remains important, many significant developments take place outside it. The most notable events have been reforms in social security financing and impending tax reform, both of which took place independent of the budget process. The periodic raising of the debt ceiling has become a routine occasion for gaining of political advantage. The executive has also had more frequent resort to deferrals of funds.[56]

Third, in the prevailing complexity, it has been very unclear what budget figures really do mean.[57] Outlay figures and revenue estimates upon which deficit projections depend are particularly hazy, sensitive to economic miscalculation and political manipulation. Estimates of savings, especially where projected many years ahead, are confusing and misleading. There are also highly complex forms of expenditure used by agencies that are virtually incomprehensible to the lay person.

Fourth, for several years the president's budget has been pronounced "dead on arrival," and Congress has put together its own starting position for budgetary debate. Far from being the initiator and driving force in the budgetary process, the executive budget has been a tentative "opening shot." While reiterating a firm belief in a balanced budget, the president's budget has consistently proposed ever higher deficits. After presentation of his budget, the president has simply reacted to congressional proposals, set out positions from which he would refuse to retreat, and intervened vigorously in negotiations where the political issue was important to him.

Finally, from a general sense of frustration and with the support of the executive branch, Congress passed the

Gramm-Rudman-Hollings Act, which attempted to take budgetary decisions out of the hands of both legislature and executive. If a budget could not be agreed upon in which deficit reductions would reach a specified target each year, there would be automatic sequestrations from appropriations across the board in all programs not exempt from the Act.[58] The calculations and implementation of these provisions would lie neither with legislature nor executive, but with the General Accounting Office. Speculation as to the exact reasons why participants chose to pass or accept this legislation, its technical constitutionality, or its ultimate consequences lie beyond the scope of this article. But it is a sad commentary on the fate of the executive budget.

Conclusion

One of the most striking characteristics of rapid change in human affairs is the concomitant development of language. Not only are new terms created to describe new phenomena, but existing words may also change in meaning. For some, this deviation from exact form represents linguistic deterioration, inadmissable imprecision, and plain wrong use of words. Others accept expansion and modification of language as positive developments, evidence of flexible adaptation and enhancement of conceptual capacity.

Political institutions are subject to similar considerations. According to one view, institutions, processes, and procedures *shape* politics and determine political outcomes. Institutions are relevant and their definition, design, and integrity are crucial. From another point of view, institutions *reflect* politics and develop and respond to the demands of political participants at any given time. They have little validity of their own and constitute a mere starting point in the political battle. In particular, the United States Constitution has left open political outcomes without prejudicing them by stipulating rigid institutional relationships.

The enigma of the executive budget lies in the argument between these two perspectives. According to the first, the substantive intent of the institution provides the source of criteria for judgment. There are a number of criteria. If the budget is seen as an entirely executive prerogative, because it is a purely managerial category, then there has never been a federal executive budget as this concept was never accepted. At the other extreme, it would also be misleading to think of the executive budget as simply a proposal put together by the executive for the disposal of Congress, since the president had sole power to present estimates, to veto appropriations, and to implement the budget. The executive budget has not been treated as a self-contained document, but has always involved relationships with Congress and with the administration. Its utility has been justified not only in terms of management, but with the erosion of the policy-administration dichotomy, with policy as well. As an institution it carried within it the potential for breakdown through the possibilities of deadlock (where the legislature rejects a presidential program but the president continues his term in office) and executive irresponsibility (where an executive thwarted by Congress uses whatever means are available at his disposal). Both these possibilities spell institutional breakdown, since the minimum condition for the executive budget—responsibility in budgeting—no longer fulfills expectations.

From the second perspective, the concept of the executive budget looks quite different. The executive budget has little meaning beyond its form, a document produced by the executive as advice to Congress, drawing upon the resources of the executive branch. It shares the ambiguities of the United States system of government, where the executive-legislature relationship has been deliberately left fluid. The notion of the executive budget may be traced back to the Constitution, and its emergence was evolutionary in nature without a sharp break in practice (irrespective of reform rhetoric). It has since developed because it has been perceived as useful. If there is any breakdown, it is a political breakdown to be mended by political means. The executive budget remains available to be employed as and when participants feel it would serve their purposes.

Both perspectives have validity. Institutions are important: they structure the rules and conventions by which the political game is played. They do develop and their purposes and effects change over time. The executive budget is an elusive concept, and short of radical constitutional reform, it is likely to remain so. But it should be noted that where words get left behind the reality they seek to describe, where meanings are confused or distorted, and where they arouse expectations that are no longer fulfilled, the purposes of language are defeated, form and substance diverge, and judgment is clouded.

ENDNOTES

1.   Frederick C. Mosher, *A Tale of Two Agencies: A Comparative Analysis of the General Accounting Office and the Office of Management and Budget* (Baton Rouge: Louisiana State University Press, 1984), p. 14.

2.   *The Federalist Papers* (New York: Mentor New American Library, 1961), p. 308.

3.   *Ibid.*, pp. 435-6.

4.   Mosher, *op. cit.*, p. 16.

5.   Woodrow Wilson, *Congressional Government: A Study in American Politics* (New York: Houghton Mifflin, 1925), p. 180.

6.   *Ibid.*, p. 135.

7.   *Ibid.*, p. 148.

8.   *Ibid.*, p. 181.

9.   Carolyn Webber and Aaron Wildavsky, *A History of Taxation and Expenditure in the Western World* (New York: Simon and Schuster, 1986), p. 369.

10. *Ibid.*, p. 405.

11. Personal letter from Allen Schick.

12. H. Landon Warner, ed., *Reforming American Life in the Progressive Era* (New York: Pitman, 1971), p. 10.

13. *Ibid.*, p. 4.

14. Peri E. Arnold, *Making the Managerial Presidency: Comprehensive Reorganization Planning 1905-1980* (Princeton: Princeton University Press, 1986), p. 20.

15. Rene Stourm, *The Budget* (New York: Appleton, 1917).

16. Arnold, *op. cit.*, p. 15.

17. William F. Willoughby, *The Problem of a National Budget* (New York: Appleton, 1918), p. 29.

18. *Ibid.*, p. 30.

19. *Ibid.*, p. 32.

20. *Ibid.*, p. 39.

21. *Ibid.*, pp. 145-6.

22. Dwight Waldo, *The Administrative State* (New York: Ronald Press, 1948), p. 105.

23. Webber and Wildavsky, *op. cit.*, p. 403.

24. *Idem*; Arnold, *op. cit.*, p. 403.

25. *Ibid.*, p. 14.

26. Report of the President's Commission on Economy and Efficiency (Taft Commission), *The Need for a National Budget* (Washington; United States House of Representatives, Document No. 854, June 27, 1912).

27. *Ibid.*, p. 27.

28. *Ibid.*, p. 10.

29. *Ibid.*, p. 11.

30. *Ibid.*, p. 141.

31. *Ibid.*, p. 143.

32. *Ibid.*, p. 145.

33. *Ibid.*, p. 136.

34. *Ibid.*, p. 139.

35. *Ibid.*, p. 141.

36. *Ibid.*, p. 145.

37. Willoughby, *op. cit.*, pp. 145-6.

38. Louis Fisher, "Congress and the President in the Administrative Process: The Uneasy Alliance," in Hugh Heclo and Lester M. Salamon, eds., *The Illusion of Presidential Government* (Boulder: Westview Press, 1981), pp. 23-4.

39. Hugh Heclo, "Introduction: The Presidential Illusion," in Heclo and Salamon, *op. cit.*, p. 6; Richard Neustadt, "Presidency and Legislation: the Growth of Central Clearance," *American Political Science Review*, vol. 48 (September 1954), p. 643.

40. Neustadt, 1954, *op. cit.*, pp. 644-646.

41. *Ibid.*, p. 647.

42. "Report of the President's Committee on Administrative Management," *Public Budgeting and Finance*, vol. 1 (Spring 1981), p. 85.

43. There is a huge literature on the growth in power and prestige of the president. An excellent summary may be found in William Andrews, "The Presidency, Congress and Constitutional Theory," in Aaron Wildavsky, ed., *Perspectives on the Presidency* (Boston: Little Brown, 1975), pp. 24-45.

44. See Herbert Kaufman, "Emerging Conflicts in the Doctrines of Public Administration," *American Political Science Review*, vol. 50 (December 1956), pp. 1057-1073. See also Herbert Kaufman, "End of An Alliance: Public Administration in the 1980s," John Gaus Lecture

delivered at the Annual Meeting of the American Political Science Association, Washington, DC, August 29, 1986, in which he argued that the fundamental inconsistency between neutral competence and executive leadership is now being revealed.

45. See Richard Nathan, *The Administrative Presidency* (New York: John Wiley, 1983).

46. Louis Fisher, *Presidential Spending Power* (Princeton: Princeton University Press, 1975).

47. Allen Schick, *Congress and Money* (Washington: Urban Institute, 1980), p. 22.

48. *Ibid.*, p. 48.

49. See *ibid.*; for a brief account see Naomi Caiden, "The Politics of Subtraction," in Allen Schick, ed., *Congress and the Making of Economic Policy* (Washington: American Enterprise Institute, 1984), pp. 100-130.

50. Louis Fisher, "Ten Years of the Budget Act: Still Searching for Controls," *Public Budgeting and Finance*, vol. 5 (Autumn 1985), pp. 4-6. See also Allen Schick, ed., *Crisis in the Budget Process: Exercising Political Choice* (Washington: American Enterprise Institute, 1986), pp. 20-21.

51. Dennis L. Ippolito, "Reform, Congress and the President," in W. Thomas Wander, F. Ted Hebert, and Gary W. Copeland, eds., *Congressional Budgeting: Politics, Process and Power* (Baltimore: Johns Hopkins, 1984), pp. 134-5.

52. Allen Schick, "The Problem of Presidential Budgeting," in Heclo and Salamon, *op. cit.*, pp. 92-3.

53. Much of the section that follows draws heavily on Joseph White, "What Budgeting Cannot Do: Lessons of Reagan's and Other Years." Paper presented at the Annual Meeting of the American Political Science Association, Washington, DC, August 28-31, 1986.

54. See Allen Schick, *Reconciliation and the Congressional Budget Process* (Washington: American Enterprise Institute, 1981).

55. See David Stockman, *The Triumph of Politics* (New York: Harper and Row, 1986).

56. *Washington Post* (March 3, 1986); p. A 10; *Los Angeles Times* (March 12, 1986), Part 1, p. 11.

57. See Mark S. Kamlet, David C. Mowery, and Tsai-Tsu Su, "Who Do You Trust: An Analysis of Executive and Congressional Forecasts"; John Ellwood, "Budget Authority vs. Outlays as Measures of Budget Policy." Papers presented at the Annual Meeting of the American Political Science Association, Washington, August 28-31, 1986.

58. See Charles W. Washington, "The President's Budget for Fiscal Year 1987," *Public Budgeting and Finance*, vol. 6 (Summer 1986), pp. 3-26.

CHAPTER TEN

Computers and the Constitution: A Helpful, Harmful, or Harmless Relationship?

KENNETH L. KRAEMER AND JOHN LESLIE KING[*]

Early in 1986, while discussing the lawsuit challenging the constitutionality of the Gramm-Rudman-Hollings deficit reduction law, Congressman Michael Synar, primary sponsor of the suit, said he was compelled to challenge the law because he believed Congress may not delegate its constitutional responsibility to a computer. With the enactment of general revenue sharing in 1972, and with each successive renewal of aid over the following decade, critics decried the "politics by printout" arising from district-by-district computer printouts showing aid distribution based on

[*] **Kenneth L. Kraemer** is a professor in the Graduate School of Management and the Department of Information and Computer Science and director of the Public Policy Research Organization, University of California, Irvine. He is the coauthor of *People and Computers* (Columbia University Press, 1986), *The Dynamics of Computing* (Columbia University Press, 1985), *Modeling as Negotiating* (Ablex, 1985), and *Datawars* (Columbia University Press).

John Leslie King is Chair of the Department of Information and Computer Science and an associate professor in the Department of Information and Computer Science and the Graduate School of Management, University of California, Irvine. He is a coauthor of *The Dynamics of Computing* (Columbia University Press, 1985) and *Datawars* (Columbia University Press).

complex formulas. And with the enactment of the Deficit Reduction Act of 1984, scholars argue that Congress has, in effect, reversed the 1974 Privacy Act by requiring all states to participate in file merging, matching, and linking programs to verify the eligibility of beneficiaries of social welfare programs.[1] Despite such concerns, the tendency towards computerization continues unabated with federal agency budgets for information technology reaching $15.2 billion in fiscal year 1986, and forecast to reach $23.8 billion by 1988.[2]

Computers have taken on a highly visible role as tools of government and as symbols in the ongoing debate about how government ought to function. Far to one side in this debate, computers form part of a demonic vision; an Orwellian nightmare in which autocrats eliminate democratic government and individual freedom through computerized surveillance. This view has been prominent over the years, beginning in 1964 with Vance Packard's popular book, *The Naked Society*, and it remains a strong theme in both popular literature and scholarly works such as Kenneth Laudon's recent book, *Dossier Society*.[3] Far at the other side of the debate, computers form part of a beatific vision of efficient, effective, and truly democratic government. While seldom articulated in a single place, this vision is incumbent in works that laud the computer's role in eliminating waste, fraud, and abuse; streamlining the functions of government; and permitting electronic voting and plebiscites.[4] These end points embrace a spectrum of widely divergent views about the role of computers in democratic government and raise the basic question of whether computers and computerization are altering or will alter the functioning of American constitutional government. A less common perspective that is orthogonal to these two, which raises equally serious questions, is Huxley's *Brave New World* view of technology as a seductive force leading to complacence in which liberty and freedom are given up to a benign and helpful social order facilitated by the technology.

As part of this special 200th anniversary observance of the American Constitution, this paper assesses the implications of computers within the constitutionally-defined structure, processes, and function of government in the United States. This topic is especially interesting because the original Framers of the Constitution could not have foreseen the introduction and massive deployment of computer technology, so they established no precedent to guide the use and influence of such technologies within the governmental system.

Making Sense of the Terms

Computers, in this article, refer to substantially more than the basic machines associated with computing. Computer technology is a "package" which encompasses a complex, interdependent system comprised of *people* (computer specialists, users, managers), *equipment* (hardware such as computer mainframes, peripherals, and telecommunications gear; software such as operating systems and application programs; and data), and *technique* (management science models, procedures, organizational arrangements). As suggested above, we include the expanding functional intersection of computing and communications technologies in our definition because computers and telecommunications are increasingly intertwined in the everyday functioning of computer-based systems at all levels of government. Other information technologies, especially mass communication technologies such as radio, television, and print, have implications for democratic government, but we do not include them in this analysis. We focus on computers and those key information technologies which tend to be closely linked with computers—namely, telecommunications and management science models for decision-making.

The Constitution refers to the documents and the ongoing mechanisms of constitutional government that maintain the operations of the U.S. federal system. The most important of these are the original Constitution, its Amendments, and the landmark constitutional interpretations of the Supreme Court.[5] Three structural features of the Constitution are especially relevant to computers: (1) it establishes the three branches of the federal government and specifies their duties and constraints (the separation of powers doctrine); (2) it defines the functions which the federal government must perform, can perform, and cannot perform, thereby leaving the rest of the states and the people (federalism); and it (3) specifies relations between the government and the people, mainly the First, Fourth, Fifth, and Fourteenth Amendments.

Interrelation of Computers and the Constitution

In a broad sense, the issue of computers and the Constitution involves the sensitivity of the federal system, as established in form and function by the Constitution, to technological change. Four major nexes of the federal system are generally considered to be particularly susceptible to disruption via technological change:

1. Interactions between the relative power among the branches of the federal government—legislative, executive, judicial—in the context of their performance of their constitutional duties and the role they play in governmental affairs. One of the fundamental principles of the Constitution is to check the central power of the national government by dividing it into three essentially equal, independent, and sometimes competing branches. However, the differential rate of computerization among the three branches has the potential to undermine the constitutional checks and balances by providing substantive, procedural, functional, or symbolic advantage to one or more branches.[6]

2. Interactions between and relative power among the national government and other governments in the federated governmental system. The construction of national information systems such as those in criminal justice and the growing linkage of federal-state-local information systems such as employment, tax, and welfare systems is viewed by some as increasing the power of the national government and nationalizing, or at least delocalizing, state and local policy and programs.[7]

3. Interactions and relative power distribution between "government" and the "people," both individuals and groups. The increased sharing of computer-based information on individuals and groups within the society by all branches of government is viewed as having the potential to subtly and pervasively undermine individual freedoms.[8]

4. Functions of the political processes that result in the election and appointment of office holders under the

structure provided by the Constitution. The exploding use of computer technology in political activity, including political party management, fund raising, public opinion monitoring, and direct-mail campaigning, has the potential to change the balance of power among various factions in the political system even if it does not change the constitutional structure of the government system.[9]

Computers and Federal Interbranch Relations

Ever since the introduction of computers in the national government, the public press has been rife with speculation that power shifts would result from who has more computers, more information, more analytic capacity, and/or more technical staff. In general, it has been argued that the executive branch would gain advantages over the legislative and judicial branches because of its relatively greater computerization. A recent example of this kind of speculation is provided by an article that appeared in the *Washington Post* by Michael Schrage entitled, "How you can profit from the coming federal InfoWar."[10] Schrage's article consisted of a lengthy list of winners and losers from the advent of computers, particularly microcomputers. Winners ". . . bask in the advantages that clever exploitation of information technology can provide." Losers ". . . may be doomed to an impotent existence of technological obsolescence." The idea underlying all these speculations is that "the agency with the most computer and information firepower wins." More broadly, this idea lies at the heart of arguments that computers and information systems provide strategic or competitive advantage.[11] While thought provoking, these kinds of analysis suffer from serious weaknesses when viewed in terms of the constitutional separation of powers among the branches of government.

The essence of the separation of powers doctrine is that each branch has separate functions, each is constitutionally and politically independent of the other, and each has inviolate recourse through which to check the others. Information technology does not and cannot fundamentally change these constitutional relationships, although it might occasionally tip the balance at the margins. Three examples serves to illustrate:

Example 1. The executive branch gains advantage over the legislative branch as a result of computerized information systems. It is most frequently asserted that the executive branch gains power over the legislative branch as a result of the executive's greater computerization.[12] The actual exploitation of computer-based information requires highly sophisticated software and people, easy access to the information, and powerful computers for processing the information. Such capability is most likely to reside in the executive branch because of its size, greater experience with computing, and relatively monolithic bureaucracy. Consequently, the executive branch would gain in power over the smaller, less experienced, and diffuse bureaucracies supporting the legislative branch. The power gain supposedly stems from the greater computing, information, and analytic capabilities available to the executive branch that allow the president to better defend administration policies and better control the bureaucracy, while at the same time withholding information from Congress and thereby weakening its influence with the bureaucracy.

Even if such power gains were to occur, the executive's advantage would be temporary because Congress has several responses available to it. First, Congress can limit and control executive branch computerization. It can stop executive purchase of new computer systems by legislation; it can "order" the executive branch to jump through many procurement hoops on equipment, software, and staff; and it can delay acquisitions by directing the General Accounting Office to look in to questions of faulty procurement, cost overruns, mismanagement, and threats to privacy resulting from executive computerization.

Second, Congress can enhance its access to executive branch information by linking terminals to executive agency databases. Few in the executive branch want this because it potentially gives away too much of the executive branch's power to Congress. From a constitutional standpoint, one would say this potentially impairs the "independence" of the executive branch. However, Congress can always request data from executive agencies under the Freedom of Information Act; and agencies are usually only too willing to provide data in exchange for favorable treatment of their appropriations. Congress can also gain direct access to computer databases of the executive branch where they share functions as in the budgetary process. Though the executive branch initially resisted on the grounds of executive privilege, it now regularly shares its computerized budget plans with Congress in the interest of timely congressional review and completion of the budgetary process.[13]

Third, Congress can increase its independence from executive information, expertise, and analyses by buying its own computers, developing its own information systems, and operating its own analytic models with its own staff. In this way, Congress can achieve parity with, as well as independence of, the executive branch. Congress has repeatedly found that if it has its own capabilities and people, members can get better determinations, analysis, support, models of legislation, drafts of legislation, tracking of bills, and monitoring of executive actions. Congress has moved increasingly in this direction in this century by establishing the Congressional Research Service, the General Accounting Office (GAO), the Office of Technology Assessment (OTA), and the Congressional Budget Office (CBO). Although a latecomer, Congress has added extensive computer technology and technologists to its expert staff and library tools.

For example, Congress has added considerable computer modeling capability to its Congressional Budget Office and committee staffs. In 1974, the professional staff of the House Ways and Means Committee became concerned about evidence that the Nixon administration had attempted to use the Internal Revenue Service for political purposes. Congress decided that it could not longer trust Treasury Department computerized models that enabled it to evaluate the possible consequences of new tax proposals. The Committee therefore brought the model in-house and developed an independent ability to examine tax proposals through the same base data by the Treasury.[14] In 1976, in response to the Treasury's Office of Revenue Sharing having a computerized model, CBO developed the capability to simulate the effects of different revenue sharing formulas on congressional districts, regions, states, and specific locales.[15] And today, CBO works with OMB and Treasury to insure that each uses the same base data and econometric models of the U.S. economy but develops independent economic forecasts.[16] Although these examples illustrate that Congress has been largely reactive, getting the capability to use computers and models to equalize temporary imbalances of power between the executive and legislative branches, they also illustrate the inherent ability of Congress to restore the balance prescribed by the Constitution.

Example 2. The executive branch tries to influence judicial review or overload the judicial branch with data from its vast stores of computer databases. The judiciary is the least computerized of the three branches of government and so is considered most vulnerable to the information that the executive branch can amass in support of its legal and policy preferences. However, the Judiciary also has several powerful responses it can employ in legal proceedings. First, the Judiciary, by virtue of its tremendous power to grant or deny standing of parties and materiality of information, can declare all or part of the executive branch's information to be "non-information" and therefore inadmissible. In a profound sense, the Judiciary can define what information "is."

Second, the Judiciary can require the executive to provide the information it wants, when it wants it, and in the form it wants it; and, the Judiciary can do so regardless of whether the information yet exists or what it costs the executive to get it. The Judiciary wields this power over all parties in litigation, as illustrated in the decade-long IBM antitrust suit. The Court would allow only a small portion of IBM's warehouse full of information to be admitted into evidence, while at the same time it felt free to require IBM to submit new information not readily at hand. Milton Wessel describes the situation as follows:[17]

> The U.S. government's antitrust case against IBM had its tenth anniversary on January 16, 1979. At that point, ". . . the government had reviewed 60 million pages of IBM documents and IBM had inspected 26 million pages of government documents. By its fourth anniversary of actual court trial—on May 19, 1979, in addition to 1,309 witness depositions, there were some 90,000 pages of trial transcript, with the end nowhere, even remotely, in sight. Then, on June 15, 1979, the judge directed IBM to produce what it estimated to be an additional five billion documents, which

IBM claimed would involve 62,000 man-years of work and $1 billion production cost."

Although IBM eventually won the case, company lawyers were generally unsuccessful in their attempts to influence what the Court would consider as evidence in the hearings.

Third, where violations of federal law may be involved, the Court can overcome executive branch attempts to withhold information under claims of "executive privilege." The most dramatic example occurred during the Nixon administration in the Supreme Court's order to the President to turn over the "Watergate tapes" to those investigating the incident.

In summary, because of the Judiciary's powers over executive branch actions the vast banks of computers, huge databases, and sophisticated analytical models of the executive branch have little substantive effect on the balance of power between the executive branch and the Judiciary.

Example 3. The legislative branch seeks to gain advantage over the executive through the use of computers for oversight. Although computers had been used by the Congressional Research Service in support of Congress since the mid-1960s, computers first really came to Congress in the early 1970s with the creation of the House and Senate information systems offices. Since that time computerization has primarily focused on the day-to-day operations of Congress including writing and tracking bills, tallying votes, publishing reports, paying staff, conducting research into social issues (through computer-based polling), and communicating with constituents.[18]

Congress has developed a renewed interest in oversight since the mid-1970s. This interest can be attributed to a post-Watergate disenchantment with executive power, the rise of a "new breed" of legislators, and the promise of computers to make comprehensive oversight feasible. Because of the computer revolution, many legislators and scholars believe that it is now possible to gather significant data about what really goes on within the bureaucracy. For example, Frantzich concludes that computer technology has ". . . put Congress in an enhanced power position relative to the executive branch."[19] With respect to oversight and budget review in particular he says:

> The Member Budget Information System (MBIS)
> provided by HIS [House Information Systems]
> allows the user to look at actual expenditures for
> previous years and get a feel for consistent
> patterns of surplus or deficit. The Program
> Review System developed by the Senate Computer
> Center takes the Office of Management and
> Budget tapes and identifies the line items for
> which each committee and subcommittee is
> responsible. This allows the committees to know
> exactly what they are responsible for very early
> in the process and less can be slipped by with
> little or no review. During the Budget process,
> the Comparative Statement of Budgetary Authority
> (CSBA) tracks the President's budget as it goes
> through Congress to provide a "snapshot" of an
> appropriations bill at any given point in time.
> Each of these make the Congress better informed
> on its dealings with the executive branch and
> thereby increases its relative POWER.[20]

Frantzich also cites a study by Worthley which found that "legislatures with developed information systems do indeed function more influentially vis-a-vis the executive and the bureaucracy."[21]

However, a recent study of computerized systems for legislative oversight in state governments by Miewald, Muller, and Sittig[22] concluded that none of the leading states have the "ideal" information system for legislative oversight—a centralized, comprehensive, regularized process of administrative review based upon independent information. Moreover, the legislature's concern for oversight is limited, with individual legislators preferring to rely upon particularistic oversight vital to their constituents and to good press (Frantzich agrees). The legislature is not anxious to create an independent body of information because most legislative staffs find agency data to be reliable and meaningful and because they are interested in ensuring that legislative and executive information systems do not become incompatible. Finally, computer technology has not significantly changed the nature of legislative oversight or vice versa. Miewald and his colleagues indicate that budget review, which is the oldest form of oversight and the most heavily computerized, ". . . may be one more elegant toccata and fugue on incrementalism." Thus, it seems that substantial power-enhancing effects of computer technology for legislative bodies remain in question.

Even if an "ideal" computerized system for legislative oversight were in place, the executive responses can be many. These range from stalling in the provision of information, to provision of misinformation and disinformation, to outright refusal to provide information requested by Congress. But the most powerful response of the executive branch is the ability to present the president's viewpoint directly to the American people, thereby marshalling popular support and potentially nullifying the effects of oversight by Congress. Thus, we believe that computers are unlikely to produce power shifts from the executive to the legislative branch in this area either.

Other examples of the interrelations of computers with the constitutional powers of the three branches of government are possible but not necessary. What is clear from the foregoing discussion is that as long as the branches are able to check one another, for example, by the Supreme Court deciding what is information and what is not, Congress granting or denying funds for acquisition of pieces of the computing package, or the President having a fireside chat with the American people to make a point on a given issue, no *lasting* power shifts will occur among the branches of government as a result of computers. However, temporary shifts in the balance of power could occur, as the foregoing examples illustrate. Because such shifts are often incremental, subtle, and difficult to discern, the cumulative effects of many small changes could create an imbalance threatening to the constitutional separation of powers. Thus vigilance and systematic observation of computing use is needed.

Computers and Intergovernmental Relations

A number of scholars have pointed to the possibility that acquisition of vast computer databases gives the federal government exceptional power over states and localities or that clever state or local use of computing can do the reverse. For example, Benjamin says that:

. . .the location in Washington of a preponderance
of computer expertise and of resources to obtain
the new technology and make it available, condi-
tionally, to other levels of government may
enhance already evident centralizing tendencies.
. . . Federal incentives, if sufficiently large, may
result in centralization of information networks in
some policy areas, as in the case of law enforcement. State mandates may occasionally result in
forced uniformity for local jurisdictions because
of the technical requirements of statewide
systems.[23]

This nationalization (or delocalization) of issues is somewhat
more plausible than the interbranch power shifts above,
since the U.S. Constitution does not spell out a clear
relationship between the federal government and the states
or localities. Federalism, or the balance of power between
federal, state, and local governments, refer to the question
of who shall define the goals, finance, and administer
government programs and, ultimately, who shall monitor and
conduct oversight of programs. According to Laudon, the
last 50 years have demonstrated that federalism is evolving:

The specific balance of power between federal and
state governments changed beginning in the 1930's
with the development of the Social Security
Administration, and the initiation of federal
responsibility for welfare and economic development programs. These early federal programs
were administered by the federal government and
only loosely articulated with state programs. By
the early 1960's the relationship between federal
and state governments was characterized by some
as a new "creative federalism." In this period the
federal government rapidly expanded funding and
program responsibility, while the states and
localities were given day-to-day administrative
responsibility. In the Reagan period, the
pendulum has swung towards less federal government involvement, and a greater reliance on state
and local governments.[24]

What, then, is the role of computer technology, and what is its likely effect on federalism? In general, we conclude that the technology will not concentrate power in the hands of one level of government over another. Whatever their evolution, the institutional arrangements of federalism have historically ensured a dispersion of power among levels of government. There is no reason to believe that this will change in the near future. Therefore, the distribution of computer technology throughout the federal system will reinforce rather than change this distribution. There are several reasons for this conclusion:

First, the national government already has the supremacy of federal law on its side. It does not need computers to obtain what it already has. The states' powers are not coordinate with those of the federal government because the laws and treaties of the latter are, in the explicit words of the Constitution, "the supreme law of the land, anything in the constitution or laws of any state to the contrary not withstanding." Moreover, the states are not independent of the national government nor it of them. The states have wide powers of autonomous action (i.e., the residue of powers not conferred by the Constitution upon the federal government), but not independence.

Second, most intergovernmental relations do not involve the federal government "ordering" state and local governments to implement particular policies of programs. Rather, they involve the federal government (1) paying for national programs such as unemployment and social welfare which are implemented by state or local governments, or (2) holding out carrots and sticks to induce state and local governments to adopt particular policies or programs that the federal government would like to see implemented, but which it cannot or chooses not to order them to do. However, the careful use of computers could permit the federal government to be more heavy-handed in its superior role.

For example, as part of a campaign to reduce fraud in federal welfare programs, the Reagan administration is requiring states to investigate the backgrounds of welfare applicants before adding them to federal benefit rolls. Under regulations published early in 1986, states must establish income verification programs by fall. The programs will enable social workers to check a welfare applicant's finances by examining state unemployment wage and benefit records, Social Security wage records, and some Internal Revenue Service records. Pete Earley argues that while technically the federal government cannot require a state to computerize its records, "the White House's Office of Management and Budget has written its income verification programs so stringently that it will be difficult and expensive for states to comply without using a computer."[25] Thus the administration is not only requiring that states implement income verification programs but, indirectly, it also is requiring that they computerize them. When all 50 states have complied, the administration will have created a *de facto* national social surveillance system through the states. What is interesting about this case is that the administration is being heavy-handed in its superior role. It is requiring states to implement "income verification programs"; these programs enforce federal standards for welfare applicants. By requiring income verification, the administration is also creating an information system which will enable it to assess state compliance with federal standards. While this information system affects intergovernmental power relations only at the margins, it nevertheless enables federal agencies to better monitor state compliance with national standards.

Third, as the foregoing example illustrates, there could be a slow but significant shift over time toward the aggregation of federal government ability to administer policies and programs at the state and local level more effectively than in the past. But the current trend is mostly in the opposite direction. It is conceivable that at some time in the future the federal presence in service delivery at the local level could be intensified. For example, improvements in data acquisition at the local level, communication of those data upward to federal policy makers, and use of those data by policy makers in Washington with computer-aided models designed to identify deviations from federal norms could conceivably permit the federal government effective control of local program implementation. Laudon argues that this is already happening with law enforcement and perhaps social welfare.[26] However, the dominant trend of federalism at present seems to be the opposite—toward more devolution of funding, administration, and oversight responsibility to state and local levels. Moreover, federal presence at the local level in the near future is unlikely; the bigger the federal government presence, the bigger target that presence becomes for growth-stoppers and budget cutters. It is likely that much of the explanation for state governments' recent emergence as the fastest growing sector of government lies in their comparatively low profile among the citizenry who are busy watching Washington and City Hall.

Computers and Relations Between Government and the People

No area of speculation about the impact of computers on constitutional matters has received as much attention as the relationship between government and the people. The Constitution was designed by the Founding Fathers in large measure to protect citizens from government tyranny, thus the concern is basic. At issue is whether the use of computer technology will give government the power to overwhelm constitutional safeguards against abuse of individuals or groups. The question is problematic because it requires a distinction between government as an entity and government as an agent of "the people." The Constitution clearly intends to protect citizens from abuse by a monolithic government, and given the power limitations on the separate branches and levels of government discussed above, computer use will not create a monolithic government. There is much greater ambiguity on the appropriate balance between the rights of individuals and the rights of a government that represents the will of the people. The issue is not whether individuals are imperiled by a faceless government armed with computers, but whether duly elected representatives, working through appropriate constitutional mechanisms, will engender computer-dependent abuse of individual rights.

Most of the concern over this issue is expressed in the debate about computers, databanks, and personal privacy. A voluminous literature deals with the issue of privacy in its own right, and a sizable component deals with the impacts of computers and communications technologies on privacy.[27] Much of the literature generates speculation and scenarios about the potential problems for privacy due to the computerization of government record-keeping activities. In contrast, there has been much less empirical evaluation of the privacy-related consequences of computerization.[28] The debate has at times been intense spurred by concern that the building of databases containing personal information may be the first step toward the complete abolition of personal privacy.[29] Of course, no one advocates building databanks for the purpose of reducing personal privacy, and therefore the counter-arguments to these concerns are essentially defenses of the status quo. The status quo, in turn, is continued discussion and modest legislative action aimed at privacy, on one hand, and continued construction and interconnection of computerized data bases containing personal information on the other.

In the absence of widespread privacy invasions to cite as cause for immediate action, the alarms over computers and privacy issue are largely ideological. A cogent articulation of the ideological issue is provided by James Rule in his description of the "surveillance potential" created by the establishment of large computerized databases of personal information on individuals.[30] With enough data and the right computer systems, authorities become able to monitor the behavior of large numbers of individuals in a systematic and ongoing fashion. Surveillance has always been possible, but it has been expensive. Technology makes it possible to monitor many people inexpensively, thus lowering the costs of surveillance that once imposed a natural limit on the government's ability to monitor individuals. Lowering or eliminating that cost limit places the protection from unwarranted surveillance in the comparatively weak realm of law and policy. The issue is no longer what authorities can do, but what they choose to do in surveillance of the population. Rule and others argue that the establishment of systems with massive surveillance cannot be permitted because their potential for abuse is too great and the conventional legal constraints to contain abuses are insufficient to deal with this threat.[31]

Again we ask whether the Constitution, as our most basic set of laws, is sufficient to counter the concerns raised by the computers and privacy issue? We believe it is, but not as an *automatic* matter. Privacy as a concept is not well established. Although privacy has played a key role in past issues of constitutional significance, including the highly controversial *Roe vs. Wade* decision legalizing abortion, privacy is also a matter of continuing interpretation. For example, in the 1965 case of *Griswold vs. Connecticut*, the Court defined the right of privacy as implicit in the Constitution and covering very personal conduct such as marriage and procreation. In the 1976 case of *Paul vs. Davis*, the Court reaffirmed the individual's right to privacy but held that privacy did not extend beyond the bedroom, e.g., criminal justice agencies were not required to keep confidential matters that are recorded in official records. Most recently, in *Howard vs. Becker* (1986), the Court took privacy away from the bedroom when it determined that consenting adults could be arrested for performing illegal sexual acts. These cases also illustrate that although the Supreme Court is buffered form day-to-day political activity, it is influenced by the moods of the electorate. And although existing uses of computerized data banks have not yet abridged personal privacy sufficiently to require constitutional action or even substantial Supreme Court action on the matter, mass computer matching may yet require it. While constitutional remedies remain available for the time being, the privacy issue is being played out in the realms of rhetoric, legislation, and executive action.

It is likely that the controversy will persist for two important reasons. The first is the increasing creation and interconnection of large systems containing personal information. Many large government information systems such as those of Social Security, the IRS, and the FBI contain sensitive personal information that can be used for social surveillance—tracking individuals or groups by linking data about them from such systems. Despite provisions made to limit the dissemination and use of data in these systems at the time they were established, the inter-connection of these systems is eroding these safeguards.

The linkage of government information systems began in earnest as a response to rising crime rates in the mid-1960s, with efforts to interconnect criminal justice information systems at the local, state, and federal levels. Now, despite the lack of evidence about the cost-effectiveness of interconnecting these systems, linkage among other systems is being expanded.[32] Recently, concerns have arisen in response to both back-end and front-end computer "matching" of personal data across welfare, tax, and unemployment systems. For example, the Parent Locator system uses Social Security data to locate parents who are delinquent in child support payments; similar systems are being implemented to locate individuals who have defaulted on student loans or defrauded welfare programs. In the name of income verification, systems for front-end matching of records are being proposed for "families whose children apply for low-interest college loans from the government, veterans who check in at VA hospitals, retired coal miners who request black lung benefits, and young families who ask the Farmers Home Loan Administration for a mortgage.[33] Such systems can greatly increase surveillance potential, and the creation of these integrated systems is actively being pursued by the current administration.[34]

The second cause for continued controversy over the privacy issue is the weak enforcement of existing privacy legislation. Proponents of linking systems argue that legislative, and if necessary, constitutional remedies will be able to control abuse of such systems. But these remedies must be enforced and maintained. According to David Flaherty, who has studied privacy legislation and enforcement in many western countries, the enforcement of privacy laws in the United States appears to be lacking in comparison to the situation in Canada, West Germany, Japan, and the United Kingdom.[35] The major national law, the Privacy Act of 1974, was never provided with either a Privacy Protection Commission (similar to the Civil Rights Commission) or a specific executive agency to see to its implementation. Instead, responsibility for oversight was handed to OMB and to Congress. Flaherty maintains that under the current administration, OMB has stopped paying much attention to privacy or to the requirements of the Privacy Act. The 1974 law needs updating, but the administration and Congress are preoccupied with other matters, and such a revision is not expected soon. Laudon and Earley point out the irony in the current situation where OMB, the primary executive agency for privacy oversight, has become the primary advocate for computer matching and national information systems, which in the name of governmental efficiency, pose serious threats to individual privacy.[36]

The federal government has not as yet established a single, comprehensive system facilitative of surveillance of the population. It has, however, increased the use of multiple national and state systems to track individuals to such an extent that it may be creating a *de facto* national social surveillance system. This surveillance potential created by linking government information systems, and the weak record of privacy law enforcement, warrants cause for continued concern and systematic study of the privacy issue. The privacy issue may yet warrant definitive Supreme Court rulings or perhaps even a constitutional amendment.

The Constitution does not directly address what is possible in government/citizen interactions. Instead, it comments on what is and is not allowable. The amendment process permits the creation of constitutional amendments to accomplish desired goals. It would be possible, as Westin has suggested, to amend the Constitution to classify certain kinds of data as simply "untouchable" for any use other than that for which they were collected. This would make questionable actions involving government use of personal data more difficult to commit and much easier to challenge.

Computers and the Political Process

The Framers of the U.S. constitutional government took great pains to design a political system that worked well for encouraging freedom and constraining tyranny. But the Constitution is more than a road map for government function; it is an embodiment of specific and ongoing debates about the nature of democratic government and the means necessary to preserve it. Contemporary views of the Constitution are a product of the thoughts and writings of the Founding Fathers, coupled with past experience and the realities of the current era. As noted in previous sections, the vision of the Founding Fathers has stood a remarkable test of time, and technological advancements in information handling do not appear as serious agents of change in the constitutional structure which that vision promulgated.

There is a chance, however, that computer technology will have a substantial influence on political processes that lead to the election of representatives and the mobilization of national political movements. The Founding Fathers were careful about creating a stable government that would represent the will of the people and ensure the rights of citizens. But they could not foresee the changes in technology that would reshape the processes by which public opinion is formed and guided. Much has been written about the effects of communications media, particularly mass media of radio and television, on political contests.[37] The addition of advanced forms of public opinion sensing and computerized direct-mail systems has created a package of tools that may transform the nature of the political process.

At one level, these new means of conducting political races are immaterial. Competing political groups have always sought to avail themselves of the latest tools and technology, and they have been quick to imitate their competition's use of such tools. In a healthy pluralistic system, the equilibrium is quickly reestablished. But at a different level, there is concern that the extensive manipulation of public moods through the use of technology will decrease overall electoral awareness of the issues and increase the tendency toward the election of individuals on the grounds of media image and single-issue direct mail advertising. The ultimate concern is the deliverance of the role of political opinion making, and thereby the mobilization of political bias, into the hands of technicians who stand between actual political leaders and the electorate. This can result in reduced influence of the electorate over political leaders and, potentially, the means for wholesale distortion of the issues by political leaders with skilled "image-making" technocrats.[38]

To a greater degree than with the issues discussed earlier, the impact of computers on political fund raising and campaigning could prove to have significant effects on the functioning of the constitutional system. This would not come about due to any particular weakness of the Constitution itself or as a result of changes in the structure of function of the governmental system. Instead, the changes would be part of larger effects of automation on the mobilization of bias among interest groups in the population. The existing examples of application of computing to political campaigns are not terribly significant in their own right. Their incidence is small as yet, and though some credit the use of such systems to unexpected political upheavals, such uses have not jeopardized the two-party system or the electoral process. Nevertheless, the concept of constitutional democracy depends on an informed electorate, capable of discriminating among candidates based on their overall strengths. Neil Postman contends that extensive use of television in campaigns has already decreased the quality of debate and reduced attention to the issues.[39] Highly targeted, single-issue fund raising and campaigning conducted through computer-assisted direct mail or targeted telephone solicitation could contribute to such a trend. This is a speculative point, and experience with use of such systems has been insufficient to determine the effects. Nevertheless, the potential for significant change in the processes of constitutional government exist because the Constitution only specifies what the offices of government are, how they are to be filled, and who can be enfranchised to vote. The Constitution does not address the means by which campaigns should be conducted or the grounds on which voters should make electoral judgments.

Although we cannot provide direct evidence of the effect of computers on our political process, a highly instructive lesson about our point can be drawn from the financial sector of the economy. In the past three years, major brokerage houses have invested millions of dollars in computerized securities trading analysis systems to help them capitalize on market movements. As the major institutional investors who control hundreds of millions of shares adopt such systems, some market watchers have begun to fear that they will force small investors from the marketplace, and more importantly, turn an important capitalization mechanism into a form of gambling.[40] Clearly, differences exist between the securities market and the country's political process, but the experience with computerized trading systems illustrates the power of computing technology to alter the behavior of complex social systems comprised of large numbers of individual decision-makers.

Computers and the Constitution: A Relationship That Requires Vigilance

Our overall conclusion is that computers have had very little effect on constitutional issues to date, but they might have considerable effect in the future. Relations between the branches of the federal government supersede issues of computing and even, to a remarkable degree, issues of relative information access. Since no effective way exists for one branch to gain a sustained monopoly on information, the technology to handle it, the expertise to manipulate it, or the right to determine when it will be applied, the question of computer impacts on the separation and checks and balances of powers appears moot.

Intergovernmental relations appear similarly unaffected by computerization. This is largely because the role that could be played by computer technology is subordinated to the existing constitutional definition of authorities and the political and practical nature of federal-state-local interactions. There is not much potential for computer technology to change this arena except at the margins.

Relations between government and the people are a somewhat different matter. The potential for abusing individual right to privacy is substantial and rapidly growing as a direct result of computer-based surveillance and action. Computer matching and national information systems are currently directed towards perpetrators of crime and fraud, but they could be directed more broadly. This potential for abuse poses a serious threat, especially given the instability of the privacy concept in the courts and the lackluster implementation, if not overturn, of the Privacy Act by the major U.S. monitoring agency. These conditions may require direct intervention by the Supreme Court, or possibly a constitutional amendment, to strengthen protection against governmental abuse of information in aggrandizing power over individuals.

Computer use can and probably will affect the political processes by which people are elected to public office. It is too early to tell what the actual effects will be. But since the Commission itself addresses only the major offices and issues of enfranchisement, and not the protocols of party behavior or campaigning, it is possible that computing-based changes in the conduct of political contests will eventually have an effect on the ways the Constitution is interpreted and implemented.

Our analysis suggests three reasons why computer technology has had relatively little effect on constitutional issues to date. First is the relatively insignificant role computing plays in such affairs. Computer technology is a powerful tool, but it is only one variable among many in the larger social and political processes of society. Also, the effects of computerization are not immediate and therefore are not immediately observed. Computers are introduced into organizations incrementally, and their effects evolve. Computing is a social movement that makes a slow and gradual passage through a web of economic, legal, organizational, social, and cultural constraints. In the process, the technology itself is shaped to fit the character of the adopting organizations to a remarkable degree. Even when it appears that computer technology is having an effect, the effect can be difficult to pinpoint and measure.

Second, computerization efforts do less than their promoters suggest they can under the best of circumstances. A cursory reading of GAO reports over the last ten years readily shows that the history of executive branch computerization is replete with examples of poorly conceived systems, frequent implementation failures, and extraordinary cost overruns. While many proposed systems are technically feasible, others are not, and all of them turn out to be very, very expensive. These large costs tend to brake federal computerization efforts and certainly dampen whatever potential effects computerization might have on constitutional processes and functions.

Third, aside from the technology itself, the very objective of information management is political and will be treated politically. As Alan Westin has noted, "Information is a power resource that no one gives freely. We can set boundaries and control access in very, very effective ways."[41] Moreover, we can actually improve information control and responsibility in computerized systems more effectively than in manual ones. Most importantly, computers have not changed power distributions within government, or within society more generally; if anything, they have reinforced existing power distributions.[42] Even though the technology may be applicable to various purposes, which groups in society get to use a new technology and which social ends get served are preeminently political questions. The past high cost of computers and telecommunications restricted their availability to large, powerful organizations such as government and business. Historically, information technology has been shown to be a power-enhancing tool; its costs of production and operation have guaranteed that it would be used first by elites, and that elites would dominate its use for as long as beneficial.

Some scholars suggest that the microcomputer could bring about a dramatic change in the traditional elitist domination of computing, thereby altering power relationships among groups within society.[43] They view the microcomputer as a power-distributing force in contrast to the mainframe computer which was largely a power-enhancing force. They suggest that microcomputers could be a major liberating force by democratizing computing access, information access, and decision influence, thereby providing the possibility for individuals and small groups to make their mark too. They cite the growing use of personal computers for work at home, for professional and technical group communication, and for mass mail mobilizations on political and social issues as contributing elements and embryonic illustrations of the potential.

While possible, we consider this scenario extremely unlikely· for the reasons given in the foregoing analysis. In addition, recent research clearly indicates that microcomputer use in organizations tends to follow the trends set by mainframe computing. Although the distribution of microcomputers encompasses more users than did mainframe technology, the proportionate distribution of microcomputer use among different groups within organizations is identical with that of mainframe use over the past two decades. Also microcomputer use in the home presently is dominated by middle-aged, high income, well-educated people in technical professions although students and the elderly are discernible minority users.[44] However, microcomputers have only begun to be deployed and networks that facilitate more horizontal information sharing have only begun to appear. It is possible, therefore, that these current tendencies towards reinforcement could evolve into other patterns that are power-distributing.

The effects of computing on constitutional government clearly avoid popular, extreme characterizations of technological impact. They clearly do not suggest the demonic vision of George Orwell's *1984*, in which technology permits malevolent autocrats to eliminate democratic government and individual freedom.[45] They do not even approach the unpleasant but less horrific visions of the mechanical society seen in Yevgeny Zamyatin's *We*, E.M. Forster's *The Machine Stops*, or Kurt Vonnegut's *Player Piano*. On the other hand, we do not see computers yielding the beatific vision of expanding freedom and democracy made possible through the beneficence of technological advancements that banish want and encourage understanding among people and nations.[46]

In all, computer technology seems to be having a less decisive impact on constitutional government than these visions would suggest. Rather, the impact involves dynamic tension between what the technology makes possible and what the Constitution, the Amendments, the Courts, and our own experience tells us is wise. We have not been able, in this paper, to present the contention, conflict, and compromise involved in balancing these interests. For purposes of exposition and argument, we have treated these balances as historical fact. In reality, they are just the tally at the end of a day's trading in a political market; tomorrow is a new trading day. Consequently, we and most academic observers tend to have a cautious view of the potential changes, though generally it is a positive, incremental one.[47]

There is a view of technology and its impact on social life that is orthogonal to this continuum, and that reflects another threat to our constitutional democracy. It encompasses the issues raised by the application of computing to mass surveillance, national information systems, and political campaigning; and, in particular, to the question of what is really important in the determination of who should govern. This concern is manifest in Aldous Huxley's *Brave New World*, in which technological advancements have been deliberately, and to a large measure democratically, applied toward elimination of need and stabilization of the social order. The new world is the epitome of successful technocracy to the point where circumstances that give rise to jealously are preempted through ubiquitous use of technology. Technology is used not to give expression to our most malicious and destructive tendencies, but to our best-intentioned efforts to eliminate the causes of strife. In the process, it seems, the removal of strife has eliminated existential choice and thereby freedom. Technology has maximized efficiency in exchange for unavoidable limitations on individual privacy, choice, and freedom.

The metaphor we find in the story is useful to our analysis of computers and constitutional government. The world depicted by Huxley evolved over a protracted period of time, and each step along the way posed a choice: live with the contradictions of the present or remove them with a technical solution. To the extent that American constitutional government is threatened by the application of information technology, the threat does not come from weaknesses in the Constitution or the government it shapes. Rather, the threat comes when the governed fail to protect and defend their rights to personal privacy and due processes. Whether the growing use of information technologies in mass social surveillance or in partisan political contests is leading to this end remains to be seen. However, this paper gives sufficient evidence to warrant renewed concern and increased monitoring of government computing activity.[48]

ENDNOTES

1.   See Sarah Fritz, "Synar Energetic, Willing to Take Risks," *Los Angeles Times* (February 8, 1986), Part I, p. 20; Rochelle L. Stanfield, "Playing ·Computer Politics with Local Aid Formulas," *National Journal*, vol. 10 (December 1978), pp. 1977-1981; and Kenneth C. Laudon, *Dossier Society* (New York: Columbia University Press, 1986).

2.   Office of Technology Assessment, *Federal Government Information Technology: Management, Security, and Congressional Oversight* (Washington: Office of Technology Assessment, 1986), p. 280.

3.   Vance Packard, *The Naked Society* (New York: David McKay Co., 1964) and Laudon, *op. cit.*

4.   U.S. Department of Justice, Bureau of Justice Statistics, *Information Policy and Crime Control Strategies* (Washington: M.S. Department of Justice, 1984); Ted Becker, "Teledemocracy," *The Futurist*, vol. 15 (December 1981), pp. 6-9.

5.   Edward S. Corwin and Jack W. Peltason, *Understanding the Constitution* (New York: Holt, Reinhart and Winston, 1964).

6.   David Burnham, *The Rise of the Computer State* (New York: Random House, 1983), p. 29.

7. Gerald Benjamin, "Innovations in Telecommunications and Politics," in Gerald Benjamin, ed., *The Communication Revolution in Politics* (New York: The Academy of Political Science, 1982), pp. 1-12; Laudon, *op. cit.*

8. Burnham, *op. cit.*; David H. Flaherty, "The Need for an American Privacy Protection Commission," *Government Information Quarterly*, vol. 1 (February 1984), pp. 235-258; James Rule, *Private Lives and Public Surveillance* (New York: Schocken, 1974); Laudon, *op. cit.*; Alan F. Westin and Michael Baker, *Databanks in a Free Society* (New York: Quadrangle Books, 1972).

9. Charles Roll, "Private Opinion Polls," in Benjamin, *op. cit.*, pp. 61-74. Extensive news coverage of these uses appeared during the 1984 election period. For a more colloquial view of this matter, see the following articles by David Burnham in the *New York Times*, "When an Ethnic Name Makes a Voter Fair Game" (April 17, 1984), p. 18; "Use of Computers for Dossiers Prompting Concern" (June 10, 1984), p. 38; "Mondale Campaign Ahead of All Others in Use of Computers" (January 28, 1984), p. 1; "Have Computer, Will Travel the Campaign Trail" (September 22, 1983), p. 10; "Reagan's Campaign Adds Strategy Role to Use of Computers" (April 22, 1984), p. 1.

10. Michael Schrage, "How You Can Profit from the Coming Federal Infowar," *Washington Post* (September 29, 1985), B-1, p. 4.

11. Warren McFarlan, "Information Technology Changes the Way You Compete," *Harvard Business Review*, vol. 84 (May/June 1984), pp. 98-103.

12. Theodor D. Sterling, "Democracy in an Information Society," *Information Society* (forthcoming).

13. Steven E. Frantzich, "Congressional Applications of Information Technology," Draft report prepared for the Office of Technology Assessment Proposal US 84-10/16, Congressional Data Associates, 1984. See also earlier

works by Frantzich, "Communications and Congress," in Gerald Benjamin, ed., *The Communications Revolution in Politics* (New York: The Academy of Political Science, 1982), pp. 88-101, and *Computers in Congress* (Beverly Hills: Sage Publications, Inc., 1982).

14.   David Burnham, "Computer is Leaving a Wide Imprint on Congress," *The New York Times* (April 13, 1984), p. 10.

15.   Stanfield, *op. cit.*

16.   John Leslie King, "Successful Implementation of Large Scale Decision Support Systems: Computerized Models in U.S. Economic Policy Making," *Systems Objectives, Solutions,* vol. 3 (November 1983), pp. 183-205; John Leslie King, "Ideology and Use of Large-Scale Decision Support Systems in National Policymaking," *Systems Objectives, Solutions,* vol. 4 (April 1984), pp. 81-104; Kenneth L. Kraemer, Sigfried Dickhoven, Susan Fallows Tierney, and John Leslie King, *DataWars: The Politics of Computer Models in Federal Policy Making* (New York: Columbia University Press).

17.   Milton R. Wessel, *Science and Conscience* (New York: Columbia University Press, 1980), p. 16.

18.   Burnham, *op. cit.,* April 13, 1984; Frantzich, *op. cit.,* 1982, 1984.

19.   Frantzich, *op. cit.,* 1984, p. 3.

20.   Frantzich, *op. cit.,* 1984, p. 29.

21.   John A. Worthley, *Legislatures and Information Systems: Challenges and Responses in the States* (Albany, NY: Comparative Development Studies Center, 1977), p. 427.

22.   Robert Miewald, Keith Muller, and Robert Sittig, *State Legislative Use of Information Technology in Oversight.* Draft report prepared for the Office of Technology Assessment (Lincoln: University of Nebraska, 1984). A distinction is made by the authors between true

oversight by Congress as a whole, and intrusive access encompassing the sum total of individual and committee contacts with the administration. The application of computers is considered to be the best way of converting intrusive access into true oversight, wherein all legislators would have access to the same body of independent (i.e., nonexecutive branch) information about the issues of budgeting, post-audit, program evaluation, rules and regulations, and administrative behavior. See also, M.E. Ethridge, "Legislative-Administrative Interaction as 'Intrusive Access': An Empirical Analysis," *Journal of Politics*, vol. 43 (May 1981), pp. 473-492.

23. Benjamin, *op. cit.*, 1982, pp. 6-7; Laudon, *op. cit.*, 1986.

24. Laudon, *op. cit.*, 1986, p. 15.

25. Pete Earley, "Watching Me, Watching You," *Washington Post Magazine* (May 11, 1986), p. 10.

26. Laudon, *op. cit.*, 1986.

27. The literature on privacy, particularly related to computerized data banks, is extensive. Major milestones include, Alan Westin, *Privacy and Freedom* (New York: Athenum, 1967); Arthur Miller, *The Assault on Privacy* (Ann Arbor: University of Michigan Press, 1971); Alan Westin, "Civil Liberties Issues in Public Data Banks," in Alan Westin, ed., *Information Technology in a Democracy* (Cambridge, MA: Harvard University Press, 1971); U.S. Department of Health, Education and Welfare, *Records, Computers and the Rights of Citizens* (Washington: U.S. Government Printing Office, 1973); Alan Westin and Michael Baker, *op. cit.*, 1972; Rule, *op. cit.* 1974; Privacy Protection Study Commission, *Personal Privacy in an Information Society* (Washington: U.S. Government Printing Office, 1977); James Rule, Douglas McAdam, Linda Stearns, and David Uglow, *The Politics of Privacy* (New York: Mentor, 1980); and Burnham, *op. cit.*, 1983. A comprehensive bibliography is provided by David Flaherty, *Privacy and Data Protection: An International Bibliography* (London: Mansell, 1984).

270   COMPUTERS AND THE CONSTITUTION

28. The major empirical studies are Alan Westin and Michael Baker, *op. cit.*, 1972; and the data collated by the Privacy Protection Study Commission, *op. cit.*, 1977. Public opinion surveys related to the issue include American Federation of Information Processing Societies, *A National Survey of the Public's Attitudes Toward Computers* (New York: Time, Inc., 1973) and Louis Harris and Associates, Inc. and Alan Westin, *The Dimensions of Privacy: A National Opinion Research Survey of Attitudes Towards Privacy* (New York: Garland, 1981).

29. Burnham, *op. cit.*, 1983.

30. Rule, *op. cit.*, 1974; Rule, *et al., op. cit.*, 1980, pp. 132-138.

31. For more detailed explications of the issue of appropriate and inappropriate applications of computing in human affairs, see Joseph Weizenbaum, *Computer Power and Human Reason: from Calculation to Judgment* (San Francisco: W.H. Freeman, 1976) and Abbe Mowshowitz, *The Conquest of Will: Information Processing in Human Affairs* (Reading, MA: Addison Wesley, 1976).

32. Laudon, *op. cit.*, 1986; Kent Colton, *Police Computer Technology* (Lexington: Lexington Books, 1978); Kenneth C. Laudon, *Management of Criminal History Information Systems in the United States* (Washington: Office of Technology Assessment, U.S. Congress, 1980); Kenneth C. Laudon, "Environmental and Institutional Models of System Development: A National Criminal History System," *Communications of the ACM*, vol. 28 (July 1985), pp. 728-734; Kenneth C. Laudon, "Data Quality and Due Process in Large Interorganizational Information Systems," *Communications of the ACM*, vol. 29 (January 1986), pp. 4-11.

33. Earley, *op. cit.*, 1986, p. 21.

34. This has been a controversial issue, as several newspaper articles by David Burnham in the *New York Times* show, "Private Computers' Income Data to Aid

IRS in Hunt of Evaders" (August 28, 1983), p. A-1; "IRS Rejected in Hunt for Estimated Income Lists" (October 30, 1983), p. A-1; "U.S. to Urge Census Bureau to Share Its Personal Data" (November 20, 1983), p. 1; "White House Kills Plan to Share Census Data" (November 23, 1983), p. A-16; "IRS Starts Hunt for Tax Evaders Using Mail-Order Concerns' Lists" (December 24, 1983), p. 1; "IRS Seeks Links to County Computers in Texas to Find Debtors" (March 12, 1984), p. A-23; "Senate Backs Bill Requiring IRS to Share Income Data" (May 3, 1984), p. 15; "IRS to Seek Clues From States' Data" (June 6, 1984), p. 21; "Diverting Refund to Child Support Raises Tax Cheating, Study Finds" (June 7, 1984), p. 29.

35. David Flaherty, *op. cit.*, 1984.

36. Flaherty, *ibid.*, p. 245; Laudon, *op. cit.*, 1986; Earley, *op. cit.*

37. Benjamin, *op. cit.*, 1982.

38. Astute discussions of the issue of technology and political action appear in the work of Langdon Winner. See in particular, Langdon Winner, "Do Artifacts have Politics?" *Daedalus*, vol. 109 (Winter 1980), pp. 121-136; and Langdon Winner, *Autonomous Technology: Technics-out-of-Control as a Theme in Political Thought* (Cambridge: MIT Press, 1977), pp. 135-172. The latter, in particular, contrasts two complimentary visions contained in Don Price's *The Scientific Estate* (Cambridge: Harvard University Press, 1965) and John Kenneth Galbraith's *The New Industrial State* (New York: New American Library, 1968). Both provide extensive commentary on the emergence of technocratic skill as a key component in the service of elites, and, potentially, the emergence of new technocratic elites.

39. Neil Postman, "The Contradictions of Freedom of Information." Paper presented at the Annenberg Scholars Conference on Creating Meaning: The Literacies of Our Times, Annenberg School of Communications, University of Southern California (February 16-18, 1984). mimeo. 31 pp.

40.   Traditionally, decisions to trade securities rested
       mainly on evaluations of the companies whose stock
       was being traded, as well as background information
       about the conditions of the market and the economy.
       The new computerized analysis programs have begun to
       turn securities into commodities through manipulation
       of securities futures, which are essentially bets on the
       direction of the market. These computerized systems
       "watch" the market, looking for anomalies that suggest
       a trend in the market, and when the appropriate
       signals are released, they notify their operators who
       shift dollars from securities into futures or vice versa.
       In this way, profits are made from speculation when
       the market readjusts prices to equal the inherent value
       of the securities. See James Flanigan, "New 'Program'
       Trading Alters Face of Market," *Los Angeles Times*
       (September 16, 1986), Part IV, pp. 1, 4 and Debra
       Whitefield, "Program Trading, and Its Effects on the
       Stock Market, Under Scrutiny," *Los Angeles Times*
       (September 21, 1986), Part IV, p. 2.

41.   Alan F. Westin, "Privacy, Technology and Regulation,"
       in Dennis P. Donnelly, ed., *The Computer Culture*
       (Rutherford: Fairleigh Dickenson Press, 1985), p. 147.

42.   Kenneth L. Kraemer and William H. Dutton, "The
       Interests Served by Technological Reform,"
       Administration and Society, vol. 11 (November 1979),
       pp. 1-15.

43.   See, for example, Richard Bingham, "The Wired City,"
       Urban Affairs Quarterly, vol. 20 (December 1984),
       pp. 265-72; Westin, *op. cit.*, pp. 136-148; and Theodore
       Lowi, "Blurring of Sector Lines: Rise of New
       Elites—From One Vantage Point," *Information
       Technology: Some Critical Implications for Decision
       Makers* (New York: The Conference Board, 1972),
       pp. 131-148.

44.   The trend in organizational distribution of
       microcomputers is from Kenneth L. Kraemer, John
       Leslie King, Debora Dunkle, Joseph P. Lane, and Joey
       George, "Microcomputer Use and Policy," *Baseline Data
       Report*, vol. 17 (January 1985). The trend in

microcomputer use in the home is from Nicholas P. Vitalari, Alladi Venkatesh and Kjell Gronhaug, "Computing in the Home," *Communications of the ACM*, vol. 28 (May 1985), pp. 514-515. An extended refutation of the redistribution hypothesis, based upon several empirical studies of microcomputers, is contained in Chapter 12 of James N. Danziger and Kenneth L. Kraemer, *People and Computers: The Impacts of Computing on End Users In Organizations* (New York: Columbia University Press, 1986).

45. Postman, *op. cit.*, 1984, contains an extended discussion of this set of metaphors. It is always useful to point out that the use of Orwell's *1984* as a mirror of contemporary society is risky because the setting of the book is the world after general nuclear war—a circumstance that surely would alter many aspects of society.

46. A sampling of these visionaries includes Alvin Toffler, *The Third Wave* (New York: Morrow, 1980); John Diebold, *Making the Future Work: Unleashing the Powers of Innovation for the Decades Ahead* (New York: Simon and Schuster, 1984); Simon Nora and Alain Mince, *The Computerization of Society* (Cambridge, MA: MIT Press, 1981); Lewis Branscomb, "Information: The Ultimate Frontier," *Science*, vol. 203 (January 12, 1979), pp. 143-147; and Harland Cleveland, "The Twilight of Hierarchy: Speculations on the Global Information Society," in Bruce Guile, *Information Technologies and Social Transformation* (Washington: National Academy Press, 1985).

47. A range of middle-of-the-road views about the impacts of information technology can be seen in several documents, including Herbert Simon, "Applying Information Technology to Organization Design," *Public Administration Review*, vol. 33 (May/June 1973), pp. 268-278; "Designing Organizations for an Information-Rich World," in Martin Greenberger, ed., *Computers, Communications and the Public Interest* (Baltimore: Johns Hopkins University Press, 1971), pp. 37-52; Anthony Oettienger, "Communications in National Decision Making," in Greenberger, *op. cit.*, 1971,

pp. 73-114; Alan F. Westin, "Foreword," in D. A. Marchand, *THe Politics of Privacy, Computers, and Criminal Justice Records* (Arlington, VA: Information Resources Press, 1980), pp. v-viii; John Leslie King and Kenneth L. Kraemer, *The Dynamics of Computing* (New York: Columbia University Press, 1985); Laudon, *op. cit.*; and Kenneth C. Laudon, *Computers and Bureaucratic Reform* (New York: John Wiley and Sons, 1974); Lowi, *op. cit.*; Theodore Lowi, "The Third Revolution Revisited" (unpublished paper prepared for The Conference Board, 1985); and Thomas E. Patterson, "Toward New Research on Communications Technologies and the Democratic Process," Report of the Aspen Institute Conference on Communication Technologies and the Democratic Process (New York: Aspen Institute, 1985).

48.   Specifically, we suggest the following issues receive continued assessment and monitoring: (1) the real effect of computers on the efficiency and effectiveness of government; (2) the actual cost-effectiveness of computer matching and other national information systems in reducing crime or preventing fraud; (3) the extent of change in control, oversight, and accountability of public bureaucracies due to computerization; (4) the effect of computerization on political campaigns and their outcomes; (5) the effect of computerization on the distinction between public and private sector responsibilities and prerogatives; (6) the opportunities and limitations of using computerization to enhance democratic processes via information dissemination and public opinion assessment; and (7) the effects of widespread computerization on centralized versus decentralized political power and effectiveness.

CHAPTER ELEVEN

Public Administration in the Third Century of the Constitution: Supply-Side Management, Privatization, or Public Investment?

JAMES D. CARROLL[*]

Following ratification of the Constitution, Alexander Hamilton raised a fundamental question about the new system of government not directly addressed in the Constitution: What is the appropriate role of the federal government in the economic and social development of the nation? As secretary of Treasury, Hamilton advocated strong policies, and strong central administration of those policies: assumption by the federal government of debts of the states and of the United States; payment of debts through taxes; and establishment of a national bank to carry out these and related policies. According to Charles Beard,[1] Hamilton's program was a capital formation program designed to promote economic growth in the new nation.

Hamilton's program was enacted by the first Congress and signed into law by President Washington. It contributed

---

[*] James D. Carroll is a senior staff member in the Center for Public Policy Education of the Brookings Institution. He has served as director, Government Research Division, Congressional Research Service, the Library of Congress; professor and chairman, the Department of Public Administration, the Maxwell School, Syracuse University, and director, the Advanced Study Program, the Brookings Institution.

to the development of a central administrative organization of the new government.[2]   Hamilton's justification of his program significantly affected constitutional history.   It was adopted by Chief Justice John Marshall "almost word for word" in Marshall's decision in 1819 upholding the power of Congress to charter a bank.[3]   Marshall's decision served as precedent for the exercise of substantial economic and administrative powers by the federal government later in the nineteenth and twentieth centuries.

Hamilton's program raised but did not definitely answer a question recurrently debated ever since: To what extent and in what ways should the federal government be responsible for economic and social development in the United States?   Through what forms of action? How important is strong federal administration to the future of the nation?

As the United States begins its third century of constitutional experience, the roles and responsibilities of the federal government in the economy and society are again under intensive reexamination, particularly in an international context.   Productivity and economic growth, international competitiveness, the management and development of complex technologies, and social equity are important elements on the national agenda.   How important will public administration be in addressing these concerns?

In the most fundamental sense, the function of federal public administration in the American constitutional system is likely to continue to be what it has been—a struggle to create a measure of order out of the disorderly pluralism and dispersion of power in the system in order to carry out the public's business.   Designed to protect liberty, pluralism, fragmentation, and dispersion of power, the Constitution created the conditions and tasks of federal administrative organizations—integrating and reconciling fragmented, competing processes and values into more or less coherent courses of action, e.g., making the air traffic control system work.   These competing processes and values are based in political, economic, legal, managerial, scientific and technological, and cultural systems of belief and action. Changes in these processes influence the substance of demands and policy directives integrated into, reconciled, and administered through public administrative organizations.

Changes in national and international economic and technological systems today are raising new questions about the role and responsibilities of the federal government and public administration.

This article outlines three directions which public administration may take in response to different resolutions of the question of the federal role in the economy and society: (1) a continuation of the status quo of policy restraint and budgetary gridlock that now characterizes the Reagan era, symbolized by the Gramm-Rudman-Hollings Act and a supply-side management approach to federal operations; (2) further privatization of public functions; and (3) new and renewed policies and actions directed to both public and private investment. While these directions are not entirely inconsistent with each other, as a matter of emphasis and degree each has different implications for public administration.

Direction One: Supply-Side Management

The Reagan administration took office in 1981 with a well articulated set of objectives:

- reduce the size, scope, and influence of the federal government in American life;
- strengthen defense;
- reduce inflation;
- balance the budget;
- stimulate economic growth; and
- reaffirm certain traditional moral values.

The administration has pursued various initiatives to achieve these objectives. These have included:

- budgetary and personnel reductions in many domestic agencies;
- increases in defense and intelligence agencies;
- reductions in marginal tax rates as incentives to work, save, and invest;

- tax reform to make the tax code fairer, to reduce tax expenditures as instruments of social and economic policy, and to reduce the "distortion effects" of tax incentives on economic behavior;

- regulatory reform through budgetary and personnel reductions in regulatory agencies and increases in powers of the Office of Management and Budget;

- shifts of programmatic and regulatory responsibilities to state and local governments and other organizations;

- appointments to the federal judiciary of judges committed to judicial restraint.[4]

The supply-side economic policy of the administration was designed to increase saving and investment by reducing marginal tax rates and reducing the size of the federal government.   In keeping with its supply-side economic strategy, the administration has pursued a supply-side management approach to the conduct of the federal government's business.[5]   This approach has involved centralizing budget authority in the Office of Management and Budget (OMB), reducing policy planning and managerial staffs in domestic agencies, shifting as much management and programmatic responsibility to other organizations as possible, increasing contracting out, and emphasizing business management in federal operations.

In the sixth year of the Reagan era, results of the administration's policies are mixed.   The administration's economic policies have had to compete with other policies, particularly the defense buildup.   The size of the federal government has increased, measured by outlays as a percentage of gross national product—from about 22.7% in fiscal year 1981 to about 23.4% in fiscal year (FY) 1986.[6] The number of civilian executive branch employees has increased from 2,843,404 in January 1981 to 2,984,755 in January 1986.[7]   (These figures include the Postal Service.) Defense spending has increased from 23.3% of federal outlays in FY 1981 to 27.1% in FY 1986, and from 5.3% of gross national product (GNP) in FY 1981 to 6.3% in FY 1986. Spending for nondefense has decreased from 76.8% of outlays, FY 1981, to 72.9% in FY 1986, and from 17.4% of GNP in FY 1981 to about 17.0% in FY 1986.   Spending for the warfare state has in part added to and in part replaced spending for the welfare state.

Total receipts have declined from 20.1% of GNP, FY 1981, to 18.5% of GNP, FY 1986. The budget deficit has increased from 2.5% of GNP in FY 1981 to 5.2% in FY 1986. Payment of net interest on the federal debt has increased from 2.3% of GNP in FY 1981 and 10.1% of outlays to 3.4% of GNP in FY 1986 and 14.6% of outlays. Financing the deficit and debt, to the extent they are financed from domestic sources, requires a substantial share of net saving in the United States, measured as a percent of GNP. Net saving has averaged about 7% for several years but has declined to 5 to 6% in the mid-1980s. Pressure on domestic saving has been partially relieved by foreign investments. Foreign investments to finance the deficit have contributed to total United States international debt. The United States is now the largest borrower nation in the world, with a negative international balance of $107.4 billion at the end of 1985, compared with a $6.3 billion surplus in 1981.[8]

Analysts disagree about long-term prospects for the administration's efforts to increase saving and investment through tax cuts and implications of reform of the tax code.[9] The surge in increased saving, investment, and economic growth anticipated by supply-side advocates has not occurred. Many believe that large deficits have contributed to high interest rates by increasing competition for funds and discouraging capital formation. Reductions in deficits eventually could result in supply-side growth as envisioned by the administration.

Viewed in political terms, the administration's policies and Congress's response have produced gridlock. The Balanced Budget and Emergency Deficit Reduction Act of 1985—Public Law 99-117 (The Gramm-Rudman-Hollings Act)—is an attempt to resolve through procedural means differences over priorities that cannot be resolved through political bargaining and agreement. One result of this political gridlock is that new domestic policy initiatives with the exception of tax reform have largely been shut off. Many interest groups are struggling to maintain the status quo.

Evidence is that the American people continue to support a substantial role for the federal government in defining and acting upon domestic problems.[10] At the same time, the pressure of the deficit and lack of political agreement on how the deficit should be reduced are making new initiatives unlikely.

Some evidence shows that the federal public service is becoming demoralized and that highly qualified people are not being attracted to some federal agencies.[11]   Program cuts, pressures to do more with less, and erratic budget allocations are increasing uncertainty, limiting the capacity of some agencies to plan and act, and eroding confidence in the capacities of some agencies to carry out their missions.

Prospects for change are uncertain. For the remainder of its term, the Reagan administration seems committed to exercise further restraint on federal domestic programs and agencies through continuing opposition to tax increases and perhaps through stronger efforts toward privatization.

Direction Two: Privatization

To some critics of the Reagan administration's effort to reduce the size and influence of the federal government, the administration has pursued a flawed strategy. To these critics, further privatization of federal operations is needed.

"Privatization" can be defined in at least two ways.[12] First, it can be defined as an administrative approach to the conduct of public business. Second, it can be formulated as a theory of political economy and the responsibilities of government. Privatization as a theory of political economy has significant implications for public administration. If carried out, it would greatly reduce the size, scope, and functions of public administrative organizations in the federal government.

Privatization has not been a dominant element in the Reagan administration's approach to government.[13]   The administration has advanced several proposals and has taken limited forms of action in the name of privatization. First, it has endorsed in principle the Grace Commission's assertion that thousands of federal jobs can and should be privatized.[14]   The Grace Commission's estimate was in the order of 500,000 jobs, or 15 to 20 percent of federal civilian administrative positions. The Grace Commission asserted that many federal functions can more efficiently be performed through market-oriented operations than through public administration.

Second, the administration has expanded contracting out under OMB circular A76. It estimates that it has contracted out approximately 30,000 federal jobs.[15]

Third, the administration has recommended—that in a very modest way achieved—more extensive use of vouchers and user fees, e.g., increases in the price of government publications.

Fourth, it has recommended the sale of several major federal physical assets and operations, such as the power marketing operations, the naval petroleum reserves, and the National Technical Information Service.[16]

Finally, it has announced a plan to privatize an array of federal commercial-like operations and to give stock to federal employees who would become part owners and employees of the new corporations.[17]   The corporations would compete for federal business on a market basis.

These efforts and proposals have had mixed results. Contracting out has been largely an intensified extension of policies pursued in previous administrations. Proposals to sell federal assets and operations have not been received well by Congress or the public.   Plans to establish corporations in which former federal employees would hold stock remain in a formative stage. The administration *has* introduced experimentation with and consideration of privatization techniques which could prove effective in the future.

Viewed as a theory of political and administrative economy, as distinguished from a limited set of administrative techniques, privatization has a broad appeal to those who believe federal operations inhibit economic growth, are inefficient, unnecessarily distort market operations, and constrain political liberty. To Stuart Butler,[18] the supply-side strategists of the Reagan administration have pursued the right objectives but have used some wrong methods. The objective is to reduce federal spending, the size of the federal government, and the burden of the federal government on the economy. The Reagan administration has attempted to achieve this through spending cuts. "The initial and fundamental mistake of the administration was its assumption that the only way to control and cut the budget is to seek legislation to reduce the supply of dollars flowing out of Washington. This led the White House to view spending in aggregate terms and to regard the budget problem solely as one of managing and restraining expenditures."[19]

This view of the budget process, according to Butler, ignores the demand side of the political equation. "It overlooks the subtle process by which government programs grow and the fact they are sustained by powerful coalitions. When this process is examined, it becomes clear why no administration is likely to succeed in reducing the size of the federal budget by the conventional approach of seeking to win congressional backing for substantial budget cuts."[20]

To advocates of a broad privatization strategy, the critical point is that the federal government is dominated by spending coalitions. These coalitions consist of beneficiaries and would-be beneficiaries, service providers, public administrators, and political activists. These coalitions dominate the federal government across the spectrum of federal activities—the ownership of federal assets, such as public housing; human services; defense; social security and other entitlements; and the like. The fatal flaw in the Reagan administration's supply-side approach, according to Butler, was that it failed to weaken the coalitions that drive federal spending and to alter the political dynamics that give spending coalitions their immense power. The result has been large deficits. What is needed is a strategy to address the *demand side* of the political equation, the combination of forces that causes Congress to create new programs and to expand their funding.

A privatization strategy addressed to limiting demand should be based on four key principles.

The *first* is to establish the government as a facilitator, not provider, of goods and services. Government can require that services be provided, e.g., mandating enrollment in a retirement plan. It can encourage private action, e.g., through tax incentives. It can also encourage private provision, as though deregulation. The essential point is that government does not have to and should not serve as a provider.

The *second* principle is to divert demand into the private sector. The key to doing this is to design public policies that make private alternatives more attractive, by altering relative prices through tax incentives, impossible user charges on public services, and other means.

The *third* principle is to detach groups from spending coalitions and thus weaken such coalitions. Discounts to tenant buyers, for example, can weaken resistance to sale of public housing.

The *fourth* principle is to create private sector coalitions that are the mirror image of public spending coalitions. This can be done by structuring incentives to beneficiaries, providers, and private administrators.

As a theory of political economy, privatization is a challenge to the bureaucratic-interest group pluralism that usually is regarded as dominating federal operations. At a minimum, it holds some promise for changing the way some of the federal government's business is conducted. Its effectiveness as a broader political approach remains to be seen.

Direction Three: An Investment Approach

An investment approach to public policy and administration entails a more positive role for the federal government in the economy and society than continuation of the supply-side approach, or privatization. It asserts that many federal policies, agencies, and programs are investments in the nation's economic growth and technical progress, international competitiveness, capacity to manage technology, and continuing pursuit of social equity. It suggests a greater emphasis in the future upon public administration of investment than upon public administration of consumption. It raises the question of what kinds of public investment are needed. In recent decades public administration of consumption has crowded out public administration of investment. In both public and private activities, greater emphasis upon investment is necessary.

Lester Thurow explains one of the major reasons for this as follows: "The deficit of the U.S. government is almost entirely the result of financing public consumption; the major expenditures are made for national defense and social security or medicare. The public investment part of the federal budget is shrinking. Such a transfer from investment to consumption slows any country's long-run rate of growth and leads its productivity, international competitiveness, and standard of living to fall relative to those countries who are saving and investing more."[21]

Consumption and Investment Policies and Programs

From the perspective of an investment approach to public policy and administration, federal activities can be classified into two categories, those oriented to consumption and those oriented to investment. Investment activities yield long-term benefits, while consumption activities yield immediate benefits. For example, most transfer payments such as unemployment insurance benefits are oriented to consumption, while most education and training activities are oriented to investment.

Historically, the federal government had made investments in both physical facilities, e.g., the national highway system, and less tangible capital, often knowledge capital, e.g., agricultural research and development, development of the computer, and nuclear power.[22] It has done so for several reasons:

- regional and national economic development, e.g., national navigation and rail systems in the nineteenth century;

- coordination of inter-regional and national activities, e.g., the air traffic control system;

- externalities, e.g., construction of wastewater facilities in one locality to prevent pollution discharges in others;

- social welfare, e.g., medical research;

- military strength and international power and competitiveness, e.g., nuclear power, space;

- improvements in public systems, e.g., support by the Post Office of the development of aviation; and

- long-term economic growth, e.g., support of basic research by the National Science Foundation.

State and local government have also made large investments, particularly in physical facilities and public education.[23] Some of these have been funded in part through federal programs.

Since the early 1970s, federal consumption-oriented programs have grown relative to investment-oriented programs, particularly entitlement and transfer payment programs for individuals: Social Security and railroad retirement, federal employees retirement and insurance, unemployment assistance, medical care, assistance to students, housing assistance, food and nutrition assistance, public assistance and related programs, and other payments to individuals, both direct and through grants to other organizations. According to the Office of Management and Budget, payments to individuals amounted to approximately $446 billion in FY 1986, out of a total of federal outlays of $980 billion.[24]

In David Stockman's view, Social Security and other social insurance programs *are* the welfare state: "In 1954, they cost about $25 billion (1986 dollars), or 1.5 percent of GNP. By 1980, they cost $230 billion, or 6.5 percent of GNP. Those numbers tell the story of the modern welfare state in a nutshell; they were the megabucks that made Big Government appear so big in 1980."[25].

While often viewed critically, federal consumption programs are consistent with a larger, underlying reality—the propensity of American society to consume rather than save. The saving rate of the United States is low, compared with the saving rate in several countries that have become competitors of the United States.[26]

Analysts disagree over which federal programs should be classified as investment and which should be classified as consumption. By OMB measures, about 23 percent of federal outlays in fiscal year 1986 were of an investment nature. About half were military programs.[27]

Charles Schultz analyzed alternative measures of federal investment outlays for fiscal year 1984.[28] Schultz stressed that no market test can be imposed on public investment. He excluded from the investment category activities for which there is general agreement that the yield in the category falls below the cost of capital and activities that do not contribute to the growth of measured GNP, e.g., pollution control investment. He also excluded defense spending. By these measures, he found that civilian investments declined from 16 percent of civilian budgets in 1964 to approximately 8 percent in 1984.

In a related analysis, Donald Nichols[29] found a decrease in Reagan administration spending, up to 1984, on federal activities most likely to stimulate economic growth; research and development, human capital formation, physical construction, and the environment.

Robert Eisner has challenged conventional economic definitions of investment.[30] On several conceptual and analytical grounds, he argues that a substantial amount of government spending is productive investment:

Capital formation includes far more than what we traditionally measure in business spending for plant and equipment or the somewhat wider but still narrow category of gross private domestic investment. It also includes investment in tangible capital by government and government enterprises, households, and nonprofit institutions. . . . And most important, investment in health and education and the basic skills and capacity of human labor involves some of the most fundamental accumulation of the capital necessary for output and economic growth.[31]

In the course of developing a "Total Incomes System of Accounts," Eisner concluded that narrowly defined business investment in plant and equipment has been no more than 14 percent of total capital formation in the United States in recent years.[32]

Elements of an Investment Approach

An investment approach to public policy and administration would strengthen both public and private activity designed to yield long-term benefits to the nation. It would have several elements:

- a stable macroeconomic policy to reduce the distortion effects of deficits on the economy, particularly the absorption of savings to finance the deficit and debt;

- tax, research and development, monetary, regulatory, intellectual property, antitrust, and trade and trade adjustment policies designed to encourage private investment, training, and technical innovation;

- organizational policies to promote cooperation among government, business, universities, and research and development organizations to increase the productive efficiency of labor and capital particularly through the development of know-how and technology;

- policies to recognize, increase, and improve public investments in people, research and development, technology, education and training, natural resources and the environment, and the national infrastructure, e.g., dams, bridges; and

- policies to strengthen and improve the analytical, managerial, and organizational capacities of public organization to manage the mix of public-private programs which now characterizes much of public action, particularly technological programs and public investment programs—including regulation of health, safety, and the environment.

An investment approach would not be based solely upon criteria of economic efficiency and productivity, but would also encompass concerns with organizational and managerial capacity, environmental quality, and social equity.

Functions of an Investment Approach

An investment approach to public policy and administration would promote the strategic development of both private and public investments to address the productivity slowdown and lagging economic growth; international economic competitiveness; the development, management, and regulation of technology; and persistent concern with social equity.

The productivity showdown and economic growth. By almost any measure, productivity in the United States is in a stage of prolonged slowdown. Using the measure of national income, Edward Denison[33] observes that growth fell sharply after 1973 and even more after 1979. Despite some improvement following the 1982 recession, productivity growth continues to lag.

With many other analysts, Denison stresses that the sustained productivity slowdown is a cause of serious concern. National income measures the output which the economy makes available for both private and public consumption, including provisions for education and national security and for additions to the capital stock.

The implications of continuation of the productivity slowdown can be expressed in stark terms. By one account, adjusted for inflation, average weekly earnings per worker (held down slightly be a shorter work week) declined 14.3 percent, 1973 to 1984. Median household income—$26,433 in 1984—declined from 1973, after adjustment for inflation.[34] While many workers entered the workforce, they often entered in low paying jobs. Investment is only one factor affecting the productivity slowdown, but most analysts agree it is an important one.[35]

An investment approach to public policy and administration requires a strategy of growth and equity based on developing and employing both public and private investments—particularly public investments in people, research and development, education and training, technology, and the environment. It would mean strengthening public activities with the greatest potential for contributing to growth.

International economic competitiveness. Concern with competitiveness is related to but distinct from productivity.

The President's Commission on Industrial Competitiveness has stressed, as have many others, that the standard of living in the United States and the leadership of the United States in the free world will depend upon the capacity of the United States to compete in the new international economy. "Competitiveness for a nation is the degree to which it can, under free and fair market conditions, produce goods and services that meet the test of international markets while simultaneously maintaining and expanding the real income of its citizens. Competitiveness is the basis for a nation's standard of living."[36]

The Commission concluded that competitiveness can be measured by four indicators: labor productivity; real wage growth; real return on capital; and position in world trade. By these measures, the ability of the United States to compete in world trade is eroding.

Until 1971, the United States had a positive balance of trade. In the late 1980s it is running a record merchandise trade deficit. While affected by several factors such as the strength of the dollar and the policies of other nations, the "deterioration of our trade balance began more than a decade ago, when the dollar was widely thought to be weak. In industry after industry, U.S. firms are losing world market share. Even in high technology—often referred to as the "sunrise" industries—the United States has lost world market share in seven out of ten sectors. Electronics posted an overall trade deficit in 1984, and our bilateral electronics trade deficit with Japan is likely to surpass our deficit in automobiles."[37]

The Presidential Commission on Industrial Competitiveness avoided the controversial questions raised by proposals for more explicit industrial policies and various versions of protectionist policies.[38]   It recommended a strategy that would require greater cooperative effort among business, governments (including state and local governments), labor, and academia: creation, application, and protection of technology through cooperative efforts; reduction of the cost of capital to industry; development of a more skilled, flexible, and motivated work force; and recognition of trade as a national priority.

The Commission asserted that "Government cannot legislate success" but can and should act to develop understanding and agreement on public and private policies that will be essential to the further development of America's competitiveness.   Government can act to provide stable fiscal and monetary policies, to protect technological innovation, to change antitrust and export administration policies, and to increase America's investment in research, education, and training.

An investment approach to public policy and administration would pursue these policies.

Management and regulation of science and technology. The report of the Rogers Commission[39] on the Challenger disaster makes clear the central importance of adequate investment in the managerial, scientific, and technological capacity of public organizations responsible for the development and deployment of complex technologies—in space, defense, and civilian matters as well, e.g., the national air traffic control system.   These systems are complex sets of public and private activity and technology, requiring strong investments in people, knowledge and know-how in the public and private organizations involved.

While many factors contributed to the Challenger disaster, NASA was a system under pressure prior to the Challenger flight on January 28, 1986.   It was pursuing a schedule designed to achieve economy.   The result was disaster: "In establishing the schedule, NASA had not provided adequate resources for its attainment. As a result, the capabilities of the system were strained. . . . One effect of NASA's accelerated flight rate and the agency's determination to meet it was the dilution of the human and material resources that could be applied to any particular flight. . . . It was falling behind because its resources were strained to the limit."[40]   Under political and economic pressures, NASA was consuming rather than building its human and technological assets.

The task of managing the nation's defense, space, and public civilian technology systems requires mobilization and organization of some of the nation's best managerial, scientific, and technical manpower into complex patterns of public/private action. This task requires extensive investment in public as well as private organizations.[41] This is equally true for agencies responsible for regulating complex technologies—nuclear power, toxic chemicals, biotechnology. In the words of a recent study, the goal is "averting catastrophe."[42]

The scientific basis for regulating science and technology—identifying, assessing, and reducing risk—is limited by current limits of science itself.[43] The United States' system of regulating risky technologies has averted catastrophe, but "How much further improvement will be achieved depends largely on whether those groups and individuals concerned with health and safety can manage to win the political battles necessary to extend and refine the strategies now being used."[44] Without continuing investment in the development of the knowledge and know-how needed to regulate dangerous technologies, it is questionable how long the nation will be able to "avert catastrophe."

Social equity. Despite extensive criticism, the nation's system of trying to help the poor and the most vulnerable parts of the population—e.g., the chronically mentally ill—also represents a substantial investment, an investment in social equity, as well as long-term economic productivity. According to some evidence, the Reagan administration's objective of reducing dependency on government programs has increased the suffering of some of the most vulnerable parts of the population.[45] Poverty in the United States in the 1980s has increased, imposing high costs on both the individuals affected and on public education, health, and other systems. In 1983, 22.2 percent of all children in the United States were living in poverty, according to current Census Bureau definitions of poverty.[46] These children constitute 40 percent of all poor people in the United States. If children represent the future of a nation, it is difficult to conclude that the nation is making an adequate or effective investment in its own future by failing to reduce child poverty. Despite debates over alternative approaches to decreasing child poverty—"what works?"—a great deal has been learned about the effectiveness—and degrees of uncertainty—of various approaches.[47] Can the

United States afford not to invest more extensively and effectively in the development of the 22 percent of its youth that is in need?

Conclusion

Almost 200 years ago Alexander Hamilton raised a question that continues to confront the nation: What is the appropriate role of the federal government in the economic and social development of the nation? Are strong public administrative organizations needed? Hamilton realized, as did many others, that the answer to the question would significantly affect distribution of powers and responsibilities in the constitutional system. He also realized that the question has significant implications for the development of public administration in the United States.

The future of federal public administration in the United States will to some degree depend upon how the nation responds in the new international economic and technological order to the questions raised by Hamilton.

Supply-side management and privatization are both directed to limiting public administration. As an alternative, an investment approach would increase the potential of both public and private organizations to contribute to the resolution of national and international problems. It would de-emphasize consumption and shift federal budgetary and other priorities in the direction of investment. It would emphasize the value of investing in strong public organizations and a strong public service to meet economic, technological, and social challenges to the nation in its third century of constitutional experience.

ENDNOTES

1. Charles A. Beard, *Economic Origins of Jeffersonian Democracy* (New York: Macmillan, 1915), pp. 108-195.

2. For the development of federal public administration in this era, see Leonard D. White, *The Federalists* (New York: The Macmillan Company, 1956).

3. Carl Brent Swisher, *American Constitutional Development* (Cambridge: Houghton Mifflin, 1954), p. 74.

4. See John L. Palmer and Isabel V. Sawhill, eds., *The Reagan Record* (New York: Ballinger Publishing Co., 1984), and the 26 other volumes in the Urban Institute's Changing Domestic Priorities Series. See also "Reagan Is As Intent As Ever On Making Over the Courts," *New York Times* (June 1, 1986), p. E5.

5. James D. Carroll, A. Lee Fritschler, and Bruce L. R. Smith, "Supply-Side Management in the Reagan Administration," *Public Administration Review* (November/December 1985), pp. 805-814. See also Charles H. Levine, "The Federal Government in the Year 2000: Administrative Legacies of the Reagan Years," *Public Administrative Review* (May/June 1986), pp. 195-205.

6. The data in this section, with the exception of personnel data, are from Office of Management and Budget, *Historical Tables, Budget of the United States Government, Fiscal Year 1987* (Washington: U.S. Government Printing Office, 1986), various tables.

7. "The Growing Government," *The Washington Post* (April 30, 1986), p. A23 (reporting unpublished OMB data).

8.   See the discussion in Sidney L. Jones, *Federal Budget Deficits: False Perceptions and Real Problems* (Washington: The Brookings Institution, July 1986, processed).

9.   E.g., see Charles R. Hulten and Isabel V. Sawhill, eds., *The Legacy of Reaganomics* (Washington: The Urban Institute Press, 1984), and Murray L. Weidenbaum, "Dealing a One-Two Punch to Growth," and John H. Makin, "Don't Blame the Bill if We Have A Slump," *New York Times* (August 24, 1986), p. 2F.

10.   See Thomas Ferguson and Joel Rogers, "The Myth of America's Turn to the Right," *Atlantic Monthly* (May 1986), pp. 43-53.

11.   Irene S. Rubin, *Shrinking the Federal Government* (New York: Longman, 1985); Carl Brauer, *The Quiet Problem of the Civil Service* (Cambridge: Harvard University, July 1986, processed); Haynes Johnson, "Customs Service Tries To Do More with Less," *The Washington Post* (August 24, 1986), p. 1; (August 25, 1986), p. 1; (August 26, 1986), p. 1.

12.   See Ted Kolderie, "The Two Different Concepts of Privatization," *Public Administration Review* (July/August 1986), pp. 285-290, and the works cited therein.

13.   See the discussion in Office of Management and Budget, *Management of the United States Government, 1987* (Washington: U.S. Government Printing Office, 1986), particularly "M. Performance of Commercial Activities," pp. 71-75, and "O. User Fees," pp. 79-81. On the proposed sales of federal assets see *The United States Budget in Brief Fiscal Year 1987*, "Reduce Competition with the Private Sector," pp. 23-24, and *Major Policy Initiatives Fiscal Year 1987*, Privatization," pp. 25-48.

14.   President's Private Sector Survey on Cost Control, *War on Waste* (New York: Macmillan, 1984).   This is a commercially published version of the two summary volumes of the President's Private Sector Survey on

Cost Control. The 47 volumes produced by the survey were not published commercially.

15. On June 6, 1986, President Reagan signed into law the Civil Service Retirement Act of 1986, reducing federal retirement costs about 5 percent. On August 8 1986, OMB Director James C. Miller III suspended all contracting out of federal jobs until OMB could determine that contractors could perform the work for less money, as required by various legal provisions.

16. See, e.g., "Sale of Federal Agency Debated," *The Washington Post* (August 24, 1986), p. H2.

17. United States Office of Personnel Management, *Federal Employee Direct Corporate Ownership Opportunity Plan* (Washington: Office of Personnel Management, July 1986). See also "Going Private," *Management*, vol. 6 (No. 1 1986).

18. *Privatizing Federal Spending: A Strategy to Eliminate the Deficit* (New York: Universe Books, 1985).

19. *Privatizing Federal Spending*, p. 9.

20. Idem.

21. Daniel Bell and Lester Thurow, *The Deficits: How Big? How Long? How Dangerous?* (New York: New York University Press, 1985), p. 92.

22. Congressional Budget Office, *Federal Policies for Infrastructure Management* (Washington: U.S. Government Printing Office, 1986). See also Richard Nelson, ed., *Government and Technical Progress* (New York: Pergamon Press, 1982).

23. This is a vast subject in itself and is not addressed in this paper which focuses on the federal role. Many federal programs work through and assist state and local governments. For some recent studies related to this subject, see Ronald F. Ferguson and Helen F. Ladd, *Economic Performance and Economic Development Policy in Massachusetts* (Cambridge: John F.

Kennedy School of Government, Harvard University, May 1986, processed); *Leadership for Dynamic State Economies* (New York: Committee for Economic Development, processed, May 14, 1986); R. Scott Fosler and Ronee A. Borger, *Public-Private Partnership in American Cities* (Lexington: Lexington Books, 1982); and Harvey Brooks, *et al.*, eds., *Public-Private Partnership: New Opportunities for Meeting Social Needs* (Cambridge: Ballinger, 1984).

24. Office of Management and Budget, *Historical Tables, Budget of the United States Government, 1987* (Washington: U.S. Government Printing Office, 1986), p. 11.3 (12).

25. *The Triumph of Politics* (Cambridge: Harper and Row, 1986), p. 409.

26. According to Lester Thurow, "In 1982 American investment was less than half that of Japan and 25 percent below that of most other industrial countries." Bell and Thurow, p. 92. For an extensive discussion of different concepts of "saving" and alternative measurement and data systems, see John B. Shoven, "Saving in the U.S. Economy," in Michael L. Wachter and Susan M. Wachter, eds., *Removing Obstacles to Economic Growth* (Philadelphia: University of Pennsylvania Press, 1984), pp. 187-223.

27. "Federal Investment and Operating Outlays," Special Analysis D. Office of Management and Budget, *Special Analysis: Budget of the United States Government, Fiscal Year 1987* (Washington: U.S. Government Printing Office, 1986), pp. D1-29.

28. "Alternative Measures of Federal Investment Outlays," in Charles R. Hulten and Isabel V. Sawhill, eds., *The Legacy of Reaganomics* (Washington: The Urban Institute Press, 1984), pp. 175-178.

29. "Federal Spending Priorities and Long-Term Economic Growth," in Hulten and Sawhill, eds., pp. 151-174.

30. *How Real Is the Federal Deficit?* (New York: The Free Press, 1986).

31. Eisner, p. 154.

32. "The Total Incomes System of Accounts," *Survey of Current Business* (January 1985), pp. 24-48. See also George M. Von Furstenberg, ed., *The Government and Capital Formation* (Cambridge: Ballinger Publishing Company, 1980), particularly Attiat F. Ott and Jang H. Yoo, "The Measurement of Government Saving," pp. 177-241, and Attiat F. Ott and Thomas D. Austin, "Capital Formation by Government," pp. 265-317.

33. *Trends in American Economic Growth, 1929-1982* (Washington: The Brookings Institution, 1985).

34. "The Average Guy Takes It on the Chin," *New York Times* (July 13, 1986), section 3, p. 1, and "Average Family's Income Up Little Over 11 Years," *The Washington Post* (August 25, 1986), p. 1.

35. See Edward N. Wolff, "The Magnitude and Causes of the Recent Productivity Slowdown in the United States: A Survey of Recent Studies," in William J. Baumol and Kenneth McLennan, eds., *Productivity, Growth and U.S. Competitiveness* (New York: Oxford University Press, 1985), pp. 29-57.

36. President's Commission on Industrial Competitiveness, *Global Competition: The New Reality* (Washington: U.S. Government Printing Office, 1985), p. 12.

37. President's Commission on Industrial Competitiveness, pp. 13-14.

38. See Chalmers Johnson, ed., *The Industrial Policy Debate* (San Francisco: Institute for Contemporary Studies, 1984).

39. Presidential Commission on the Space Shuttle Challenger Accident, *Report to the President* (Washington: Presidential Commission, June 6, 1986).

40. Presidential Commission on the Space Shuttle Challenger Accident, p. 164.

41. See Martin Binkin, *Military Technology and Defense Manpower* (Washington: Brookings, 1986), for an analysis of the complexities of military technology from an operational point of view.

42. Joseph G. Morone and Edward J. Woodhouse, *Averting Catastrophe* (Berkeley: University of California Press, 1986). For an assessment of the positive results of health, environmental, and safety regulations, see David Bollier and Joan Claybrook, *Freedom From Harm* (Washington: Public Citizen and Democracy Project, 1986).

43. See Ted Greenwood, *Knowledge and Discretion in Government Regulation* (New York: Praeger Publishers, 1984); Robert W. Crandall and Lester B. Lave, eds., *The Scientific Basis of Health and Safety Regulation* (Washington: The Brookings Institution, 1981); Sandar Panem, ed., *Public Policy, Science, and Environmental Risk* (Washington: The Brookings Institution, 1983); National Research Council, *Risk Assessment in the Federal Government* (Washington: National Academy Press, 1983). See also, for a case example, *Formaldehyde: Review of Scientific Basis of EPA's Carcinogenic Risk Assessment* (Hearings before the Subcommittee on Investigations and Oversight of the Committee on Science and Technology, U.S. House of Representatives, Ninety-seventh Congress, Second Session, May 20, 1982).

44. Monroe and Woodhouse, p. 175.

45. Martha R. Burt and Kanen J. Pittman, *Testing the Social Safety Net* (Washington: The Urban Institute Press, 1985).

46. See the extensive analyses by the Congressional Research Service and the Congressional Budget Office, published as one integrated study in *Children in Poverty* (Washington: U.S. Government Printing Office, 1985) (Committee on Ways and Means, U.S. House of

Representatives, Ninety-ninth Congress, First Session, Committee Print WMCP:99-8, May 22, 1985).

47.　Sheldon H. Danziger and Daniel H. Weinberg, eds., *Fighting Poverty: What Works and What Doesn't?* (Cambridge: Harvard University Press, 1986); Congressional Budget Office, *Reducing Poverty Among Children* (Washington: CBO, 1985). For an excellent historical review and perspective, see James T. Patterson, *America's Struggle Against Poverty 1900-1985* (Cambridge: Harvard University Press, 1986).

CHAPTER TWELVE

Time and Public Administration

LUTHER GULICK[*]

The commemoration of 200 years of the U.S. Constitution presented in this volume and in hundreds of other events across the nation reflects a focus—perhaps temporary—on time, which is unusual in American society. Two-hundred years is an extremely short social history in the "course of human affairs." The opportunity for the Founding Fathers to create a government on blank paper, drawing more from the theorists of the day than from the history and traditions of a society, was unique and helps account for our tendency to underestimate the importance of time and history. In the first hundred years of the nation, openness to newcomers, Jeffersonian faith in universal education, and Benjamin Franklin's adage that "time is money" set the stage for remarkable progress through which more complex aspects of time could be taken for granted. Even remarkable recovery from the destructive civil war could be accomplished without formal plans. But at the end of the second century of the Constitution, the lessons of a

---

[*] Luther H. Gulick is Chairman Emeritus of the Institute of Public Administration. He was IPA president, 1920-1962; IPA chairman, 1962-1982; city administrator of New York, 1954-1956; and a member of the President's Committee on Administrative Management, appointed by President Franklin D. Roosevelt in 1936. He was the Eaton Professor of Municipal Science and Administration, Columbia University. He is a lecturer and author, and he has served as consultant to governments throughout the world.

maturing industrial society, environmental exhaustion, massive immigration, and international wars are lessons in the importance of time none can overlook.

Time is a crucial factor in every event. Without it, there is no change, no growth, no cause and effect, and no responsibility for management. But the importance of time has been neglected in public administration as well as in politics. Examination of leading texts on government and management today yield little on the topic. One finds only three standard texts that refer at all to time as a subject, and not one that deals penetratingly with the significance of time for management.

Episodes

Action research is a current term for learning while doing. History is time, and it is through personal action in events of American history that my concern for time emerged. The importance of time in management was first impressed upon public administration when Frederick Winslow Taylor came to the Training School for Public Service of the New York Bureau of Municipal Research one day in 1915 to introduce the eager students to his ideas about time and motion in factory work. As he talked, he brought out the stop watch which he always carried, and he called attention to time wasted by us students taking off our raincoats after we arrived in the office instead of performing that motion in the elevator on the way up. With this as his starting point, he went on to show how every act in the office or assembly line could be analyzed, measured, standardized, and fitted into a work-flow chart. He was an intense and creative man, a true missionary. After contact with him, one was never the same; consciousness of time captured one's attention whatever the circumstances.

I next experienced significant revelations concerning time in World War I, in the statistics branch of the general staff, U.S. Army. We statisticians, chiefly borrowed from the Russell Sage Foundation, gathered information from all sources and issued a weekly top secret report for the president, secretary of state, and a very few others, summarizing the measurable units of the American war effort. The charts and summaries on which I worked dealt with manpower. While this endeavor proved that the military resent "outside" reporting, we also learned that (1) coordinated timing among interdependent units is a crucial factor; (2) each program must have a planned time allowance, a safety margin allowing for unpredicted events such as accidents or a flu epidemic or a sudden shift in enemy strategy; and (3) improvement in turn-around times (e.g., in loading and unloading at ports) is just as important as building more ships. Indeed, time equalled ships.

Another lesson in timing came to me in New York after the war when working with various committees of the New York State Legislature. One of these committees produced the New York State income tax; another, the great expansion of state aid to local governments—especially for educational equalization; and a third started the state old age pension program which laid the basis for the federal social security act. (I still have the pen given to me by Governor Franklin Delano Roosevelt after he used it to sign the Old Age Pension Act.) The success and subsequent influences of these public policy innovations were rooted in their timing: the political climate was favorable *after* careful education not only of the public, but also of political and civic leaders and welfare groups. As Frank Moore (Nelson Rockefeller's mentor during his first years as governor) often pointed out, in democracy timing is the hallmark of statecraft because leaders are sensitive and voters are fickle. William Shakespeare put it eloquently, some time before us:

> There is a tide in the affairs of men,
> which, taken at flood, leads on to fortune.[1]

The importance of foresight was a crucial lesson of World War II. In 1938, I was convinced that war was approaching. Frederick Kepple, director of the Carnegie Endowment and former assistant secretary of war, provided a grant for me to go to Washington, D.C. with an open-ended mission to help develop useful approaches to preparedness. Working with the army to review the experience of World War I—particularly the civic and economic aspects, I was able to help General Somervell with the unification of supply services. I learned once more how much leadership and energy are needed to overcome natural tendencies to focus exclusively on the present. Ultimately I joined the staff of the War Production Board as director of Organizational Planning, where under the hand of Robert Nathan skilled planning began to alert Franklin Roosevelt and the economic command to the need for expanding production of aluminum, synthetic rubber, and other basics and for sustaining the threatened civilian economy. Long-range planning was a precondition to eventual victory in war. The essential element we saved was *time*.

After the close of the war, I wrote the following about its management problems:

Through administrators have always been driven to meet deadlines imposed by budget dates, fiscal years, legislative sessions, tax calendars, and periodic reports, administration has seldom faced the pressures of such crucial force as during World War II. The landing in Normandy itself might have been impossible three months later as the rockets came into full play and as German war industry went underground. What if we had taken our time at a leisurely pace, while Germany developed the atomic bomb? Those were deadlines indeed!

The element of time was found to be not just something on the clock or the calendar, but it was the precise equivalent of steel, cooper, and aluminum. It was ships, aircraft, 100-octane gas, and rubber. In the allocation of these critical materials, upon which the date of the invasion itself depended, a million tons in one month was found to be only 500,000 tons in two months; it was time that made the difference. But it was precisely time which we had to allocate and apportion along with aluminum and steel and manpower.

Time came into the administrative picture in another way. It put great premium on the elimination of red tape, as in personnel practices and procurement procedures, and in encouraging direct action across the hierarchical lines by administrative subordinates, as reflected in General Brian Somervell's famous order to do away with "layering."[2] (General Robinson and I drafted that order.)

Aspects of Time

Five important aspects of time emerge from these episodes. The first is *time as an input,* that is, as a resource used by management, along with manpower, energy, machinery, and other elements, to produce a desired end. The second is *time as an output,* that is, as a resource saved, and thus created, as by completing a task ahead of schedule or substituting a less time-consuming procedure. Third is *time as the flow of events,* interrelated or in sequence like falling dominoes, provided by design, as in an assembly line, or mandated by nature, especially by the growth process of living matter. Fourth is *time as a gap between* two or more significant events or processes. And finally, fifth is *timing as a management policy* designed as in taking advantage of changes in wind, tide, or economic and political cycles or in varying the starting times of differently timed processes.

There are other aspects of time, but in management these are the basic elements: time as an input, time as an output, time as an assembly line, time as a gap, and timing as a strategy.

Theories

Mankind has had difficulty in nailing down a single, simple meaning for time primarily because our consciousness and vocabulary reflect a three-dimensional world. We have no simple words for dealing with or thinking about the fourth dimension. Only the mathematicians are at home with a four-dimensional world. Yet time is the fourth dimension of everything we encounter and is deeply embedded in patterns of culture and religion. Time determines how people experience their society, the way they think about it and dream about it.

The ancient Hindu idea of time is related to belief in reincarnation, picturing time as running "round and round," but also in a broad river which flows to final enlightenment. The Greeks, impressed by the rising and setting of the heavenly bodies, with the earth at the center, also saw time and history running in a circle. Certain African tribes even now arrange their time in sharply defined and disconnected historic blocks, the central episode of which is a great tale of an isolated heroic event.

The modern West has a cultural bias derived from our Judeo-Christian heritage. St. Augustine wrote to his God in 400 A.D., "What then it time? If no one asks me, I know. If I wish to explain it to one who asketh, I know not."[3] But medieval Christians became more sure of their vision of time. For them the world was created by God in the year 4004 B.C., and time marches on in a straight forward line from that date through the Great Flood in 2348 B.C., to the birth of Jesus of Nazareth in 4 B.C., and then to the second coming, the "last judgment," and the establishment for the redeemed of God's Kingdom in Heaven. At this point in history all time ends, and heaven lasts forever.

While Copernicus, Newton, Darwin, Einstein, and Bell[4] have pulled the oriental rug out from under this beautiful picture, the western world still acts on the belief that time goes straight ahead, up and up, bigger and better, as far as we can see. Despite intellectual understanding of the relativity of space-time, Ben Franklin's very American definition still has more immediate meaning to us.

Despite our western commitment to straight line, everlasting, upward progress, encouraged by the spectacular technological advances of the past century, some western economists have quietly but insistently called attention to the reality of cycles, for example, of periodic depressions and painful reorganizations. The economic recession of the early 1980s can be interpreted as a period of political-economic "rest" and reorganization inherent in the technological evolution of human institutions. This contrasts with a straight-line, progress-oriented interpretation which seeks to blame situational human leadership for setbacks and to credit it for economic growth. Unquestionably, coordination of fiscal, tax, and energy policy with monetary policy and flexible response to global price movements would have moderated economic setbacks, but dramatic worldwide shifts in climate, trade, inflation, and employment would not have been eliminated.

Fundamental developments may be more accurately pictured as cycles spiraling through history, as wave motions in time. Cycles are composed of time and cannot be discussed in human affairs except against a background of months, years, and centuries. If regular cycles can be proved to exist, they will be time to time, in a way which limits and prescribes what we can do to moderate them, to ride their tides and values, and to guard against their destructive forces.

The perplexing mysteries of time in the universe are limitless. There is no absolute and universal time for our universe. All times are relative and differ not only with motion, but also with emotion and the requirements of entities which exist and act in space. But in the context of 200 years of social experience under the U.S. Constitution, time goes one way only. It cannot be reversed or stopped, though we can apparently sense it as speeded up or slowed down within limits. On this earth- and clock-bound time, events can be simultaneous, or they can happen at different times, one before, or after, the other. With action and response, cause and effect, the action or the cause always comes before the effect. The gap between is one of the mysterious phases or our kind of time. The length of the distance between the act and its result is determined by the nature of the action and the environment or culture in which it takes place. No event causes itself, nor can events occurring at the same time cause each other. Time by itself does not go "up" or "down," it merely goes "on" in company with the curvature of space.

It is not possible for us to know the beginning or end of time, *nor is it necessary*. It is our destiny to live and work in the small span of time which falls hundreds of millions of years after the start, if there was a start, and probably hundreds of millions of years before the end, if indeed there be an end. Our span is, for us, all we need or can hope to comprehend or influence.

Thus, our time is a fixed point, a date, a gap between cause and effect, a duration between events, and a resource, not like steel and electricity, subject to the laws of physics and chemistry, but an intellectual identification of the relative gap which exists in nature between arbitrarily selected states of being in a mass continuum of dynamic interrelations. As such it is essential in the growth process and creates the only opportunity available to management in its effort to modify the future.

Two highly significant differences distinguish the past and the future. The past is **RELIABLE** which the future is not, and the future is **FLEXIBLE**, which the past is not.

Nothing that actually happened in the past can be doubted or changed. The things made were made, the words spoken were spoken, the beliefs held were accepted. Not one jot or tittle can now be changed. The past is finished and frozen.

No man has seen this more clearly than the Persian Omar Kayyam when he wrote:

> The moving Finger writes, and, having writ,
> Moves on; nor all thy Piety nor Wit,
> Shall lure it back to cancel half a line,
> Nor all your Tears wash out a line of it.[5]

Neither nature with its built-in evolutionary drive nor man with his managerial genius can go back in time to change the record. No management decision can change history.

In all this rigidity there is a significant value; the historical record generally tells the truth even where manipulators seek to pretty up their careers and to falsify their deeds or motives. Thus the true history of man though beyond redoing is a reliable storehouse of information and advice.

The future is a different matter. It is filled with expectations. This concerns tomorrow, next spring, next year, the next decade, the third century of our Constitution. As such, it is filled with hopes and fears, with specific personal wants, with prestige and dreams. There are anticipated rewards for hard work, and expected punishment for bad, goals for striving and the justification for suffering and sacrifice. These are the immediate concerns for management and the dynamics of human action. Thus, expectations for the future cast their shadows back upon the present as though time were reversed by the action of the mind. This is no small matter as unfulfilled expectations are the most dangerous and explosive force known to modern governments.

Once the "present" is recognized as an imaginary point or line in time which has no material body, it is easier to see what the "present" means for management. First, it is the end of gathering new information. Standing at this point, the manager must be prepared to act with what he has in hand of facts, resources, and ideas. This makes the decision process a major function of the "present."

Decisions are made in the "present," not the past or the future. The moment a decision is made, it is both an end of the past and a beginning of the future in that particular arena or time.

Second, while it is important to have in hand the basic information and resources for a management decision, to postpone action can be to lose opportunity wherever added information is unavailable or useless. Needless postponement is bad management.

Finally, it is hardly necessary to repeat that each "present" is the beginning of the future. No decision can be made in the "present" without a prior exploration of its side effects and long-range implications. This is a quest inherent in every "present."

Implications

The practical implication for public administration of this view of time is significant. It means that the "principles" of management and administration are eternally tied to the culture in which they arise, and that culture must evolve appropriately in most cases well before major changes in human organization can be successfully undertaken.

It means, for example, that the time gap between tribalism and the modern national industrial state must be recognized and regarded as a socio-biological growth process.

It forces us to recognize that most changes in institutions must be brought about through step-by-step growth and that growth, expansion, and the release of energy, which are explosive and destructive when they occur instantaneously, may be beneficent and useful when they occur slowly. A major difference between a destructive revolution and a wholesome evolution is the speed of the change, i.e., time.

It makes us realize that we in administration are dealing primarily with the near future and that this is conditioned in each culture by expectations, the fulfillment of which calls for the effective management of all resources including both time and expectations.

It means that we must never look at a problem in government, or private management, without carefully considering the timing and the time requirements of any contemplated changes.

Since timing involves dovetailing of partly independent programs, each with its own schedule, managers need to remember that such timing depends on the knowledge of, and sympathy for, correlated or competitive agencies or forces.

It means that we can never turn the clock back. With the passage of time, every significant new law or changed arrangement results in unexpected side effects. These may be beneficial or may, at times, devalue the entire program. Management must be alert to such developments.

In view of the importance of time for any human activity, should we not reconsider the description of organizations as though they were machines? If so, should we not be careful when we use organizational charts? In the standard organization chart, all you have is a flat, static skeleton, a collection of bones for the archaeologists. Left out are the muscles, the power system, the neural system with its sensing organs, communication, memory, information storage, coordination, and command. Where is the "dual supervision" which Macmahon and Millett exposed? Where is Likert's "informal organization" and the social and psychic structure emphasized by Mary Follett and the Hawthorne studies? The truth is, an organization of men and women working together for a defined purpose cannot be symbolized meaningfully by a two-dimensional skeleton. An organization of people is a social and symbiotic organism, swimming in the river of time.

The tragic events in Iran are perhaps the most dramatic signs of what can happen if we ignore the imperatives of time. We blame the Shah for moving too fast: for neglecting recommended "infrastructures." The magic word should have been "ante-structures," not "infra." Not only must the investment in roads, rails, schools, health, diet, and such come before or along with the financial changes and institutions, they must allow for the time gap to nurture the growth processes and for appropriate evolution of community values.

Finally, the concept that time is essential for any organization, because an organization is not a machine, but an organism, makes it clear that we can never again offer once and for all time to "solve" organizational, managerial, or economic and social "problems."

In a universe based on ceaseless change, from the atom up or down to sentient bundles of matter and whirling stellar systems, restless change is predestined, all of which will shift with the spirals of time.

We present not a utopia with solved problems; we offer humankind a better future in a changing world. For this, the fourth dimension, time, must get into our bones to make them strong and into our minds to make them wise.

Conclusion

Technological and economic progress must be integrated in time with human values and social structures. Our enormous capacities for technological invention and destruction must be reconciled with the organic pace of social and moral change. The visions of 200 years ago are valid—visions of freedom, openness, adventure, and local capacity. But they must yet be translated into new forms of organization with capacities for strategic use of time as input and output, statesmanlike leadership which educates as it innovates, and the foresight and wisdom of long-range planning and short-range flexibility. This is the responsibility of public administration.

Time must become a central strategic and moral concern in public management for the third century of our Constitution. The past cannot be changed, although through interpretation and reinterpretation it can be translated into wisdom or foolishness. The present is not a tangible thing, but a mental construct, a precious interval between past and future, where decisions are made by living creatures in response to their inherent drives, fears, and expectations. The future is all we have to work on. Government must plan and work with this flow *in* time and *for* time.

ENDNOTES

1.   *Julius Caesar*, Act III.

2.   Luther Gulick, *Administrative Reflections from World War II* (University: University of Alabama Press, 1946), p. 105.

3.   St. Augustine, *Confessions* (New York: Pocket Books, Inc., undated), pp. 224-232.

4.   See Gary Zukov, *The Dancing Wu Li Masters* (New York: Morrow and Company, 1975), pp. 271, 305, 133, 323.

5.   Omar Kayyam, *Rubiyat*, stanza 79.